PASSING the TORCH

The Influence of Economic Incentives on WORK and RETIREMENT

Joseph F. Quinn
Richard V. Burkhauser
Daniel A. Myers

1990

W. E. UPJOHN INSTITUTE for Employment Research

Library of Congress Cataloging-in-Publication Data

Quinn, Joseph F.
    Passing the torch : the influence of economic incentives on work
and retirement / Joseph F. Quinn, Richard V. Burkhauser, Daniel A.
Myers.
        p.   cm.
    Includes bibliographical references.
    ISBN 0-88099-091-0 : $22.95. — ISBN 0-88099-092-9 (pbk.) : $13.95
    1. Old age pensions—United States. 2. Retirement income—United
States. 3. Retirement age—United States. 4. Age and employment—
United States. 5. Aged—Employment—United States. 6. Labor
mobility—United States.   I. Burkhauser, Richard V. II. Myers,
Daniel A. III. W.E. Upjohn Institute for Employment Research.
IV. Title.
HD7105.35.U6Q55   1990
331.25'2'0973—dc20   ∞   90-12352
                                                                                    CIP

THE INSTITUTE, a nonprofit research organization, was established on July 1, 1945. It is an activity of the W. E. Upjohn Unemployment Trustee Corporation, which was formed in 1932 to administer a fund set aside by the late Dr. W. E. Upjohn for the purpose of carrying on "research into the causes and effects of unemployment and measures for the alleviation of unemployment."

The facts presented in this study and the observations and viewpoints expressed are the sole responsibility of the authors. They do not necessarily represent positions of the W. E. Upjohn Institute for Employment Research.

To Diane and Ginger

Acknowledgments

We are very grateful to the W. E. Upjohn Institute for Employment Research for funding this research. We would also like to thank Eric Kingson and John Williamson of Boston College, Herbert Parnes of The Ohio State University, and an anonymous referee for very helpful comments on an earlier draft of the entire manuscript. Robert Clark, Alan Gustman, Richard Ippolito, Elizabeth Johnson, Olivia Mitchell and Thomas Steinmeier offered helpful suggestions on parts of the text, and John Turner provided some unpublished Department of Labor statistics. We also owe thanks to Judy Gentry, Allan Hunt, Robert Spiegelman and Steve Woodbury of the Upjohn Institute for support and assistance along the way.

Policy Summary

Work and retirement patterns of older Americans, especially men, have undergone major changes during the past two decades. Policymakers need to understand how economic incentives embedded in Social Security and employer pension plans influence the short- and long-term decisions of older workers in order to craft new policy initiatives or adjustments to existing policy.

Life-cycle analysis shows that pension rights are a component of compensation and that workers base labor market participation decisions throughout their lives on retirement income at the close of a career. Research on the quantitative effects of policy, both public and private, on individual decisions of older workers shows that workers behave as though they understand and respond to the incentives they face.

A central finding of the study is that many older workers seek alternate employment after leaving career jobs that span many years. The authors show that incentives affect the way older workers leave career jobs for one of several options: self-employment, part-time work, a full-time second career, or full withdrawal from the labor force. Correlates of the various retirement transitions include health, pension and mandatory retirement status, industry and occupation, earnings and wealth.

Labor force participation rates of older workers have fallen dramatically over the last two decades, and attempts to modify that trend by changing Social Security rules alone are not likely to have more than a modest effect. Most defined benefit pension plans continue to encourage workers to leave the career job at the earliest possible retirement age. How these employer pensions respond to future labor market conditions will have a major effect on work and retirement decisions. The authors are convinced that "older Americans would respond to changed incentives in the future as they have in the past. What remains to be seen is whether the market—firms responding to labor shortages on the horizon—will introduce the appropriate changes themselves, or whether a more active government role is required."

The Authors

Joseph F. Quinn is a professor of economics and chairman of the economics department at Boston College. He received his undergraduate education at Amherst College and his doctorate from M.I.T. He has taught at Boston College since 1974, and has been a visiting professor at the Institute for Research on Poverty at the University of Wisconsin, the Graduate School of Public Policy at Berkeley, and the University of New South Wales in Sydney. He has published primarily on the economics of aging, with emphases on the determinants of the individual retirement decision, wage determination and the economic status of the elderly.

Richard B. Burkhauser is a professor of economics and senior fellow at the Gerontology Institute at Syracuse University. He received his doctorate from the University of Chicago, and has taught at Vanderbilt University and been a visiting scholar and research associate at the University of Wisconsin. He has published widely on the behavioral and income distribution effects of government policy in the labor market. He is an Associate Editor of the *Journal of Human Resources* and a member of the editorial boards of the *Journal of Gerontology* and *The Gerontologist*. He has served on the National Academy of Sciences panel on Employer Policies and Working Families and, in 1990–91, will be a visiting scholar at the Netherlands Institute for Advanced Study.

Daniel A. Myers is an assistant professor in the department of economics at Western Kentucky University. He received his B.S. from the University of Tennessee at Chattanooga, and his M.S. and doctorate from Vanderbilt University. He has been a Social Science Research Specialist at the Institute for Research on Poverty at the University of Wisconsin, and has published articles on widowhood, poverty, the retirement decision and work after retirement.

Contents

Tables

Figures

PASSING
the TORCH

– 1 –

Introduction and Overview

The artful policymaker can anticipate future crises and develop plans to ameliorate them. These plans may seem puzzling to those concerned with present and past problems who do not foresee what lies ahead. No demographic phenomenon has provided a greater continuing challenge to the policymakers' skills than the aging of the postwar babyboomers. During the 1950s, they created a demand for maternity beds and four-bedroom houses in the suburbs. As they entered school, they forced a massive increase in educational facilities and then left some painful contractions in their wake. In the 1970s, they sorely tested the economy's ability to create jobs for young adults, and they may soon clog promotion paths as they progress up the occupational ladders. In the early part of the next century, they will contemplate leaving the labor force. Their decisions on when and how to retire will have dramatic implications for the structure of society, the economy, and the financial well-being of our public and private retirement income schemes.

The demographic projections are startling. In the United States, the population aged 65 and over—about 30 million today—will nearly double over the next 40 years. In stark contrast, the population under 65 is estimated to increase by only 12 percent. As a result, the proportion of the population over age 64 is projected to rise from 12 percent today to nearly 20 percent by the year 2030. The nation then will look like Florida today.[1]

Those interested in issues of retirement finance often emphasize the aged-dependency or support ratio—the ratio of those of prime working age (20 to 64) to those of traditional retirement age (65 and over). In the United States, this ratio is nearly 5 to 1 today, but is estimated to drop to about 2.6 to 1 by the year 2030 and to 2.4 to 1 by 2060 (Aaron, Bosworth, and Burtless 1989). In fact, the actual story is even more

1

significant because 65 is no longer the age of normal retirement. As we will see, older workers have been leaving the labor force earlier and earlier, decreasing further the ratio of those employed to those retired.[2] The ratio of Social Security-covered workers to old-age and survivor beneficiaries is forecast to drop from about 3.3 to 1 today to only 2 to 1 by the year 2030 (Tobin 1988).

These changes are dramatic and extremely important. But some can be predicted—like the number of older Americans—and others—like retirement patterns—can be influenced by current and future public policy decisions. The future is not exogenous. It depends on what we foresee and how we respond to it. We will argue that individual retirement decisions depend in large part on the financial structures we have built into our public and private retirement systems. These structures frequently penalize workers who stay on the job too long—or leave too early—and thereby influence labor supply decisions in important ways. The financial incentives that currently exist may have made sense in the past, but demographic trends suggest that they will not in the future.[3] Our ability to forestall crisis depends critically on an understanding of how these financial structures work, how they affect labor supply decisions, and how they can be changed to alter retirement trends in the years ahead.

Dramatic changes in attitudes and public policy toward retirement and in the employment patterns of older workers have occurred in the United States over the past several decades. Americans are leaving the labor force earlier than ever before. As recently as 1950, nearly half of all American men aged 65 and over were employed. By 1960, this figure had dropped to a third, and by 1970 to a quarter. Today, only about one in six older men continue to work for pay.

These long-term trends in the age distribution of the population, together with large increases in real Social Security benefits and adverse economic conditions, led to a Social Security financial crisis in the 1970s.[4] Trust funds declined and were projected to disappear by the mid-1980s, and the long-run financial stability of the system was threatened.[5] As a result, the National Commission on Social Security Reform, headed by Alan Greenspan, was appointed to analyze the expected flows of funds into and out of the system and to propose changes to bring these two streams into balance. Major legislation followed in 1983, which raised the level of future Social Security contributions, scheduled an increase in the normal retirement age from 65 to 67 while increasing the benefit reduction associated with retirement at age 62 (the equivalent to an across-the-board benefit cut), and made up to half of the benefits taxable for certain higher income recipients.

At the same time, Social Security, traditionally an extremely popular program among recipients and contributors alike, was subject to increased scrutiny and criticism. Some younger workers, reacting to the increased tax levy and the lower rate of return they expected to receive on their contributions, complained about continued participation in the program. Confidence in the system's ability to pay benefits in the future waned and some analysts suggested that participation in the Social Security system should be made voluntary.[6]

Retirement trends and retirement policy leapt from the back to the front page. They continue to be matters of public debate. Interest has further intensified with concern over the federal budget deficit. Since the outlay on old-age, survivors, disability and health insurance (OASDHI) constitutes almost a quarter of all federal expenditures, Social Security is part of the deficit discussion, even though many politicians consider it off limits.

Too often in this public policy debate, specific reforms are proposed without an adequate understanding of how such changes will affect labor supply and retirement decisions. A major goal of this book is to provide an overview of the American retirement system and how it influences work across the life cycle. We will do so by reviewing what economists have learned about the retirement process over the past two decades.

As we will see, much of our increased understanding comes from two outstanding longitudinal surveys of older Americans—the National Longitudinal Survey of older men (NLS), financed by the Department of Labor, and the Retirement History Study (RHS), conducted by the Social Security Administration.[7] Because of studies based on these and other data, we now have a much better understanding of the nature and magnitude of the financial incentives facing older workers. We are

convinced that Social Security and employer pensions do influence retirement decisions and that people respond to these incentives in ways that
are consistent with economic theory and common sense.

We also have learned that public and private pension systems affect
labor market behavior *throughout the life cycle*—not only at retirement,
but before and after as well. As we will see, the literature on the actual
retirement decision is voluminous. Much less has been written, however,
on how pensions influence younger workers—long before retirement—
and those who have already left career jobs. We will show that work
after "retirement" (after departure from a career job) is a very common event and suggest that it may become even more so in the future.
Relatively little research exists on labor force behavior during this growing portion of the life cycle—the years after departure from the career
job.[8]

Our review of the literature is selective. We focus on the economic
determinants of retirement within a public policy framework. We chose
to do so for several reasons. This is the area, we believe, in which the
most important new insights have occurred. In addition, this is the arena
in which we have worked and which we feel most qualified to discuss.
And finally, these economic incentives can be changed through legislation. These are the policy levers that affect aggregate behavior. Our
focus, however, should not imply that we think that other factors are
unimportant. Mental and physical health, social support networks, attitudes toward work and leisure, and previous employment experience
obviously influence the retirement decision. But we, as authors, know
less about them and we, as a society, are less able to change them through
direct public policy initiatives.

A substantial portion of this book, then, is a detailed review of the
recent and current work of a select group of social scientists. We discuss
how views about the retirement decision have changed and where we
now stand. In the second part of the book we describe some shortcomings of this research and point out one direction that we think future
research should take.

Most of the retirement literature focuses on who retires, when, and
why. Retirement is usually modeled as a dichotomous concept—an

individual is either retired or not. Definitions of retirement vary greatly. Some researchers use labor force participation and label as retired
only those who are completely out of the labor force. Others base their
definitions on the receipt of Social Security or employer pension benefits,
regardless of the recipient's labor force status. To others, retirement
means a substantial and discontinuous drop in earnings or hours worked. Finally, some analysts rely on subjective self-descriptions by individuals themselves. Most researchers, however, use whatever definition they adopt to classify people into two or sometimes three categories
and then analyze the determinants of their retirement status.

A major theme of this book is that these traditional classifications
are inadequate to describe the wide variety of labor market changes
that older Americans are making. Although the abrupt transition from
full-time work to complete labor force withdrawal (traditional retirement) is still the most common occurrence, many older workers are
utilizing intermediate steps between the two. Some first reduce their
hours of work to part-time status. Others leave a career job and then
start on another, either full or part time. Sometimes this new job is in
the same industry and occupation, but more often it represents a new
line of work altogether. Still others decide to retire completely, but then
change their minds and return to work.

Because of these diverse exit routes, the word "retirement" may well
conceal more than it reveals. There are too many variations for one
word to describe. The different definitions of retirement lead to confusion and seemingly contradictory research results. Our approach is not
to pose the question in terms of retirement, but rather to ask how and
when people leave their career jobs and what they do afterwards.

Career jobs are a very important part of most Americans' lives. Many
workers spend a substantial number of years on a single job. It is the
transition from this job that we will study. If this exit were to take place
at age 45, few would call it retirement. The behavioral patterns of many
older workers suggest the same thing—that much of what we observe
does not look like the traditional concept of retirement.

In the remainder of this chapter, we discuss the growth of our Social
Security and pension systems in the postwar period and the simultaneous

changes in the employment behavior of older Americans. We document the changes in the labor force participation rates of older men and women. We also discuss patterns in full-time and part-time work and changes in the importance of self-employment. Finally, we document the importance of career jobs in America in order to motivate the approach we have chosen to take.

Growth of Social Security and Private Pension Plans

In 1935, the Social Security Act was passed to provide compulsory retirement insurance for workers in commerce and industry—about two-thirds of the workforce in those days. It was financed by a flat rate payroll tax of 1 percent, paid by both employees and employers on the first $3,000 of annual earnings. The act also mandated federal participation in the state-run old-age assistance, aid to dependent children, and unemployment insurance systems.

The American Social Security system grew directly out of the experiences of the Great Depression, when more than a quarter of the labor force was officially out of work.[9] Many of its features were borrowed from older systems in Europe. The program is government run and mandatory for most workers. The benefits are earnings-related (and weighted in favor of lower income workers) and financed by specifically earmarked contributions. Benefits are paid as a matter of right, and there is no means or overall income test.

Much of the motivation for retirement insurance in 1935 was to permit older workers to leave the labor force and thereby to create job opportunities for the younger unemployed. For this reason, Social Security payment criteria included an earnings or retirement test. The original legislation eliminated the entire monthly benefit for anyone with any "covered wages from regular employment" (Schulz 1988). This was soon replaced by a modest monthly disregard ($15), which retirees could earn without loss of benefits. Today, as we will see, the rules are more complex, but the earnings-test philosophy remains intact.

Over the subsequent half century, this social insurance system has grown in both scope and coverage, much of which was anticipated by the founders (Ball 1988). In 1939, the survivors' and dependents' programs were added. Disability insurance, which had been discussed in the 1930s, was introduced in 1956, and health insurance (Medicare) followed in 1965. Over these same years, compulsory coverage was extended to regularly employed farm and domestic workers (1950), the self-employed (1950 through 1965), members of the armed services (1956), the clergy (1967), and newly hired federal employees (1984). State and local government employees may enroll if both the employer and a majority of the employees agree. Mandatory coverage now includes 91 percent of all workers (Ycas and Grad 1987). Over 96 percent of all wage and salary disbursements are covered by Social Security or by analogous railroad or federal and state civil service programs.[10]

At the same time that coverage was being extended, eligibility rules were being liberalized. Beginning in 1956 for women and 1961 for men, insured workers could claim retirement benefits at age 62. (Monthly payments were reduced by about 7 percent for each year they were claimed prior to age 65.) Benefit calculation rules were adjusted frequently after 1950, usually to reflect recent changes in the cost of living. In the late 1960s and early 1970s, following a decade of economic growth, a series of benefit increases was passed that far exceeded the recent inflationary experience, resulting in large real increments.[11] These increases were then frozen in place by the introduction of automatic cost-of-living adjustments in 1975.

In the years since its initial passage, the Social Security program has grown dramatically, both in absolute terms and relative to the overall economy. Social Security payments are now the single most important source of income to aged households, providing over a third of their money income in 1987.[12] For those in the lowest income quintile, the proportion is about 80 percent (Grad 1989). Table 1.1 provides some summary statistics, at five-year intervals, on the retirement, disability, and survivors components of Social Security (OASDI).

In constant (1989) dollars, annual expenditures have grown from about $5 billion in 1950 to over $235 billion today. The benefits are distributed to nearly 40 million Americans. The initial surges of the program, as it matured, can be seen in the real annual growth rates (averaged over

Table 1.1
Summary Statistics
Old-Age, Survivors, and Disability Insurance Program
(dollar amounts in billions)

Year	OASDI expenditure (current $$)	OASDI/GNP (percent)	OASDI/federal expenditure (percent)	OASDI expenditure (1989 $$)	Annual real growth rate previous 5 years (percent)
1940	0.06	0.06	0.65		
1945	0.3	0.14	0.33		
1950	1.0	0.35	2.4	5.2	
1955	5.1	1.25	7.4	23.5	35
1960	11.8	2.3	12.8	49.4	16
1965	19.2	2.7	16.2	75.5	9
1970	33.1	3.3	16.9	105.8	7
1975	69.2	4.3	20.8	159.5	9
1980	123.6	4.5	20.9	185.9	3
1985	190.6	4.7	20.1	219.7	3
1989	236.2	4.5	20.7	236.2	2[a]

SOURCES: Social Security Bulletin, *Annual Statistical Supplement 1990* (tables 4.A1 and 4.A3) and *Economic Report of the President* (1990, tables C-1, C-58, and C-76).

a. Growth rate over the previous 4 years.

five-year periods) in the last column. In the early 1950s, real expenditures were growing at 35 percent per year as the coverage of the program expanded and disability insurance was introduced. The real annual growth rate then dropped to about 9 percent in the 1960s and early 1970s, and to about 3 percent, and recently 2 percent, since then. But even until very recently, this has been faster than the economy has grown, as can be seen in the third column. The retirement, survivors, and disability expenditures of the Social Security system have grown to equal 4.5 percent of the gross national product, and over 20 percent of all federal government expenditures.[13]

Social Security is a major institution in the United States. Nearly all workers are covered by it or by an analogous public program, and nearly all are eligible for retirement benefits when they reach age 62. The system transfers a quarter of a trillion dollars annually (excluding Medicare) from contributors to beneficiaries. As we will see below, it does so with some very interesting incentives that penalize workers who remain in the labor force too long.

Concurrent with this growth of Social Security has been the development of the private pension system in the United States. Summary statistics for the past four decades are shown in table 1.2.

Since 1950, the number of private pension plans in the United States increased from about 12,000 to well over 800,000, while the proportion of the wage and salary population covered by a private pension plan doubled from a quarter to a half.[14] Coverage of state and local government employees increased from 60 to 90 percent (Kotlikoff and Smith 1983). Most of this growth in coverage occurred in the 1950s and 1960s; the coverage ratio has increased only modestly since then. Since 1950, real private pension assets increased 25-fold, from 80 billion to almost two trillion dollars (in 1987). Private pensions now own over a quarter of the corporate and foreign bonds and a sixth of the corporate equities held by pensions, households, and other institutions in the United States (Turner and Beller 1989).

Because pension members do not receive benefits until the end of their work careers, the recipient statistics lag behind the coverage numbers. The number of pension benefit recipients has continued to

Table 1.2
Summary Statistics
Private Pension Plans

Year	Number of pension plans (000)		Percentage of workers covered		Private pension recipients/ population 65+ (percent)[e]	Private pension assets (1989 $ billion)[f]
	K&S[a]	T&B[b]	K&S[c]	T&B[d]		
1950	12[g]		24			79
1955	28		32			166
1960	64		40			286
1965	115		42			483
1970	226		45	42	16	614
1975	441	340	49	43	20	833
1980	617	590	49[h]	44	23	1131
1985		805		45	28	1681
1986		846		45	29	1875
1987		870		---	---	1956

a. Kotlikoff and Smith (1983, table 4.1.1).
b. Turner and Beller (1989, table A.3).
c. Kotlikoff and Smith (1983, table 3.1.2 [wage and salary workers only]).
d. Turner and Beller (1989, table 13.2 [all private sector workers]).
e. Turner and Beller (1989, table 13.4).
f. Turner and Beller (1989, table 6.2).
g. Data for 1949.
h. Data for 1979.

increase up to the present. In 1986, nearly 30 percent of Americans aged 65 and over received a benefit from a private pension plan.[15] The average annual amount was about $5,000 (Turner and Beller 1989). In 1987, pension benefits constituted about a sixth of all the cash income of households with a head aged 65 or over (*Social Security Bulletin Annual Statistical Supplement, 1988*).

Private pension plans are of two basic types. In *defined benefit* plans, the employer promises to pay a particular benefit, with the amount determined by an agreed-upon formula, usually based on some combination of earnings (often over the last few years of work) and years of service and age at retirement. In *defined contribution* plans, the employer makes an annual contribution to a retirement account for the worker. These funds are then invested and form the basis for benefits at retirement. The size of the benefit depends on the size of the annual contributions, but also on the performance of the fund over the years. As we will see below, the retirement incentives that economists have emphasized occur primarily in the defined benefit plans.

A new book on American pensions by John Turner and Daniel Beller (1989) documents recent trends in the coverage and composition of these plans. Between 1975 and 1985, the total number of plans more than doubled, and the number of active participants increased by about 60 percent.[16] Despite this growth, there was almost no change in the proportion of the working population with pension coverage. This is because of growth in the labor force and because, as seen in table 1.3, about two-thirds of the growth in participants stemmed from supplementary coverage. Supplemental pensions, such as profit sharing and employee stock ownership plans, provided additional benefits to workers already covered by a primary plan. Between 1975 and 1987, the number of workers participating in two or more plans increased from 21 to 40 percent.

Most pension plans in America are small, covering fewer than 100 workers. But these small plans include only about one in 10 covered workers. In 1985, the 6 percent of the plans with 100 or more workers covered 88 percent of all participants.

Table 1.3
Characteristics of Private Pension Plans and Participants, 1975 and 1985

	Number of plans (000)		Number of active participants (000,000)	
	1975	1985	1975	1985
Total plans	340 100%	805 100%	38 100%	62 100%
Fewer than 100 participants	312 92%	757 94%	4 10%	7 12%
100 or more participants	29 8%	49 6%	34 90%	55 88%
Defined benefit	107 32%	224 28%	27 71%	29 47%
Defined contribution	233 68%	581 72%	11 29%	33 53%
Primary plans	295 100%	662 100%	31 100%	40 100%
Defined benefit	107 36%	224 34%	27 87%	29 71%
Defined contribution	187 64%	437 66%	4 13%	12 29%
Supplemental plans	46 100%	144 100%	8 100%	22 100%
Defined benefit	a a	a a	a 5%	a 1%
Defined contribution	45 100%	143 100%	7 95%	22 99%

SOURCE: Turner and Beller (1989, tables 4-11 and 4-12).

a. Less than 0.5.

In primary pensions, defined benefit plans still dominate, covering over 70 percent of all participants in 1985. But this proportion has fallen significantly. The proportion of participants whose primary coverage was in a defined contribution plan increased from 13 to 29 percent between 1975 and 1985.[17] And virtually all of the supplementary coverage (which is growing more quickly) is defined contribution. Overall, the proportion of active participants (double counting those with more than one plan) in defined benefit plans fell from 71 to 47 percent by 1985.

As we will see next, the dramatic growth of the Social Security and private pension systems coincided with a significant decrease in the labor force participation rates of older American men. There are several reasons for believing that these trends are related. While the Social Security system was maturing, the demographic structure of the population permitted the relatively small number of recipients to receive benefits that far exceeded, in an actuarial sense, the current value of the contributions they had made.[18] These intergenerational transfers were financed by the relatively large number of Social Security contributors and resulted in a net increase in the wealth of older Americans. At the same time, real wages were rising, pension rights were accumulating and home equity was increasing in value. Older Americans reached normal retirement age wealthier than had earlier generations. According to economic theory, this should increase their demand for leisure and, among other things, result in earlier retirement.

In addition to this income or wealth effect, however, is a substitution effect. The benefit calculation rules of both Social Security and many private pension schemes alter the compensation patterns of older workers over time, and therefore change the terms of the tradeoff between work and leisure. At some ages, the rules subsidize work and provide a wage supplement. At other ages, they penalize continued employment by imposing a subtle pay cut. Much of the recent research that we discuss below focuses on understanding the nature and magnitude of the financial incentives that are embedded in these retirement systems. It strongly suggests that the growth of Social Security and employer pensions and the trend toward early retirement are related. There remains considerable disagreement, however, on the size of the effects that these incentives have had and on their importance in explaining aggregate retirement trends.

Trends in Employment Among Older Americans

Much of the research interest in the retirement decision stems from the dramatic changes that have occurred in the employment patterns of older American workers during the past 50 years. Among these changes are decreases in the labor force participation rates of older men, a movement from wage and salary work to self-employment, and increases in the importance of part-time employment late in the work career.

Labor Force Participation Rates

Historical Data

It is well-known that American men are leaving the labor force much earlier than they did in the past. We will document recent trends below. What is less well-known is how long these changes have been underway; in particular, whether they began prior to the growth and development of our Social Security and pension systems.

According to the conventional wisdom, employment rates among older Americans were high as recently as the late nineteenth century, but have been dropping steadily since then. Official data originally reported by the Social Security Administration show rates of "gainful occupation" among men aged 65 and over exceeding 80 percent in 1870 and dropping to below 60 percent by 1930 (Ransom and Sutch 1986). The current labor force participation rate for this group is now about 17 percent. A graph of these long-run trends (*ibid.*) suggests a very steady decline over the past 110 years, from a time when retirement was extremely rare, and over 80 percent of older American men continued to work, to one today in which the proportions are almost exactly reversed. In this scenario, Social Security and employer pensions could not have started the movement toward earlier retirement, since it had been underway for at least 50 years prior to their development. At most they might have accelerated a trend with roots much older than their own.

Recent work by Roger Ransom and Richard Sutch (1986, 1988), however, casts doubt on the accuracy of this generally accepted story. Their evidence indicates that there was virtually no change in retirement rates among American men from 1870 to 1937 and, therefore, that nearly all of the change in retirement patterns has occurred during the past 50 years, after the inception of Social Security and the dramatic growth of private pensions.

Ransom and Sutch's findings follow from two assertions: that the definition of occupation changed significantly in 1890 (and later changed back), and that the "official" statistics for 1870 and 1880 were actually based on a backwards extrapolation of trends between 1890 and 1910.[19]

Before 1890, persons were defined as "productively occupied" if they were "earning money regularly by labor . . . or appreciably assisting in mechanical or agricultural industry" (Ransom and Sutch 1986). This is very similar to what we now mean by labor force participation. In 1890, however, the Census Bureau dropped the definition based on active participation in production and adopted one based on sources of income. Persons whose income came from property holdings were classified as *employed* landlords; those with income from stock dividends or bond interest were listed as *employed* capitalists. Many of those individuals would have been defined as out of the labor force and retired prior to 1890, as they would again today. When Ransom and Sutch recalculated the statistics for men aged 60 and over, using a consistent definition of employment, they found labor force participation rates of 64 percent in 1870 and 1880, 66 percent in 1900, 64 percent in 1930, and 61 percent in 1937 (*ibid.*).

These numbers are much lower than the old official statistics, which estimated that over 80 percent of those *over 65* were working in 1870. In addition, the new numbers are virtually constant between 1870 (or at least 1900) and 1937. Since then, however, the participation rate for men *over 60* has dropped precipitously, to 55 percent in 1950, 45 percent in 1960, 40 percent in 1970, and under 28 percent today. It is during the postwar period, then, when most of the action has occurred.

The long-term trend for women is very different. According to Golden (1989), participation rates for married women increased sevenfold since 1920. Despite this, average years of work experience among employed married women remained almost unchanged, since the new entrants were women with very little experience, who kept the average down.

Current Data

Monthly Current Population Survey reports allow calculation of the labor force participation rates of specific demographic groups. In figures 1.1 and 1.2, we illustrate recent trends for older men and women in four age categories, from 1964 to 1989. The decline for all four groups of older men is clear.[20]

For the youngest group shown—men aged 55–59—the participation has dropped over 10 points, from over 90 to less than 80 percent. The next group is particularly interesting, since the age of earliest eligibility for Social Security benefits was lowered from 65 to 62 for men in 1961 (as it had been for women in 1956). Partly in response to this change and the growing availability of early retirement options in private pensions, the participation rate of men aged 60–64 has plummeted over those 25 years, from almost 80 to 55 percent. For men 65–69, the rate remained steady through the early 1970s and then decreased by nearly 20 points. It is interesting to note that substantial increases in real Social Security benefits (on the order of 50 percent) occurred over a five-year period beginning in 1969. The 1970s were also a decade of very poor economic growth. Both of these factors may have hastened the trend already underway. Similarly, the economic recovery in the mid-1980s may be responsible for the recent slight upturn for this group. Finally, the oldest group, men aged 70 and over, has followed the same general pattern, although more dramatically in percentage terms. Their participation rate has fallen by almost half, from 20 to 11 percent, over the past 25 years.

Figure 1.1

Male Labor Force Participation Rates, 1964–1989

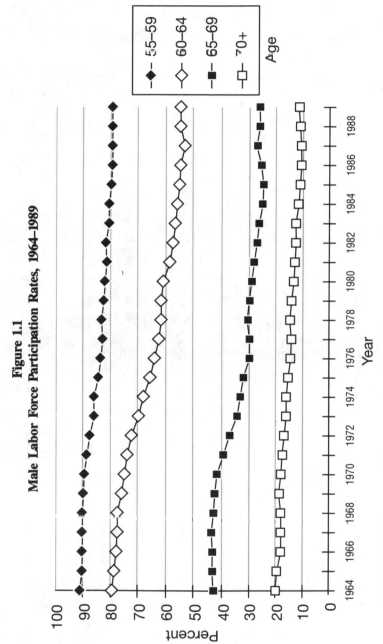

SOURCE: *Employment and Earnings* (January 1965–1990).

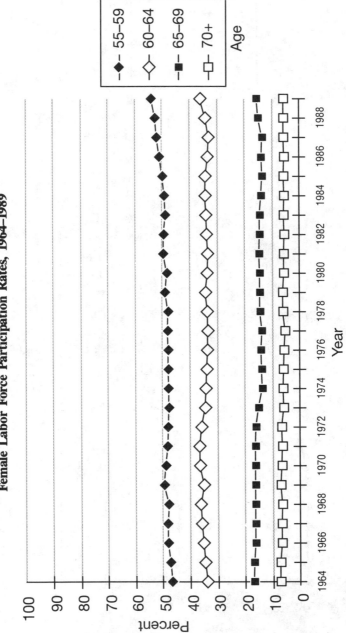

Figure 1.2
Female Labor Force Participation Rates, 1964–1989

SOURCE: *Employment and Earnings* (January 1965–1990).

The trends for older women reflect two major demographic phenomena—the decreased participation of older workers and the increased participation of women, particularly married women.[21] For the youngest group shown, aged 55-59, the latter effect dominates, and the rate has risen slightly and now is 55 percent. For those 60-64, there is very little change observed. For the older two groups, a small decline is noted. For all age categories, the participation rates are lower for women than men, with the ratio of female to male rates dropping with age.

The Department of Labor has unpublished data on labor force participation rates by individual ages. Since some of the financial incentives take effect at specific ages, these data are particularly interesting. Figure 1.3 shows the trends from 1968 to 1989, for men aged 55, 60, 62, 65, and 70. All five lines drift downward over time, but the decreases are most dramatic for those aged 62 and 65. Note also the acceleration of the decline during the 1970s. Figure 1.4 illustrates the same detail for men of each age between 60 and 65. The same overall patterns are observed, as well as the sharp differences between ages 61 and 62 (the age of earliest eligibility for Social Security benefits) and between 64 and 65 (the age of full eligibility).

Both trends, over age and over time, can be seen at the same time in figure 1.5, in which we observe four cohorts of men—those aged 55 in 1968, 1973, 1978, and 1983—and follow each group through 1989. If we ignore the multiple bars at each age, the overall macro picture shows the well-known movement out of the labor market with age. The rate of exit accelerates as people move into their 60s, with particularly large decreases at ages 62 and 65.[22] There is also a smaller, but still substantial, drop of about five points at age 60, when many pension enrollees become eligible.

The micro picture, holding age constant, is equally interesting. For nearly every single age in figure 1.5, the male participation rates decline with each successive cohort. The decreases after age 60, especially at age 62, are particularly large. This is the well-documented movement toward earlier retirement over time.

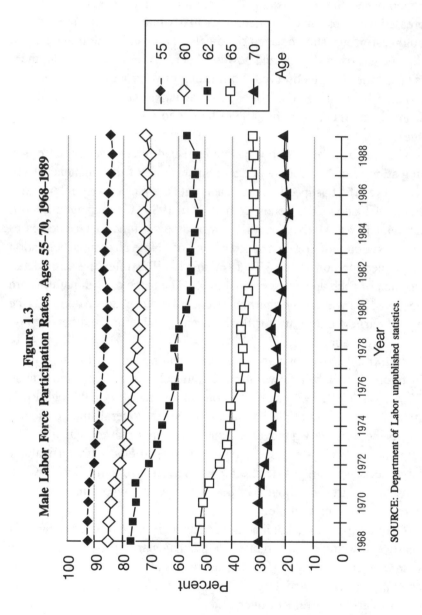

Figure 1.3

Male Labor Force Participation Rates, Ages 55–70, 1968–1989

SOURCE: Department of Labor unpublished statistics.

Figure 1.4
Male Labor Force Participation Rates, Ages 60–65, 1968–1989

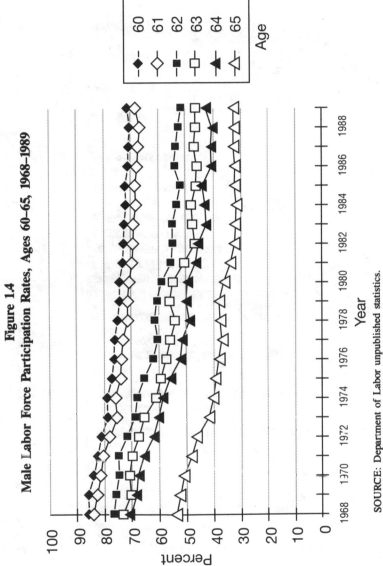

SOURCE: Department of Labor unpublished statistics.

Figure 1.5
Male Labor Force Participation Rates by Cohort and by Age

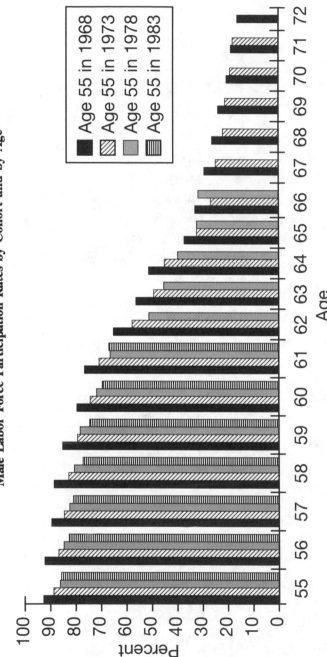

SOURCE: Department of Labor unpublished statistics.

The macro scenario for women is similar, as seen in figure 1.6. Fewer women work at older ages. But the micro story—the record over time—is different. Successive cohorts are not retiring earlier. The pattern is much more irregular, and for many ages participation rates are on the rise.

Although the movement toward earlier retirement for men is most dramatic after age 60, it is by no means confined to those ages. Figure 1.7 charts the absolute and percentage declines in the participation rates of men between 1968 and 1989, for each age between 55 and 70. The largest absolute declines are indeed found between ages 62 and 65, which certainly suggests a role for Social Security in this drama.[23] But in percentage terms, the size of the declines stays high after age 65—the age at which the Social Security reward for continued work decreases dramatically, as we will see below. The participation rate for men aged 62 in 1989 was a third lower than it was for men that age only two decades earlier. But at ages 65 and 68 it was over 40 percent below the 1968 figures.

Figure 1.7 also shows that the decrease in labor force activity starts long before eligibility for Social Security retirement benefits. The declines are substantial at age 60 (where a 17 percent decline in participation rates over these two decades is observed) and even at age 55 (where the decline is 9 percent).

The summary story, then, is one of a significant decline over time in the labor force participation of older men and a relative decline for older women, when compared to patterns of younger women.[24] At several ages important for Social Security and pension eligibility, the declines arc particularly large. Accompanying these statistics, however, are several other interesting and relevant trends.

Trends in Part-Time Employment

Not only are older Americans retiring earlier than they used to, but those who remain employed are more likely to be working part time. The proportion working part time (fewer than 35 hours per week) increases dramatically at age 65. Table 1.4 shows the distribution for persons at work in nonagricultural industries during 1989.

Figure 1.6
Female Labor Force Participation Rates by Cohort and by Age

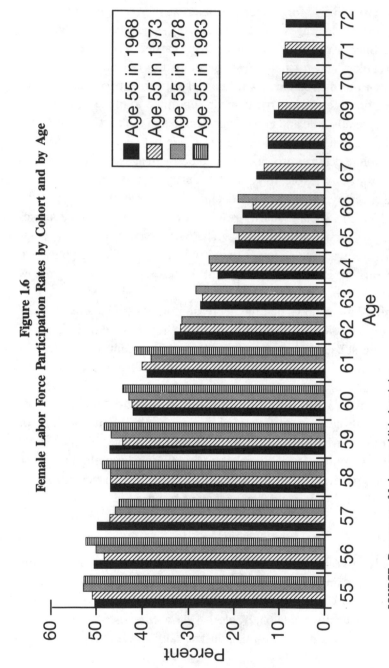

SOURCE: Department of Labor unpublished statistics.

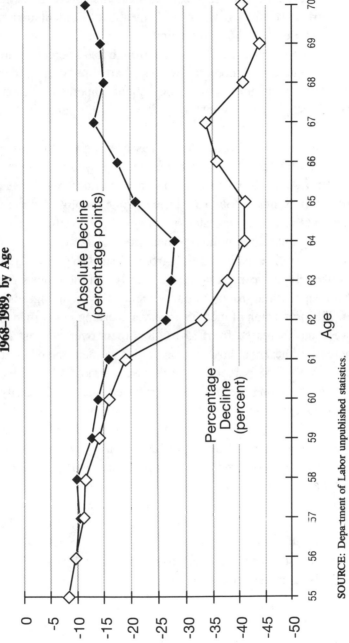

Figure 1.7
Decrease in Male Labor Force Participation Rates
1968–1989, by Age

SOURCE: Department of Labor unpublished statistics.

There is very little difference here between men aged 25–44 and those aged 45–64. Part-time work is rare. Only about 6 percent are employed part time and half of those are doing so involuntarily. But at age 65, the proportion working part time rises from 6 to 48 percent, and almost all of it is voluntary. Among the women, part-time work is more common, but the age pattern is the same—about 20 percent of those under age 65 (most of them volunteers) and almost 60 percent of those 65 and over.[25]

Over the past two decades, there has been only a modest increase in the proportion of the total workforce employed part time. As can be seen in figure 1.8, part-time workers (voluntary and for economic reasons) represented about 15 percent of the employed population in the late 1960s, when these statistics began. By 1989, the percentage had risen by only three points. When one looks only at the voluntary part time, there is even less trend, from 12 (in 1967) to 14 percent (in 1989) of those at work. Among the elderly, on the other hand, there has been significant growth in part-time employment (figures 1.9 and 1.10). The proportion of men 65 and over working fewer than 35 hours per week has increased from 35 to 48 percent over the past 20 years, an increase of nearly a third. Among older women, the proportion has risen from 50 to 58 percent. In both cases, almost all of the increase has occurred among those working reduced hours voluntarily.

Despite a fairly constant percentage of part-time work in the economy as a whole, then, the significance of voluntarily reduced hours has grown among older workers. In our empirical work below, we will pay particular attention to the importance of part-time work, since this is one logical way for individuals to ease out of the labor force. We will see that it is, in fact, a popular route of labor force withdrawal, most often on a new job for wage and salary workers, and most often on the career job for the self-employed. These transitions are ignored in labor force participation statistics and overlooked in studies that treat the retirement decision as dichotomous.

Table 1.4
Full-Time and Part-Time Status
Persons at Work in Nonagricultural Industries, 1989
(horizontal percentage)

Group Age	Total at work (000)	Employed full time	Part time for economic reasons	Voluntary part time
Men				
25-44	32,450	95%	3%	2%
45-64	15,466	93%	3%	4%
65+	1,582	52%	4%	44%
Women				
25-44	26,459	79%	5%	17%
45-64	12,509	76%	5%	19%
65+	1,232	41%	5%	53%

SOURCE: *Employment and Earnings* (January 1990, table 33).

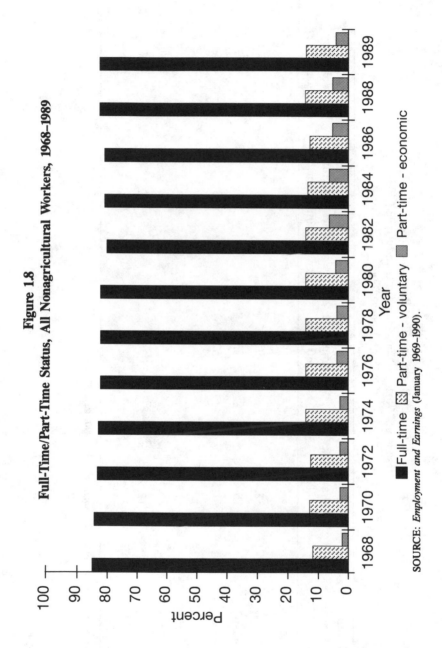

Figure 1.8

Full-Time/Part-Time Status, All Nonagricultural Workers, 1968–1989

SOURCE: *Employment and Earnings* (January 1969–1990).

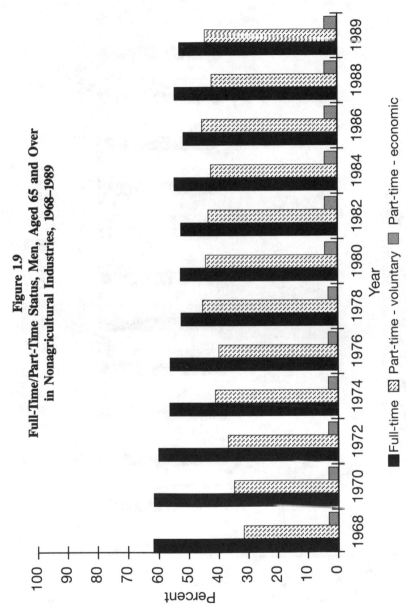

Figure 1.9
Full-Time/Part-Time Status, Men, Aged 65 and Over
in Nonagricultural Industries, 1968–1989

■ Full-time ▨ Part-time - voluntary ▨ Part-time - economic

SOURCE: *Employment and Earnings* (January 1969–1990).

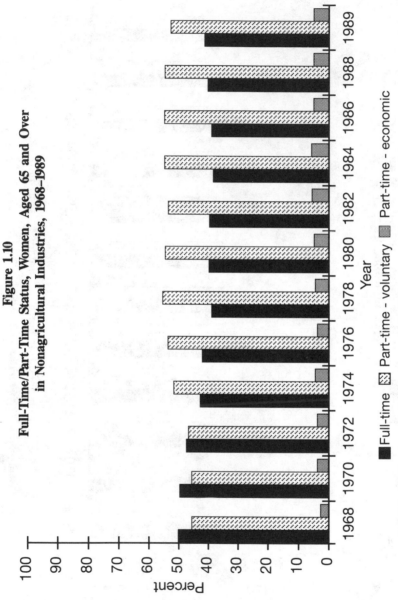

Figure 1.10
Full-Time/Part-Time Status, Women, Aged 65 and Over
in Nonagricultural Industries, 1968–1989

SOURCE: *Employment and Earnings* (January 1969–1990).

Trends in Self-Employment

Older workers are also disproportionately represented among the self-employed. As shown in figures 1.11 and 1.12, the proportion of nonagricultural workers who are self-employed rises monotonically with age—from 1 percent (age 16–19) to 24 percent (65+) for men, and from 1 to 14 percent for women. In both groups, there is a large discontinuous jump between the last two age categories. Men and women aged 65 and over are 50 percent more likely to be self-employed than are workers aged 55–64, and almost three times as likely as the general population.

According to Eugene Becker (1984), the number of the nonagricultural self-employed has increased every year since 1970, rising by 45 percent between 1970 and 1983. At the same time, agricultural self-employment has been relatively constant, resulting in a steady increase in the total number of self-employed. David Blau (1987) argued that these official statistics underestimate the size of the self-employed population.

Beginning in 1967, the Census Bureau reclassified incorporated self-employed workers as wage and salary workers, since technically they were employed by their companies, not by themselves. According to Blau, they are much more like the self-employed than they are like other wage and salary workers. Using data published sporadically in the *Monthly Labor Review,* he pieced together an adjusted series and found that the proportion of men self-employed has risen from a low of about 10 percent in the early 1970s to near 12 percent by 1982. Over the same time period, the female self-employment rate increased from 5 to 7 percent. His empirical work suggested that this recent trend is partially due to changes in tax laws and Social Security retirement benefits.

New data from the Survey of Income and Program Participation confirm that the undercount is substantial. Sheldon Haber, Enrique Lamas, and Jules Lichtenstein (1987) included the incorporated self-employed and those who report self-employment as a secondary activity, and estimated that the percentage of workers who owned businesses was 60 to 75 percent higher than the official self-employed statistics.

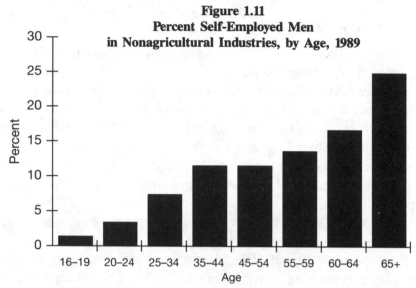

Figure 1.11
Percent Self-Employed Men
in Nonagricultural Industries, by Age, 1989

SOURCE: *Employment and Earnings* (January 1990, table, 23).

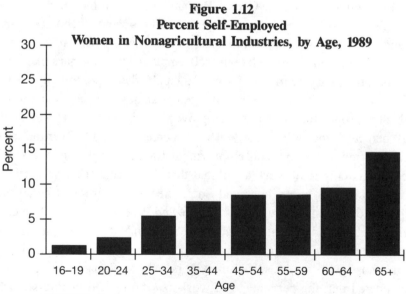

Figure 1.12
Percent Self-Employed
Women in Nonagricultural Industries, by Age, 1989

SOURCE: *Employment and Earnings* (January 1990, table 23).

The high incidence of self-employment among older workers could represent a cohort effect—the fact that these men and women began their employment experiences at a time when self-employment was more common than it is today. But this would hardly explain the discrepancy between the last two groups, born within a decade of each other. This difference must be due to two other explanations: self-employed may retire later than others, or some wage and salary workers may turn to self-employment late in life as an avenue of partial or phased retirement. Joseph Quinn (1980, 1981) found some evidence for both of these hypotheses in some early cross-sectional work with the Retirement History Study. Victor Fuchs (1982), using three waves of RHS data, confirmed them both. With the full 10 years of data now available, we will analyze the behavior of wage and salary and self-employed workers separately, and show that their retirement patterns are very different indeed.

The Importance of Career Jobs

Recent research has shown that most American men spend a considerable proportion of their work lives on long-term career jobs. This is true despite the fact that the median job tenure in the United States is quite short (3.6 years in 1978, according to Robert Hall [1982]) and completed job tenure of jobs ending at any given time is also very modest (3.9 and 2.8 years for whites and nonwhites in the early 1970s, according to George Akerlof and Brian Main [1981]). Because our research focuses on exit patterns from career jobs, it is important that we establish the importance of the career phenomenon and understand and explain the seeming contradictions above.

Research on job tenure is complicated by two issues—the distinction between current and eventual tenure and the difference between the average job and the average person on a job. The first is straightforward. Tenure on a current job is, by definition, incomplete and will eventually be longer than it now is. For example, a young person who has been in the labor market for only five years could have at most five years of tenure on the job, even if lifetime employment were the rule. The fact that there are many young workers in the labor market is largely responsible for Hall's median tenure of less than four years. When he looked at the current tenure of older workers (aged 55 and older), he found that one-third of them were in jobs of at least 20 years duration.

But even this figure is misleading. Some of these workers may have recently left jobs of longer duration. When we look at the longest (as opposed to the current) job of our Retirement History Study sample (aged 58–63 in 1969), we find that over half of the men and over a quarter of the women had a job that lasted at least 20 years. As seen in table 1.5, nearly a third of the men had held, or were then holding, jobs of 30 or more years duration, and nearly 80 percent had at least 10 years experience on their longest job.

Even these estimates are lower bounds, since a few of these older workers were still employed on their longest jobs, therefore adding to tenure when they disappeared from the sample or when the surveys ended in 1979. Hall uses statistical techniques to forecast the eventual tenure of his sample of men employed in 1978, and estimates that about half of those aged 40 or more were on jobs that would last at least 20 years.

With later data from the 1979 Current Population Survey, John Addison and Alberto Castro (1987) confirmed Hall's findings that many workers enjoy long-term employment—20 or more years with the same firm. They also found that this is more likely to be true among union than among nonunion employees.

With some new data from a supplement to the 1987 Current Population Survey, Max Carey (1988) estimated occupational tenure for the American workforce. This is defined as cumulative years in an occupation, regardless of changes of employers or other interruptions, and therefore is not directly comparable to the estimates above. Carey found that current median occupational tenure for older male workers ranged from 20 years for those aged 50–54 to 31 years for those 70 and over. There was link between this and tenure with a specific employer. Of those with occupational tenure of 25 years or more, nearly half had

Table 1.5
Job Tenure on Longest Job

Number	Men	Women
RHS sample in 1969	8,131	3,021
–those without longest job data	–313	–353
Those with longest job data	7,818	2,668
Tenure on longest job		
0–4 years	12%	29%
5–9 years	10%	15%
10–19 years	23%	27%
20–29 years	24%	17%
30–39 years	18%	6%
40 or more years	13%	5%
	100%	100%
Labor force status in 1969		
Not employed	19%	39%
Employed on longest job	63%	50%
Employed on another job	18%	11%
	100%	100%

SOURCE: Retirement History Study.

more than 25 years of tenure with their current employer and another quarter had 10 to 24 years.

Akerlof and Main (1981) cleared up another source of confusion. Although the length of the average job is very short, the average employee is on a job of long duration. The problem is that the "average job" statistic counts each job equally, despite the fact that some last much longer than others. A tenure-weighted measure gives quite a different picture.[26]

Akerlof and Main estimated the eventual completed tenure of persons employed in 1963, 1966, 1968, and 1973, and then calculated the mean tenure over these persons. They found that the average completed tenure was long (about 17 or 18 years for men, and 11 or 12 years for women) and that it changed very little over the 10-year period under study. For those aged 56 through 59, the average duration of individuals' longest jobs was over 20 years.

A career job of long duration is an important phenomenon in America. The departure from this job is therefore a significant event. It is this departure that we have studied. We will see that while many workers do leave full-time work for full-time leisure—the traditional form of retirement—many others embark on new and different careers late in life.

Outline of the Book

In the next two chapters, we review the research of selected authors who have studied the determinants of the retirement decision. We begin with the research of the Social Security Administration during the late 1930s and proceed to the present. We will see that both the research methodologies and the conclusions have changed considerably over time. The methodology has evolved from questionnaires that simply asked people why they retired when they did, to complex econometric models that draw deductions not from what people say but from what they do. The overwhelming dominance of health factors has given way to a more complex understanding of the financial environment in which retirement decisions are made. The division between chapters 2 and 3 is chronological and therefore somewhat arbitrary. In the latter chapter, which begins in the early 1980s, we describe the current state-of-the-art in retirement research.

In chapter 4, we utilize a life-cycle model to look at factors earlier in a worker's career—long before retirement. If the economic incentives embedded in our retirement systems affect labor supply behavior late in life, as considerable research suggests they do, then they may do so earlier in the work career as well. We discuss current research on the impact of pensions on labor mobility and conclude that pensions—and to some extent Social Security—are designed to make sure that workers do not stay on the job too long (the retirement issue), but also that they do not leave too early (the mobility issue).

Chapters 5 and 6 document how a sample of older American workers actually chose to withdraw from their career jobs. We find interesting and diverse patterns. Chapter 5 provides an overview of the relatively slim literature on partial retirement and then describes the actual exit patterns of our sample. Chapter 6 discusses some simple correlates of the transitions observed and compares the new jobs with the career jobs of those who changed employment late in life.

A major theme of this book is that the public policy decisions that society has made in constructing our Social Security and employer pension systems affect work behavior throughout the life cycle—before, during, and after retirement. The organization of the book can be viewed in this way. After the introductory chapter, we focus on the retirement decision—the transition from the career job. This is when the interactions between retirement income programs and labor supply decisions are most obvious. This is also the topic of the bulk of the research. We then look earlier—prior to retirement—and ask how these financial incentives might influence younger workers. Finally we discuss the end of the life cycle—work after retirement and second careers. In the final chapter, we summarize what we have learned and look ahead to what we might expect in the future.

NOTES

1. Similar changes in the age distribution will be occurring in most other OECD nations as well (OECD 1988, chapter 2 and tables A.1 and A.2).

These forecasts use baseline mortality forecasts, in which increases in life expectancy are assumed to be modest compared to those over the past decade. When more optimistic, low mortality assumptions are used (an additional 10 years of life expectancy at age 60 by the year 2030), the growth of the proportion over 64 is much more dramatic; for example it climbs to 29 percent of the U.S. population by 2050 (*ibid.*, table 7).

With a slight lag, the proportion aged 80 and above will increase significantly, from less than 3 percent of the population today to 6 percent by 2050 (and to 16 percent under the low mortality assumption (*ibid.*)).

These long-range population projections are very sensitive to the assumptions behind them. Guralnick, Yanagishita, and Schneider (1989) argue that the baseline Census projections are overly pessimistic with respect to mortality. Assuming a decline in mortality of 2 percent per year, they project that a quarter of all Americans will be aged 65 and over by the year 2040, and that the number of those aged 85 and over will increase 10-fold.

2. The early retirement trend, especially among older men, is common throughout Western Europe and North America. See Mirkin (1987) and OECD (1988) for details and some analysis.

3. Mirkin (1987) argues that one motivation for the many early retirement schemes that exist in Western developed nations was to soak up the excess labor supply that developed during the stagflation of the 1970s. These plans have now become institutionalized, and will work against societal interests if labor markets turn around and workers are in short supply.

4. Much of the short-run problem was due to an error in the benefit calculation formula. As of 1972, both the average monthly earnings (the input into the benefit calculation formula) and the formula itself were adjusting to inflation, which meant that the final benefits were overadjusted. This flaw was eliminated by the 1977 amendments. For more detail, see the U.S. General Accounting Office report (1988). In addition to this problem, the 1970s were a decade of high unemployment and slow economic growth, both of which caused Social Security revenues to fall short of benefit payments.

5. In 1946, Frances Perkins, Secretary of Labor under President Roosevelt and one of the architects of the Social Security system, wrote "even with enlarged benefits to persons reaching retirement age in the next fifteen to twenty years, there would be ample funds (in the social security system) to meet all immediate payments out of immediate income. But by any proper actuarial estimate, there would be, in the end, an accumulated deficit. The reserves would not suffice to pay benefits when those now twenty became sixty-five and eligible for retirement. . . . Perhaps in 1980 it would be necessary for Congress to appropriate money to make up a deficit." (See Perkins 1946, p. 293.) Now *that* is a prediction!

6. These issues are discussed by Tobin (1988). A number of proposals for radical change in the Social Security system have emerged, and many are critiqued in a recent book of essays edited by Meyer (1987). Starr (1988) has also written on the appropriate mix of public and private provision of old-age income support, and Aaron, Bosworth, and Burtless (1989) have discussed some of the implications of privatization.

7. Parnes *et al.* (1985) have provided a detailed description and a selection of research findings from the NLS. An analogous volume for the RHS was edited by Irelan *et al.* (1976).

8. This stage of life is growing because people are leaving their career jobs earlier and living longer than ever before. Chapman, LaPlante, and Wilensky (1986) report that the life expectancy of older Americans has been growing significantly. Between 1968 and 1980, for example, the life expectancy of men and women aged 65 has increased by between one and two months per year, mostly because of declines in cardiovascular mortality. Older people are living longer. What this means for work patterns is less clear, because there is some evidence that, even as life expectancies increase, the health of the elderly is deteriorating. These two trends may well be related, if the clinical successes of modern medicine have been able to prolong the survival of the chronically ill. Ycas (1987) provides an excellent overview of these issues.

9. Ball (1988) has published an excellent and concise description of the fundamental principles and later developments of the American Social Security system.

10. See table 5 in the *Social Security Bulletin Annual Statistical Supplement, 1986* (Washington, D.C.: USGPO).

11. In 1970, after the boom decade, nearly a quarter of those aged 65 and over were living in poverty, compared to only 11 percent of those less than 65, and 13 percent overall. Following these large Social Security increases, the elderly poverty level declined and today is less than the overall rate (Quinn 1987).

12. In 1987, Social Security provided 32 percent of the money income of multiperson families with householders aged 65 and over, and 44 percent for individuals 65 and over living alone or with nonrelatives only (*Social Security Bulletin Annual Statistical Supplement,* 1988, table 3.E3).

13. When the health insurance (Medicare) component is added, total (1989) OASDHI expenditures equal about 6 percent of GNP and over a quarter of total federal expenditures.

14. There are substantial differences in coverage by sex. In a study of new Social Security beneficiaries claiming benefits for the first time in 1982, Woods (1988) reported that only 27 percent of the women were receiving a pension, compared to 53 percent of the men. When those expecting to receive benefits in the future and those covered for potential survivor benefits were included, the coverage rate rose to 44 percent for women—about three-quarters of the comparable rate for men. In addition, the median monthly pension amount received by women was only about half that received by men.

15. According to a recent study by Ycas and Grad (1987), about a quarter of the aged units (couples and single individuals) received private pension income and 14 percent received government employee pensions in 1984. These percentages will continue to grow as new cohorts continue to retire. In 1982, for example, about half of all new Social Security beneficiaries (56 percent of the married and 42 percent of the unmarried) also received pension benefits.

16. The number of active participants in plans exceeds the number of people with pension coverage, because the former double counts those with more than one pension plan.

17. Gustman and Steinmeier (1989c) estimate that about half of the increase in primary defined contribution coverage (between 1977 and 1985) is due to employment shifts toward the types of firms historically unlikely to offer defined benefit plans, rather than firms actually changing the type of plan they offer.

18. Both Burkhauser and Warlick (1981) and Moffitt (1984) have written on the nature and size of these intergenerational transfers.

19. In a comment on the Ransom and Sutch research, Moen (1987) disputed the assertion that the definition of labor force participation changed between 1880 and 1890. Moen's reading of the instructions to the Census enumerators at the time suggests that a key Ransom and Sutch quotation refers only to the occupations of children, not adults. He also claims that Ransom and Sutch

arbitrarily excluded from the 1900 labor force those unemployed for more than six months, and that this is crucial for establishing a constant participation rate between 1870 and 1930. In a long response, Ransom and Sutch (1989) maintained that "[we] stand by our original (1900) estimate" [but] "are prepared to believe that the true labor force participation of men 60 and older was higher in 1870 and 1880 than the published census reported and higher than our benchmark estimate for 1900." Even if this is true, Ransom and Sutch have presented strong evidence that there was little change in the participation rates of older men between 1900 and 1937. What happened prior to that is of little relevance to our discussion.

20. Similar patterns are observed in most other OECD countries as well (OECD 1988).

21. A recent article by Shank (1988) documents the dramatic growth in female labor supply during the postwar period. The participation rate for women aged 25 to 54 more than doubled, from about three in 10 in 1946 to more than seven in 10 today. Department of Labor projections estimate that this will rise to eight in 10 by the year 2000. The age pattern of participation for women has also changed, from the historical M-shape (reflecting withdrawal during childbearing years) to the inverted U-shape characteristic of male participation. Currently, about two-thirds of women aged 25–54 with children under 18 are in the labor force, as are more than half of those with children under age three.

22. The absolute drop in the labor force participation rate at age 62 increases from 12 to 14, and then to 15 percentage points as we consider the first three of these successive cohorts—each five years apart. At age 65, the drops are 14, 13, and 8 percent for these cohorts.

23. Of course, the absolute changes will start to decline at some age because the initial (1968) participation rates become so small. For example, only 30 percent of men aged 70 (and 25 percent of those aged 72) were in the labor force in 1968. Even if *none* of the latter worked in 1989, the absolute decline would still be smaller than for those aged 63.

24. During the last two decades, the labor force participation rate of women aged 25–54 increased from 47 to 72 percent. For women 55–64, it was unchanged, and for those 65 and over it declined slightly. The combination of earlier retirement by men and steady participation by older women has significantly increased the female share of the older (55 and over) workforce, from two in 10 in 1950 to four in 10 today (Herz 1988).

25. See Herz (1988) for more detail on part-time and part-year work by women of different ages.

26. An analogy drawn from Bane and Ellwood (1986) may clarify the issue. Imagine a hospital with three beds, two dedicated to long-term care and one to overnight patients. Over a one-month period, each of the long-term beds has only one occupant, while the short-term bed has 30. Of the 32 total patients, 30 were admitted for only one day; hence, the *average stay* is very short. Yet, on any particular day during the month, two-thirds of the patients were on a spell of long-term hospitalization. The *average patient* on any day requires long-term care. From another perspective, of the 90 person-days of care during the month, 60 were long-term in nature.

– 2 –

The Individual Retirement Decision

As the previous chapter has documented, dramatic changes have occurred in the retirement patterns of older Americans during the past several decades. Work after age 65, once the norm, is now the exception. In 1950, the labor force participation rate of American men 65 and over was near 50 percent. By 1980, it had dropped below 20 percent, and currently only one of every six of these men is in the labor force. For women aged 65 and over, the participation rate has decreased slowly, from 11 to 9 percent over this same period.

Why have retirement patterns changed so much in recent years? Why don't older Americans work beyond age 65 anymore? Why do so many Americans claim Social Security benefits at age 62?[1] In this chapter we discuss these questions from an historical perspective, beginning in the postwar period, soon after the introduction of the Social Security system, and continuing up through the research of the late 1970s. The next chapter describes current econometric work in this area. We will see that over time the answers have changed as dramatically as the retirement patterns being explained.

We are particularly interested in the role of Social Security and employer pensions in the individual retirement decision. What is the nature of the financial incentives embedded in these programs? Do they encourage or discourage work, and at what ages? To what extent do potential retirees respond to these incentives? How have the research conclusions changed over the years?

In the early days of research on these issues, financial incentives were rarely considered to be important determinants of the retirement decision. People were assumed to work until they had to quit—forced by deteriorating health, compulsory retirement, an unexpected layoff, or a change in personal circumstances that made continued employment

41

difficult or impossible. Once they left work, they then turned to whatever retirement income sources were available—Social Security and, in some cases, employer pensions. But the thought that these retirement income sources might have *induced* the retirement behavior was largely dismissed. Voluntary retirements by able-bodied workers were thought to be rare.

Today, on the other hand, there is general agreement that Social Security and employer pensions *do* exert a significant influence on individual retirement decisions. Researchers have shown that substantial retirement incentives (or work disincentives) do exist for many older Americans and that workers respond as though they understand them. Disagreement remains on the magnitude of their influence, but all agree that they have some effect. Other factors, such as health status, job characteristics, and involuntary terminations are still considered to be important, but they are usually analyzed in conjunction with the financial tradeoffs faced by workers nearing retirement age.

This is an important and useful analytical transition. The incentives in the Social Security system and, to a lesser extent, employer pensions are subject to a greater degree of government influence than are the health status or the labor market experience (such as layoffs) of older workers. If the answers emerging from this new research are correct, then aggregate retirement trends are more responsive to public policy initiatives than we once thought.

There are at least two explanations for the changing views of retirement scholars over the past 40 years. The first is that the actual reasons for retirement may have changed and researchers have simply been documenting this transition. Retirement incentives are undoubtedly more important now than they were several decades ago. As we saw in chapter 1, our Social Security and pension systems are much larger than they used to be. Coverage and real benefits have grown over time, and so, it might be argued, has their influence.

On the other hand, the reasons for retirement may not have changed so much over time. Rather, what may be different is the ability of researchers to ferret them out. Research methodologies have changed significantly. In the early days, retirees were simply asked in questionnaires why they retired when they did. When the answers were tallied, analysts found that retirement incentives were rarely, if ever, mentioned, and concluded that they were unimportant. Modern economic research, on the other hand, pays much less attention to these subjective responses. We do not ask what retirees *say*, but rather what they *do*, and under what circumstances. This approach, with the extensive data sets and sophisticated statistical techniques that make it possible, tells a different story about the retirement decision. Those facing financial incentives to retire are more likely to do so, regardless of what they say.

This revolution has been accompanied by new ways of modeling retirement income. Economists now view Social Security and pension rights as *assets* or *stocks of wealth* rather than as annual flows. This change, along with a life-cycle view of decisionmaking, has shed new light on the choices that older workers face. There has been a timely marriage of modern economic theory, outstanding data sets, and improved statistical techniques. What has emerged is a new view of the retirement decision. In this chapter, we first review the early research and see why retirement incentives received so little attention in the past. Even in these survey questionnaires, however, we find hints that we had missed part of the story or that the reasons for retirement were changing. We then describe a simple economic model of the retirement decision and turn to the beginnings of the modern literature that developed from it. We outline the nature of the financial incentives, as we now see them, and discuss the early econometric evidence that demonstrates their importance as determinants of individual retirement decisions.

The Early Literature

Social Security Administration Research

Much of the early research on the determinants of retirement behavior was done by analysts at the Social Security Administration and published in the *Social Security Bulletin*.[2] The earliest article, by Edna Wentworth (1945), was based on a survey of nearly 2,400 male old-age beneficiaries who received benefits in 1940 and were then interviewed during 1941and 1942. These men, among the earliest Social Security recipients, were asked, "Why did you quit working before you filed for benefits?" Well over half (53 to 60 percent in various cities) said they had been laid off by their employers. Of the remainder who reported a "voluntary" retirement (that is, not initiated by the employer), about a third claimed they retired for reasons of "health." This category was broadly defined and included responses describing general fatigue and complaints about old age and the difficulty of work. (Of course, some of the involuntary retirements, at the employer's behest, may have been prompted by the deteriorating health of the worker as well.) The important point is that fewer than 5 percent of the respondents seemed to have retired voluntarily while in good health. Wentworth concluded that "the fact that only 3–6 percent of the beneficiaries retired voluntarily in order to enjoy leisure is significant in evaluating the part old-age insurance benefits have played in influencing aged workers to leave the labor market."

A few years later, Margaret Stecker (1951) reported on the Wentworth study and on three smaller surveys from the 1940s. She found that the overwhelming majority of Social Security beneficiaries left their last covered employment because they had lost their jobs or had had to quit for health reasons. Only 4 to 6 percent left because they "wanted to retire." She concluded that "most old people work as long as they can and retire only because they are forced to do so," and that "only a small proportion of old people leave the labor market for good unless they have to."

But decisions are made under constraints. Individuals who lose jobs can search for another, although, as we will see in chapter 6, they usually cannot find jobs that match their previous wage rates. Similarly, although some health conditions do absolutely preclude work, many others make it less desirable or more difficult, but not impossible. It is likely that the financial situation facing an older person who has been dismissed or fallen ill will influence the decision made. Stecker acknowledged this in discussing why people were so reluctant to retire. "The principal reason that they want to continue working, however, is that without earnings they do not have resources enough to live at the level to which they are accustomed, or even to meet the cost of basic needs." She also noted that those whose retirement incomes were the lowest were the most likely to return to work after claiming benefits. Financial incentives may influence behavior even though the individuals attribute the decision to other factors.

In 1951, the Social Security Administration conducted the first large national survey of the retired beneficiary population. The results of over 15,000 interviews confirmed earlier beliefs. Nearly 85 percent of the retired had either lost their last job or quit because they were unable to work. Fewer than 4 percent retired voluntarily in good health—an even lower percentage than in previous surveys. Most of those who quit or were dismissed for nonhealth reasons returned to the labor force. Stecker (1955) again concluded that "voluntary quitting to enjoy a life of leisure is rare among old-age beneficiaries. Relatively few who are able to work choose retirement." As we will see, this is a far cry from the situation today.

In 1963, the Social Security Administration surveyed both beneficiaries and nonbeneficiaries and included respondents as young as 62. Women had been eligible for reduced Social Security benefits at age 62 since 1956, and men since 1961. For the first time, a trend toward more voluntary retirements was observed. Nearly two-thirds of the male wage and salary workers claimed that they had decided to retire, although more than half of these did so because of health.

Of the men who had retired in the previous five years, 19 percent of those aged 65 or over and 11 percent of those 62–64 said they did so because they preferred leisure (Palmore 1964). Twenty-two percent of the retired women surveyed claimed the same (Epstein and Murray 1967). These numbers are much higher than the 4 to 6 percent observed earlier. Palmore stated that "although most men retire involuntarily—because of poor health . . . or because they have reached a compulsory retirement age—voluntary retirements are increasing." Epstein and Murray agreed that "there seem to be more and more aged men who are well enough to work and who might get some kind of job if they were interested, but who prefer the leisure of retirement."

In the 1963 survey, the question on reasons for retirement listed eight reasons plus "other (specify)." None of the eight had anything to do with Social Security or pensions. This may have been responsible in part for the rare mention of financial incentives. Those still working were asked whether they expected to stop working or work less than they currently were, and if so, why. The answer space to this question was open-ended and no specific categories were suggested. Among the men who did plan to stop or work less, the most common reason given was "becoming eligible for retirement benefits." A third of the respondents gave this reason, and another 7 percent replied "to enjoy leisure" (Epstein and Murray 1967).

Here was an early indication that retirement income eligibility might influence a worker's plans. There was no discussion of what aspect of Social Security or the pension plan might be responsible. In discussing another finding, however, Palmore (1964) suggested that "the difference [in the retirement plans of beneficiaries and nonbeneficiaries] may be due to the fact that beneficiaries under age 72 have their benefit reduced by the earnings test . . . if they earn more than $1,200 per year." Here was an early hint of an issue that has center stage today.

A 1971 article by Virginia Reno utilized a new ongoing survey of recent Social Security recipients. Those not working were asked why they had left their last jobs. Nearly half (45 percent) said health, another 27 percent gave job-related reasons, and 17 percent (the identical aggregate percentage as in the 1963 survey mentioned above) said they wanted to retire. A mere 2 percent claimed the reason was eligibility for Social Security benefits or pension. It looked like eligibility was not very important.

But in another part of the survey, respondents were asked more structured questions about leaving their last jobs. In response to the direct inquiry, "did you leave your last job because you wanted to start getting social security or a pension?" 31 percent said "yes." Perhaps eligibility was important, although not the primary reason. These responses suggest at least two conclusions: first, that there is some survey evidence that financial considerations may be significant, despite respondents' reluctance to mention them unless asked directly; and second, that the responses may depend on the form and nature of the questions asked, perhaps even of whether the questionnaire provides specific categories of answers or merely an open-ended answer blank.

Reno (1971) saw the importance of benefits in the retirement decision, and found that the proportion who wanted to retire increased directly with the size of their retirement benefits. She concluded that ". . . financial considerations often underlie the willingness with which men retire early," and that "the level of retirement benefit income had an important influence on the men's willingness to accept or initiate early retirement."

More recently, Michael Packard and Virginia Reno (1989) reported on the results of a 1982 survey of new retired-worker beneficiaries. Those no longer working (and not self-employed on their last job) were asked which of a list of factors was the most important reason for leaving their last jobs. The answers suggested that there were more voluntary than involuntary retirements. The proportion retiring voluntarily rose with the age of departure from the job, and was much higher for those eligible for a pension. Overall, about one-third (40 percent of the men and 24 percent of the women) said they just wanted to retire. This was far more than the quarter who named health.[3] Again, almost no one mentioned eligibility for Social Security or pension benefits as the primary motivation.

Sally Sherman (1985) compared the results of the 1968 and 1982 surveys for nonemployed men aged 62–64, and aggregated the answers into three categories: employer-initiated, health problems, and employee-initiated. The proportion of retirements that were employer-initiated (lost job or [rarely] compulsory retirement) remained the same over these 14 years—17 percent. The proportion due to health and employee initiation reversed. Health dropped from 54 to 29 percent, and the number of people claiming a desire to retire or (rarely) to receive retirement benefits rose from 29 to 54 percent. This is consistent with a trend toward more voluntary retirements.

Several authors have noted, however, that the importance of health generally drops with the age of benefit receipt, at least through age 65. In the 1982 survey, for example, nearly one-third of the men first claiming benefits at age 62 named health as the primary reason, compared to only a quarter of those who waited until 63 or 64, and 17 percent of those at 65. (There was an increase to 22 percent among the very small number of men who delayed receipt beyond age 65.) The pattern was less clear for women, although the 62-year-old beneficiaries were again the most likely to cite health (Sherman 1985).

Using the National Longitudinal Surveys of older men, Eric Kingson (1982) analyzed the health of "very early retirees"—those who permanently withdrew from the labor force before age 62. He found that the vast majority either had medically certified disabilities or reported health conditions that prevented or limited work. Health status was probably very important in their retirement decisions. Packard and Reno (1989) found that it was, for men at least, with a sample of very early retirees from the 1982 New Beneficiaries Survey. The proportion of men naming health as the primary retirement reason for leaving their last job declined from 35 percent among those who left before age 55, to 30 percent between ages 55 and 62, to 26 percent at age 62, and only 21 percent thereafter. It is essential to remember, however, that older Americans are an exceedingly diverse group, and that most generalizations, excluding this one, are potentially misleading. Our reading of the evidence on health is not that it is unimportant as a retirement determinant, or that it ever was, but that it is less important than it once was and less important than it may appear in surveys featuring subjective retrospective reasons for retirement.

Since Sherman's and Packard and Reno's data included only those receiving Social Security checks, they were unable to compare the circumstances of those who could and those who could not claim benefits. This would be a much more robust test of the influence of retirement benefits, and this is the approach taken in current econometric research. In addition, none of these researchers was able to test explicitly which aspects of the Social Security and pension plans might have been important. Was it the size of the benefit, the ratio of benefits to recent earnings, or the earnings test? Insights into these issues had to await a major modeling change—from viewing these benefits as flows of income to viewing them as assets or stocks of wealth.

Other Early Research

Researchers outside the Social Security Administration also shed light on the reasons for the dramatic retirement trends underway. Peter Steiner and Robert Dorfman (1957) reported on a special 1952 Census Bureau survey of approximately 3,600 men and women aged 65 and over. Although the study emphasized economic status, there were several questions on the circumstances and reasons for retirement. Steiner and Dorfman found that three-quarters of the men retired voluntarily, but primarily for health reasons.[4] All other reasons for voluntary retirement were of relatively minor importance. In particular, only a small proportion had been driven out of the labor force by retirement systems. The authors concluded that the main causes of labor force withdrawal were poor health and obsolescence of skills—a picture consistent with that painted by Social Security researchers at the time.

Clarence Long (1958) attempted to explain the decline in labor force participation by older workers in five Western industrialized countries, including the United States. He found little evidence that the trends were due to demographic changes, rising real earnings, declining physical productivity of the aged, increases in arbitrary discrimination (such as mandatory retirement provisions), or changes in technology. He suggested that the influence of Social Security and pensions was marginal and that

> . . . Social Security and pensions were far from being the main force (though they doubtless helped) in bringing about the withdrawal of elderly persons from the labor market. Indeed, there is evidence that elderly persons desire to work as late in life as their health permits, mainly because old age benefits rarely take the place of earned income even when they are comparatively generous.

The implication here is that retirement benefits could be influential, but that they were too small at the time to induce labor force withdrawal. Note that retirement rights were being viewed as annual flows, an approach that can lead to conclusions quite different from those to follow.

To what did Long attribute the decline in participation rates? He claimed that the older men were being displaced by better-trained women
who would work for lower wages. The low educational attainment of
the older generation put them at a competitive disadvantage against young
and middle-aged women. Long's answer was on the demand side of
the market.

Margaret Gordon (1963) later reported on an international study of
18 developed nations. She noted that participation rates among older
men had been declining for decades in all the countries studied. The
trend accelerated during recessions and depressions and slowed or reversed briefly during wars, but the overall declining pattern was clear.
She acknowledged that a large proportion of the retired attributed the
decision to "ill health," but noted that that phrase could encompass
a wide variety of conditions, many of which did not preclude work.
Might not the decisions of those in poor health depend on the availability
of retirement income sources? She concluded that

> [I]t seems reasonable to assume that, in a substantial pro-
> portion of cases in which ill health is the ultimate reason for
> retirement, prospective retirement income will have an im-
> portant influence on the timing of the decision to retire. There
> is scattered evidence . . . that significant numbers of elderly
> keep postponing the decision to retire, despite slow physical
> deterioration, at least partly because of the prospect of serious-
> ly inadequate retirement income.

Gordon found a significant negative correlation between the labor
force participation rate of men over 64 and the ratio of average old-
age, survivors, and disability benefits to average earnings. This is a
rough aggregate replacement rate. She also found participation rates
lower the longer the country had had an old-age benefit program and
concluded that

> . . . there is considerable evidence to suggest that prospec-
> tive retirement income has a highly important influence on
> attitudes toward retirement. . . . The findings of the present
> study suggest that, as benefit levels are improved, a rising
> proportion of elderly people will be attracted by the prospect

of retirement. . . . As old-age benefits increase, the proportion of elderly persons who choose to retire will no doubt gradually increase.

Truer words were never spoken.

The Gordon article is important for several reasons. She expressed skepticism in taking the "health" answers to retirement questions at face value. At minimum, health status is likely to interact with other factors, such as retirement income alternatives. In addition, she presented a supply-side explanation for the retirement trends: older workers were *choosing* to retire, given the alternatives they faced, rather than being forced out and then turning to whatever retirement income sources were available. And finally, in discussing Great Britain, Gordon included a long description of the impact on an individual's pension benefit of delaying retirement from age 65 to 70. She pointed out that the increase in the annual amount was insufficient to compensate for the five years of benefits foregone. This was an early preview of an issue that dominates much of the retirement literature today.

A few years later, Michael Brennan, Philip Taft, and Mark Schupack (1967) published a study titled *The Economics of Age.* They studied employment patterns by detailed occupational and age groups. Their explanation of declining elderly labor force participation rates was one of geographical and job immobility. Older workers, they claimed, found the demand for their services declining because of their decreasing productivity, greater supplementary employment costs (such as pension contributions and workers' compensation), and the substitution of female labor. Once displaced, older workers found it difficult to become reemployed, and eventually left the labor force. This prospect, which was really disguised unemployment, was the best among a very poor set of alternatives.

This is another demand-side argument. Individuals work as long as they can, until they are forced out. The authors dismissed the importance of Social Security and pensions in the decision, arguing that "retirement income . . . is simply not large enough relative to earned income to make voluntary retirement with sufficient income feasible."

Finally, in 1969, Richard Barfield and James Morgan published a research volume that focused specifically on the early retirement experience. They noted the previous increases in the coverage and benefit levels provided by Social Security and employer pensions and the liberalized early retirement benefits negotiated by the United Auto Workers in 1964. They attempted to find the factors that influenced the decision to retire voluntarily; that is, prior to mandatory retirement age and the onset of debilitating health conditions. They gathered data on a national representative sample and on a random sample of auto workers around 60 years old. The major finding of their study was that ''financial factors—primarily expected retirement income—are of principal importance in the retirement decision.'' Subjective health status, age, and attitudinal variables were also important, but financial incentives were key.

With a few exceptions, then, research through the 1960s described a drama in which Social Security and pension benefits played relatively minor roles. Many retirements were employer-initiated, and therefore involuntary. Of the voluntary departures, most seemed to be due to health problems. At least this is how retirees described their decisions when asked. Researchers had detected an increase in the number of truly voluntary retirements by healthy people who simply preferred more leisure. But these were still the minority, probably less than 20 percent. Some analysts suspected that the availability of retirement income sources was more important than the surveys suggested, but hard empirical evidence was scarce.

Circumstantial evidence, however, was abundant. Although official statistics showed labor force participation rates for older men declining since at least 1890, the size of the decline was much larger after than before the development of the Social Security system. During the 60 years between 1890 and 1950, the labor force participation rate for men 65 and over dropped about a third, from 68 to 46 percent. Over the next 24 years, as Social Security coverage grew from 18 to 67 percent of the labor force (and private pension coverage grew as well), the participation rate dropped by half (Campbell and Campbell 1976).[5]

In addition to this aggregate longitudinal evidence, cross-sectional analyses of participation rates by age showed dramatic declines at age 65, the age of eligibility for full Social Security benefits. The size of the age-65 effect grew over time, and another one appeared at age 62, after the introduction of reduced Social Security benefits (Ippolito 1990). In 1970, the male participation rate dropped by 7 percentage points between ages 61 and 62 and by nearly 25 points at age 65. By the mid-1970s, nearly half of all eligible workers aged 62 to 64 claimed early Social Security retirement benefits.

But other things were changing as well. Health status, compulsory retirement, and unexpected layoffs remained important. Pension plan coverage was on the rise. Large real increases in Social Security benefits were being legislated. The economy recovered from the recessions of the 1950s, enjoyed the economic boom of the late 1960s, and then slumped into the stagflation of the 1970s. The research problem clearly required empirical techniques that could disaggregate these various determinants and isolate their individual effects.

During this same time, two outstanding data sets were being developed. The Department of Labor was funding the National Longitudinal Surveys (NLS), one part of which would follow nearly 5,000 men aged 45–59 for 17 years—from 1966 until 1983. At the same time, the Social Security Administration was planning the Retirement History Study (RHS), a 10-year longitudinal study of the retirement process. Over 11,000 respondents aged 58–63 would be interviewed in 1969, and then again every two years until 1979. These two sources would provide the testing ground for new theories about the nature of the retirement decision.

Finally, economists were beginning to take a closer look at the choices that older Americans faced. They realized that the incentives embedded in retirement plans were very complicated and that simple, one-period models were inadequate to describe the options available. Multiperiod life-cycle models were developed and a new view of the retirement decision emerged.

Economic Models of the Retirement Decision

The Social Security Act is a very complicated piece of legislation. To describe it in all its detail would be neither enjoyable nor productive.

The goal of a model is to highlight essential details—those attributes that have an important impact on the behavior under study—and to ignore others. This yields a cleaner and more understandable description of the program, though admittedly one missing much of the rich institutional detail.

The simplest economic models of Social Security treat it as a one-period tax and transfer program. Individuals maximize utility, which depends on leisure (L) and on the consumption of a composite good (X), which is purchased with income. A person enters the period with a stock of wealth (A) and faces an exogenously determined hourly wage rate (w). If we ignore income taxes and assume that the choice of hours of work is entirely up to the worker, the task, as seen in figure 2.1, is to maximize utility subject to the budget constraint,

$$PX = A + w(T-L)$$

where P is the price of the composite good, T is the length of the time period, and (T–L) is hours worked.

Figure 2.1
Labor-Leisure Choice, Without Social Security System

Graphically, the individual chooses the point (Z_1) on the linear budget constraint (AE) that is tangent to the highest indifference curve (U_1).

A simple manipulation of the budget constraint yields a useful insight:

$$A + wT = PX + wL.$$

The term $[A + wT]$ is "full income"—the amount someone would earn by working the entire T hours. The sum is entirely exogenous in this model, since it depends on three exogenous quantities: assets, the wage rate, and the number of hours in the time period. It is not a function of the current labor-leisure choice. This "full income" is then "spent" on the two "goods"available: X , which costs P per unit, and L (hours of leisure), which costs w per hour—the opportunity cost of not working. A proportional income tax would rotate the budget constraint down (the equivalent of a decrease in the wage rate); a progressive tax would make it concave.

How does the introduction of Social Security change this model? Prior to the age of eligibility for benefits, Social Security merely taxes wages up to some maximum amount—$51,300 in 1990. Individuals earning beyond that amount have their full incomes reduced by the maximum contributions, but their marginal wage rates are unchanged. They respond as they would to any wealth loss—they purchase fewer of all normal goods, including hours of leisure. In other words, they should work more. But someone earning less than the maximum taxable amount faces a second effect. The marginal after-tax wage rate is now lower because of the Social Security contribution. Since this is the opportunity cost (the price) of leisure, leisure is now less expensive than it was. This "substitution effect" increases the demand for leisure. The income (or wealth) effect says work more because you are poorer (by the amount of the Social Security tax) than you were. But the substitution effect says work less, since leisure is on sale. Whether the income or the substitution effect dominates is an empirical question. From a theoretical point of view, the net effect is ambiguous.

When the individual becomes eligible for retirement benefits (B) at age 62, the analysis changes again. First, the zero-hours intercept of the budget constraint rises from [A] to [A+B], as seen in figure 2.2.

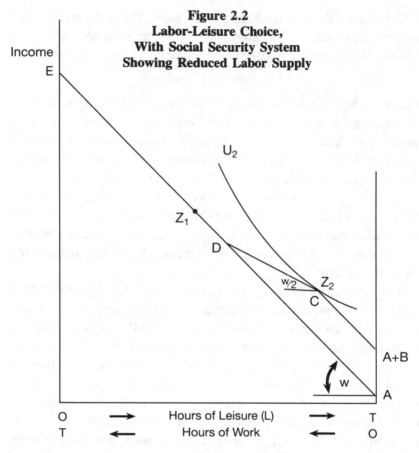

Figure 2.2
Labor-Leisure Choice,
With Social Security System
Showing Reduced Labor Supply

In addition, the marginal wage rate declines because Social Security reduces benefits by $1 for every $2 of earnings after an exempt amount.[6] In this one-period model, this is identical to an additional tax of 50 percent. If we ignore Social Security contributions and income taxes, the budget constraint is parallel to the original as long as earnings are less than the exempt amount and then has one-half the slope (along CD, reflecting the one-half benefit reduction rate) until it rejoins the original budget constraint at D. Beyond this point the individual is working too many hours to be able to collect any Social Security benefits.

The effect of these changes on the labor supply of the individual is unambiguous—the person should work the same amount or less. Because of the potential benefit (B), the individual is richer, and therefore can buy more of all normal goods including leisure. This is the income effect. In addition, the price of leisure has been reduced in that range (CD) where the 50 percent Social Security benefit reduction rate is in effect. The reward to work (the opportunity cost of not working) is less than it used to be. The substitution effect implies that the individual will purchase more of the good (leisure), whose relative price has decreased. The income and substitution effects work together. The Social Security incentives after eligibility will reduce hours of work, unless the individual was already retired (working 0 hours) or continues to work along DE and declines Social Security benefits altogether.

Some people who used to work at Z_1 will find that the tangency between the new budget constraint and their highest indifference curve (U_2) is now along CD; say, at Z_2 in figure 2.2. The combination of the income guarantee (B) and the dramatically reduced marginal wage rate (the reward for work) has reduced their labor supply. For others, the highest indifference curve may now intersect at Z_3—zero hours of work, as depicted in figure 2.3. These workers have been *induced to retire* by the Social Security incentives.

This simple one-period analysis was popular in the early retirement research by economists, which is reviewed below.[7] But it has a fatal flaw. It ignores an essential ingredient in the Social Security system. Although Social Security does resemble a tax and transfer system in many ways, it also has some features of a savings program. In particular, the benefits that one eventually receives depend upon the earnings (and therefore the contributions) made earlier. Social Security taxes today increase benefits tomorrow. And delaying retirement after the age of eligibility does the same. This changes the analysis in fundamental ways that cannot be seen in a one-period framework.

A life-cycle model of work and consumption behavior differs from a one-period model in several essential ways. Decisions made in any one period depend on past and present circumstances and on expectations about the future. People can transfer purchasing power over time—consuming income before it is earned by borrowing, or saving it for later consumption by lending. In the simplest models, with no uncertainty, individuals are assumed to foresee what lies ahead—future wage and interest rates, future Social Security rules, and the lengths of their lifetimes.

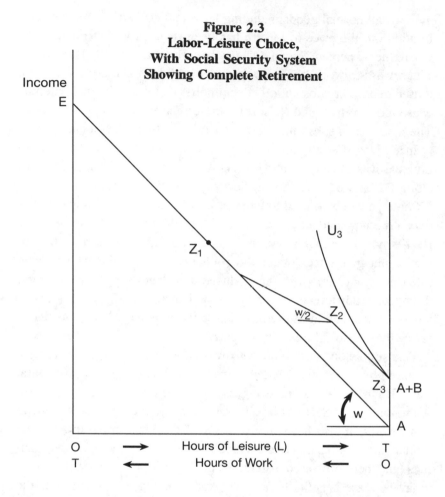

Figure 2.3
Labor-Leisure Choice,
With Social Security System
Showing Complete Retirement

From a life-cycle perspective, Social Security contributions are *not* just taxes. They are taxes today, but they generate larger benefits in the future. The net impact on one's lifetime wealth may be positive, negative, or zero, depending on whether the future increments exceed the taxes. If the rules are actuarially fair or neutral (the present discounted values of the benefits and taxes are equal), then the introduction of the Social Security system should have no effect at all on labor supply behavior. It is merely a mandatory savings program that one could offset by lending and borrowing.

Considerable research, however, suggests that for all the cohorts that have retired thus far, the Social Security system has not been actuarially fair. Rather, benefits have vastly *exceeded* the amounts that prudent investment of the contributions would have provided.[8] What looked like an earnings *tax* was really an earnings *subsidy*, since a dollar of contribution withheld provided well more than a dollar (in present discounted value terms) of future benefits. Rather than lowering the slope of the budget constraint (the wage rate) at younger ages, the Social Security rules had actually raised it.

The impact of the life-cycle view is even more dramatic once the age of eligibility for Social Security benefits (age 62) is reached. In figure 2.2, we implicitly assumed that benefits foregone by those earning beyond the exempt amount were lost forever. But this is not true for two important reasons.

Social Security benefits are based on one's average indexed monthly earnings (AIME), a complicated function of covered earnings over the lifetime.[9] Another year of earnings will usually raise this average and result in higher Social Security benefits in the future. In addition to the benefit recalculation, there is also an actuarial adjustment that can have dramatic effects. Between the ages of 62 and 65, benefits are reduced by five-ninths of 1 percent for each month prior to age 65 that one claims benefits. This implies a 6.67 percent reduction for each year of early retirement, or a 20 percent reduction for retiring the maximum three years early. Viewed from the other end, the 80 percent benefit at age 62, the rules provide a bonus—a delayed retirement credit—for each additional year of work between the ages of 62 and 65. (An adjustment is actually made for any *month* in which benefits are reduced or foregone, and differs slightly depending on whether one has yet claimed benefits at all (Clark and Gohmann 1983).) The adjustment, which applies to all future benefits, is compensation for claiming fewer checks.

The choice of whether to work another year after age 62 is now more complicated. With respect to Social Security, it is not simply a choice between a benefit of B_1 if one retires and 0 if one does not. Rather, it is a choice between one *stream* of benefits (B_1, B_1, B_1 . . .) beginning now and another *stream* (0, B_2, B_2 . . .) beginning in a year, with

B_2 larger than B_1. Which of these streams is worth more? Adding the benefits is inappropriate, since they arrive at different times. What must be compared is the *present discounted value* of the streams, where

$$PDV_1 = B_1 + B_1/(1+r) + B_1/(1+r)^2 + B_1/(1+r)^3 \ldots$$
$$= \Sigma \; B_1/(1+r)^t, \text{ and}$$
$$PDV_2 = 0 + B_2/(1+r) + B_2/(1+r)^2 + B_2/(1+r)^3 \ldots$$
$$= \Sigma \; B_2/(1+r)^t.$$

The present discounted value of a stream of future payments is merely the stock of funds today that, if invested at interest rate r, could yield the stream in question. Although B_2 exceeds B_1 (annual benefits are higher if you work another year), PDV_2 may or may not exceed PDV_1 because the first B_2 is 0.

Note that Social Security rights, which guarantee a stream of income in the future, are viewed here as an *asset* or a type of *wealth,* not as a monthly benefit. A present discounted value is a stock, like a savings account, not a flow, like a monthly salary. The value of this asset can rise or fall as one delays retirement, depending on the extent of the benefit recalculation and the actuarial adjustment. This modest change of framework, from a flow to a stock, has dramatic implications for one's view of the financial incentives embedded in the Social Security legislation.

Suppose, for example, that the present discounted values above are equal. This is an actuarially fair or age-neutral system, since the asset value is not affected by the timing of retirement. In this case, the earnings test, which is still on the books, has in fact disappeared! The benefit reduction rate of 50 percent is really zero. The reason is that benefits foregone today because of additional work are not lost, as they appear to be in a one-period model, but rather are delayed and returned to the recipient in the form of higher Social Security checks in the future.

Suppose now that PDV_2 exceeds PDV_1; that is, that the future increments are more than sufficient, in an actuarial sense, to compensate for the initial benefits lost. In this case, not only are there no earnings test and no benefit reduction rate, but the system actually provides an earnings *subsidy*. The true compensation for the year equals the paychecks *plus* the increment to Social Security wealth that accrues from the additional work.

On the other hand, if PDV_2 is less than PDV_1, future increments are insufficient to compensate for the loss in benefits today. Additional work does provide a paycheck, but it also *reduces* the value of Social Security rights by the loss in present discounted value. (The loss is less than the full amount of benefits foregone (B_1), because future benefits do increase.) While one pocket is being filled, the other is being picked. In this scenario, the Social Security system has imposed a pay cut—a surreptitious one, but a pay cut nonetheless.

As we will see, one topic of debate is over which scenario most accurately describes the Social Security system for workers between the ages of 62 and 65. But everyone agrees that after age 65, the last scenario is the appropriate one. The reason is that at age 65, the delayed retirement credit drops from 6.67 percent to only 3 percent per year of delay. This 3 percent annual increment is inadequate to compensate for the benefits foregone. Therefore, those who work beyond age 65 do so at a true wage rate that is lower than they earned the year before.

Defined-benefit pension programs are similar to Social Security. They promise a stream of benefits in the future, the size of which is usually a function of one's work history. Prior to eligibility and after vesting, additional years of work add to the asset value of the pension rights. One's true compensation exceeds the paycheck by the increment to pension wealth. But after eligibility, an employee who remains on the job forgoes pension benefits. Whether pension wealth rises or falls depends on the benefit calculation rules of the particular pension plan.

Pensions are much more difficult to study than Social Security. Although the Social Security system is complicated, there is only one system, and the details are known to the researcher. In contrast, there are hundreds of thousands of employer pension plans, each with its own rules and regulations, and these are often not known to the analyst.

Larry Kotlikoff and David Wise (1989) have studied the details of nearly 1,200 plans from the Department of Labor's Level of Benefits Survey and found a wide variety of incentives. They define the *accrual rate* as the change in pension wealth following an additional year of work divided by earnings for that year. Positive accrual rates imply a wage subsidy and negative ones, a wage tax. They find considerable evidence that future pension increments are often inadequate to compensate for current benefits foregone. They conclude that:

> Typical plan provisions provide a strong incentive for retirement after the age of plan normal retirement, and a large portion of plans provide a strong incentive for retirement after the age of early retirement. . . . For example, while the average plan may provide reduced but still positive accrual after the age of early retirement, for a large proportion of plans the accrual rate after this age is a sizable negative number. Thus, it would not be unusual for the reduction in pension benefit accrual after the age of early retirement to be equivalent to a 30 percent reduction in wage earnings.

The development of this new view of retirement income rights—as *assets* whose values can rise or fall with additional work—was gradual. There is virtually no sign of it through the mid-1970s. By now, however, it is the dominant paradigm, and it has changed our views on how retirement systems work and how they influence individual retirement decisions.

Retirement Research During the 1970s

Economists are interested in incentives. We generally believe that individuals understand and respond to the economic incentives they face. There is considerable circumstantial evidence that the Social Security and pension systems have had an important influence on retirement trends. In the United States, retirement (and early retirement) rates rose dramatically as the Social Security and pension systems expanded. Noticeable changes in participation rates occur at ages important in pension and Social Security rules—60, 62 and 65. Workers' earnings are found to cluster around the levels at which the earnings test goes into effect.[10] Other factors, of course, are important—health status, mandatory retirement rules, and the state of the economy. But, as Joseph Pechman, Henry Aaron, and Michael Taussig argued in 1968:

> Within these limits, . . . the terms upon which people can retire—the loss in earnings which they suffer from not working—are very important. Since social security is the dominant retirement system in the United States, it can influence the retirement decision, both directly by altering the income choices that workers face, and indirectly, by helping to influence the other factors which determine the time of retirement.

Pechman, Aaron, and Taussig evaluated the evidence that existed in 1968 on the influence of extended Social Security coverage and benefits on the trends in labor force activity, and concluded that "unfortunately, the little evidence bearing on this point [rising benefit levels] is even weaker than the evidence on the effects of widened eligibility for benefits." In other words, economists were confident that Social Security was an important determinant, but had yet to establish it empirically. Over the next two decades, the evidence for this proposition and our understanding of how retirement income programs work would increase dramatically.[11]

One-Period Models

Michael Boskin (1977) produced one of the earliest econometric studies of the retirement decision with a small sample of white married men from the Panel Study on Income Dynamics. He defined retirement as movement to less than quarter-time work and included among his explanatory variables a measure of health status (hours ill during the year), Social Security benefits (the maximum for which the household would be eligible), the net earnings potential of the individual (net of earnings-tested benefit reductions), and income from assets. The findings were remarkable. The Social Security effect was large and statistically significant, and many times larger than the effect of income from assets.[12] Here was evidence that those elderly eligible for larger Social Security benefits were much more likely to retire than others. Boskin concluded that

> the overall impact of the social security system . . . is clearly to induce earlier retirement for a substantial fraction of the elderly population. . . . The results . . . suggest that recent increases in social security benefits and coverage, combined with the earnings test are a significant contributor to the rapid decline of the labor force participation of the elderly in the United States.

The magnitude of the effects that Boskin claimed was very large. He suggested that an "increase in Social Security benefits from $3,000 to $4,000 per year per couple raises the annual probability of retirement from 7.5 to 16 percent," and that "a decrease in the implicit tax rate on earnings from one-half to one-third would reduce the annual probability of retirement by about fifty percent!"

These large estimates were suspect for several reasons. The sample size—only 131—was very small. This may also explain why the health effect estimated was insignificant and of the wrong sign. The study completely ignored employer pensions. Since those with pensions are also likely to be eligible for relatively large Social Security benefits, the Social Security coefficients may have been picking up some pension effects. And finally, the treatment of the Social Security system was, in retrospect, unsophisticated. It was done in the context of a one-period model, and therefore ignored the impact of additional work on future retirement benefits. But this was one of the first econometric efforts to suggest that retirement income incentives are much more important than survey questionnaires had implied.

In that same year, Joseph Quinn (1977) published the results of some early research based the Social Security Administration's new Retirement History Study. He used only the initial 1969 cross section of what would eventually become a 10-year longitudinal survey of the retirement patterns of over 11,000 older Americans. In 1969, the sample was 58 to 63 years old and a substantial portion of the group had already stopped working.

Quinn defined retirement as complete labor force withdrawal and asked what objective circumstances differentiated those who were and were not retired in 1969. He considered both Social Security and pension eligibility, along with an interaction term denoting eligibility for both. Also included were variables reflecting health status, the presence of dependents, asset income, the hourly wage rate on the current or last job, local labor market conditions, and certain characteristics of the job.[13] Some interesting results emerged.

The coefficients on all three retirement income variables were large and significant. Current Social Security and pension eligibility both increased the probability of retirement, and their effects appeared to be more than additive. Social Security eligibility alone reduced the probability of labor force participation by 11 percentage points, pension eligibility alone by 7 points, and both together by 26 points. The presence of a health limitation was also very important (reducing the probability of participation by 20 percentage points), as was the presence of asset income. The one surprising result was that the wage rate on the current or last job was not a significant determinant of retirement behavior. Subsequent research has explained this puzzling finding.[14]

Quinn then disaggregated the sample by health status to see whether health interacted with the other explanatory variables. Statistical tests suggested that it did, since the explanatory power of the separate equations was significantly greater than that of the combined equation. Although the same coefficients generally remained significant in the two equations, the coefficients were much larger among those with a health limitation, suggesting that those in relatively poor health (though not bedridden or housebound—those two groups were excluded from the analysis) were more sensitive to their financial conditions.

For example, the aggregate Social Security effect on labor force participation (-11 percentage points) turned out to be an average of a very large effect on those with a health limitation (-28 points) and a small, but still significant, effect (-4 points) on those in relatively good health. The analogous pension effects were really -14 and -5, rather than the average of -7. The effects of dependents and higher asset income were also larger for those with a health problem. This is consistent with the suggestion in some of the later survey research that health is often an important contributing, but not necessarily determining, factor in the retirement decision. Those with health problems are more likely to want to retire. Whether they can afford to or not depends on the financial options they face.

In 1978, Michael Boskin and Michael Hurd published an article using the first two waves (1969 and 1971) of the Retirement History Study. They analyzed the behavior of about 1,000 white males who were employed in 1969 and who did not have a working wife. In addition to utilizing the longitudinal nature of the RHS, this research had two interesting innovations. It analyzed three transition states: continued work (without receipt of Social Security benefits), semiretirement (working and receiving Social Security benefits) and retirement (not working at all). In addition, Boskin and Hurd considered the possibility that the potential Social Security benefit is itself an endogenous variable, a function of the individual's taste for work. The authors hypothesized that those with higher potential benefits might retire *later*, not because the higher benefits induced continued work, but because both the delayed retirement *and* the potential benefits were determined by some underlying preference for work. Those with a taste for work would have worked hard all their lives (and, hence, be eligible for large benefits) and would then continue to work in old age. The appropriate econometric response to this endogeneity is a two-stage least-squares procedure in which potential benefits are replaced by predicted potential benefits based on exogenous instruments.

Boskin and Hurd's results were similar to those of Boskin (1977), mentioned above. They found a strong influence of Social Security on early retirement, and estimated that a $1,000 increment in annual Social Security benefits would increase the probability of complete retirement by about 8 percentage points (on a mean of only 12 percent). It is interesting to note that the Social Security coefficient had the wrong sign when the variable was treated as exogenous, suggesting that the endogeneity issue may be an important one.

The Boskin and Hurd analysis ignored pensions, so that some of the Social Security effect may have reflected the influence of employer plans.

In addition, their treatment of Social Security was unsophisticated, since changes in future benefits due to continued work were not considered.

Despite these shortcomings, Boskin, Hurd, and Quinn did provide some early statistical evidence that Social Security and pensions were important determinants of the labor market behavior of older American males. Some aspect of these programs seemed to induce retirement, but was it the size of the benefits, the ratio of benefits to earnings on the job, the tax rate levied by the earnings test, or actuarial adjustment rules? This early research shed little light on these issues.

Multiperiod Models: Retirement Income Rights as Wealth

In 1979 and 1980, Richard Burkhauser added an important theoretical insight that eventually changed the way most economists view the retirement decision. He emphasized the multiperiod nature of Social Security and pension rights, and argued that "it is not simply the size of annual benefits received each year but the present value of the entire stream of benefits that emerges as theoretically and empirically important" (Burkhauser 1980).

An annual benefit amount, though better than a dichotomous eligibility variable, is an inadequate description of the incentives an individual faces. This is also true for another popular summary statistic, the replacement rate, which is the ratio of post- to preretirement income. Consider two workers currently earning $30,000 per year on identical jobs and eligible for annual retirement benefits of $12,000 if they were to retire. It appears that their financial tradeoffs are the same—an increase in leisure for a substantial reduction in income. But, they may well not be.

Suppose, for example, that the first individual's benefits are indexed for future inflation, as Social Security is, while the other's are not, as is true for many private pensions. Retirement will look more attractive to the former, especially during times of expected high inflation. And suppose that the benefit calculation and actuarial adjustment provisions differ. For the second, let us assume that the annual benefit would rise from $12,000 to $15,000 per year following another year of work; whereas for the first, it would remain at $12,000. Another year of work looks more attractive if it results in higher pension benefits in the future. In fact, in the hypothetical case here, the year's worth of benefits foregone ($12,000) would be recouped in four years, and the subsequent years of benefit increments would then provide an added bonus for that additional year's work. In the second case, however, the $12,000 in benefits foregone during the extra year of work are lost forever, and there is no financial reward for work other than the current paycheck. The point here is that the retirement incentives are very different for our two workers, despite the fact that the one-period tradeoffs appear to be the same.

A worker facing a retirement decision, then, is not just choosing between a paycheck and a pension check, but rather between two different streams of income. As we described above, these alternatives can only be compared by evaluating their present discounted values (PDV). This is precisely what Burkhauser proceeded to do.

Burkhauser (1979) first analyzed a sample of 761 male auto workers aged 59 to 64, who became eligible for Supplementary Earnings Retirement Benefits under the 1965 United Auto Workers' contract. The decision he tried to explain was whether or not the worker decided to take an early pension, that is, prior to age 65. The key new variable he introduced was the difference between the (after-tax) PDV of the pension stream if taken early and the PDV of the stream that would start if retirement were delayed until age 65.

He found that the average PDV of the *early* retirement benefit streams was $18,365; whereas, the average PDV of the *normal* retirement pension streams was only $8,660. The average loss in pension wealth, therefore, was nearly $10,000. Over the same time period, the PDV of the wages that one of these workers could earn averaged over $22,000, so an income maximizer would certainly continue to work. But a utility maximizer who enjoyed leisure might not. The true net gain from working those years was not the $22,000 in pay, but $22,000 *minus* the loss in pension wealth. Only those willing to work for a net compensation of around $12,000 would remain on the job.

In his empirical work, Burkhauser found a number of interesting significant explanatory variables. In regression, probit, and logit equations, the difference between the present discounted values of the pension streams was always a very important determinant. The larger the pension wealth loss accompanying additional work, the more likely the workers were to accept the pension benefits and leave the firm. In addition, the present value of the earnings expected between early retirement age and age 65 was significant, confirming that higher earnings encourage continued work. The probability of pension acceptance also increased with age, with the amount of other financial assets, and with poor health, measured by the number of weeks of work missed during the previous year.

The main contribution of this paper was the treatment of pension rights as an *asset* whose value changes with the age of retirement. Burkhauser found that these changes in asset value were important theoretical and empirical determinants of the pension acceptance decision. He concluded that "the loss in the asset value of both private pension and social security benefits together with their constraints on market work encourages workers to take these benefits and reduce or completely stop work"; and suggested that "efforts to increase the labor market opportunities of the aged (i.e., the recent legislation to end mandatory retirement below age 70) may have little impact unless adjustments in the asset value of pensions, both private and social security, are introduced" (Burkhauser 1979).

These Social Security implications were not based on the UAW study, because it was impossible to include Social Security variables in the analysis. In 1980, Burkhauser analyzed the impact of Social Security with a sample of about 700 men taken from the Social Security Administration's 1973 Exact Match File, which contains microeconomic information drawn from the March 1973 Current Population Survey and from SSA's internal program records. These men were all eligible for Social Security retirement benefits at age 62. The advantage of this data source was accurate information on Social Security benefits. The disadvantage was the lack of any data on personal health or pension status.

The dependent variable was the decision to accept Social Security benefits at age 62. The size of the benefit was measured by the present discounted value of the future benefit stream, including the possibility of dependent and survivor benefits. Burkhauser assumed in this paper that the Social Security system was actuarially unfair (that future benefits increments did not adequately make up for benefits foregone during additional years of work) and, therefore, that the potential loss in Social Security wealth was proportional to the initial asset value. He did not calculate the wealth loss directly. This assumption of actuarial unfairness at age 62 is controversial, and the subject of a debate mentioned below.

Burkhauser found that the size of Social Security wealth was an important determinant of the retirement decision. The larger the asset value, and therefore, he assumed, the larger the potential wealth loss during years of delayed retirement, the more likely the individual was to accept benefits at age 62. High market earnings potential discouraged Social Security receipt, as did being married or highly educated.

This data source included no information on individuals' pension status. Since this is undoubtedly an important determinant in the retirement decision, Burkhauser included a very rough proxy for this by calculating the probability that each individual was eligible for pension benefits at or before age 62, or at any time. The estimates were industrywide averages for the industry in which the respondent last worked. He found that those workers with high early pension probability were more likely to accept Social Security benefits at age 62, and that those eligible only later were less likely to accept than those with no benefits at all. This may be because pension plans frequently base benefits on the earnings in the last few years of work, thereby increasing the return to working late in one's career.

These early studies established that the incentives in our Social Security and pension systems could affect people's behavior and induce retirement, and that the most appropriate way to view retirement income rights is as an asset or a stock of wealth. The value of this asset depends on when it is claimed. Retirement plans can encourage work by growing in value with continued employment. But they can also discourage work and encourage retirement by declining in value for those who remain on the job.

A Debate Over Social Security Incentives

In 1980, Alan Blinder, Roger Gordon, and Donald Wise published an article that utilized the same general approach that Burkhauser had introduced, yet reached remarkably different conclusions. They challenged the increasingly common assumption that Social Security was an important factor in the early retirement decision and claimed that the incentives hidden in the Social Security law often provided strong incentives to work, not to retire. These incentives, they argued, frequently cancelled and sometime outweighed the disincentive effects of the benefit reduction rate.

The authors began by examining a simple one-period model in which the Social Security benefits of an eligible worker are reduced by 50 percent of any earnings over the exempt amount. When this tax is added to income taxes, it appears to provide a very strong disincentive to work, since the employee keeps so little of the gross pay. But, as we explained above, this analysis misses a key point. Unlike income taxes, Social Security contributions result in higher future benefits. If the present discounted value of these future benefit increments equals the benefits "taxed" away today, then the system is actuarially fair, and the earnings test, though still on the books, is irrelevant. If the losses are more than offset, then the tax becomes a subsidy, and additional work is encouraged by the Social Security rules, not discouraged as frequently thought.

The determination of the incentives actually faced by an individual is complicated. It depends on a number of factors, including the discount rate, the age of the potential retiree, and the presence and age of a spouse and dependent children. Blinder, Gordon, and Wise calculated the actuarial adjustment (delayed retirement credit) and benefit recalculation (AIME) incentives separately. They first asked whether the actuarial adjustment compensated for the 50 percent earnings test. Using real discount rates of 1 and 3 percent and analyzing five hypothetical 62-year-old individuals, they concluded that the actuarial adjustment made up about one to one-and-a-half times the amount of the earnings test loss—the latter, obviously, turning the earnings test tax into a subsidy. At age 65, when the delayed retirement credit drops from about 7 to 3 percent per year of delay, only 10 to 60 percent of the loss was returned. The percentage of the earnings-test loss returned in the future is higher for the married individual, if the spouse does not claim Social Security benefits on the basis of his or her own record, and declines with the age of the spouse and with the presence of dependent children. But the important point is that, with rare exceptions, the true earnings-test tax was not 50 percent.

In addition, according to the authors, the benefit recalculation rules after the 1977 amendments provided additional wage subsidies as well. For the average 65-year-old married male in their sample (drawn from the Retirement History Study), the subsidy was between one-third and one-half of the wage, depending on the discount rate used. For their average 65-year-old single man, the subsidy was about a sixth of the wage.

Blinder, Gordon, and Wise did not combine the two parts of their analysis—the actuarial adjustment and the benefit recalculation. They concluded that "the earnings test for social security does not present a work disincentive for the typical worker aged 62-64 because, if he loses benefits to the earnings test, he recoups most or even more than all of them through an actuarial adjustment of his future benefits." When the estimated wage subsidy in the benefit recalculation formula is included, they claimed that "it seems likely that the social security law—*if understood by the public*—should provide work disincentives for only a small minority of individuals. It seems that social security should induce the majority of older workers to work harder."

Gordon and Blinder (1980) continued this line of research with a major empirical analysis of the retirement decisions of a large sample of white males from the Retirement History Study. Because of their analysis above, their subsequent model assumed that Social Security was irrelevant to retirement decisions. They estimated a market wage rate for each person in the sample, from a wage equation, and then derived a reservation wage from an explicit utility function. Individuals work if their market wage exceeds their reservation wage and retire (withdraw from the labor force) when the reverse is true. Age, health, pension status, education, and demographic characteristics affect the retirement decision through their influences on the market and reservation wages.

The Gordon and Blinder model did well predicting the retirement behavior of respondents aged 58 to 61, almost as well for those 62 to 64, and not very well at all for those in the 65-to-67 age category. According to their estimates, age had a dramatic impact on the decision. In their base case, the retirement probability rose from 10 percent at age 61 to above 60 percent at 67. Health and market wages were also important. They found that "pension plans—with or without associated mandatory retirement provisions—provide powerful incentives to retire at the age of eligibility for the pension (normally 65)," and that "social security . . . has a much weaker effect (if any) on retirement decisions."

Despite the sophistication of the economic model and the econometric techniques, the derivation of the pension and Social Security variables was quite simple. The Social Security effect was not estimated directly because the authors were convinced that the incentive structure frequently favored work, not retirement. The pension variables, which were large and statistically significant at age 65, only denoted coverage. Gordon and Blinder assumed that the actuarial reductions for early pension acceptance were less than actuarially fair (encouraging early retirement), and that pensions decreased in present discounted value even further when one worked beyond the age of full eligibility (discouraging late retirement). But their dichotomous variables did not permit a test of this directly.

From these two important papers, the authors concluded that it "seems unlikely that the growth of the social security system, as impressive as it has been, has contributed much to the trend toward retirement" (Gordon and Blinder 1980). They acknowledged the remarkable coincidence of the growth of Social Security and the dramatic decline in retirement ages, as well as the small (at that time) body of econometric evidence linking the two trends, and conjectured

> that many people eligible for social security benefits may not understand how their current earnings affect their future benefits. It is possible, therefore, that social security is

discouraging labor supply only because its provisions are poorly understood (Blinder, Gordon, and Wise 1980).

These articles prompted a response from Richard Burkhauser and John Turner (1981) entitled "Can Twenty-Five Million Americans Be Wrong?" They agreed with the basic framework of analysis, that the impact of current earnings on future retirement benefits is the key issue. The forward-looking life-cycle model was gaining general acceptance. But Burkhauser and Turner faulted Blinder, Gordon, and Wise for not looking backwards in a life-cycle mode. Suppose, they said, that Blinder *et al.* were correct, that the actuarial adjustment and the benefit recalculation formula more than offset the 50 percent earnings test, and therefore that Social Security provides an earnings subsidy rather than a tax between the ages of 62 and 65. If so, then the benefit recalculation formula provides *an even larger subsidy* to wages prior to age 62, when it is in effect but the earnings test is not. In other words, current earnings are likely to increase the "average monthly earnings" on which benefits are based any time late in one's work career, and it is better to generate these earnings before age 62 rather than after. The earnings test decreases net compensation at age 62, and whether it is from a large subsidy to a small subsidy or from a subsidy to a tax is not important. In a full life-cycle framework, Burkhauser and Turner argued, the Social Security system encourages the substitution of early work for late work by tilting the relative wage profile toward the former.

As Blinder, Gordon, and Wise (1981) pointed out in a rejoinder, this final conclusion is valid only if the actuarial adjustment at age 62 is less than fair. At age 62, two changes occur—both the earnings test and the actuarial adjustment go into effect. If they just offset each other, and the benefit recalculation formula remains unchanged, then there is no intertemporal wage tilt. Therefore, much of the debate comes down to the actuarial fairness of the adjustment between ages 62 and 64. Everyone agrees that the adjustment after age 65 is inadequate. Whether it is prior to 65 remains a matter of dispute.

James Kahn (1988) has added a recent contribution to the debate. He maintains that the Blinder, Gordon, and Wise results are very sensitive to the interest rate used to discount future income streams, and argues that the appropriate rate is much higher than the 1 and 3 percent they chose. The reason is that many older people are liquidity-constrained because they cannot borrow against future Social Security benefits at market rates. If so, then these retirement income rights are worth less than they would be if they were more portable over time. At a higher discount rate, the future Social Security increments from continued work are less valuable and less likely to offset the immediate benefits foregone.

Kahn demonstrates that for a sample of men ineligible for an employer pension, the Social Security incentives are almost neutral between ages 62 and 64, when a 3-percent rate is used, but become strong work disincentives at 12 percent. He also shows that the retirement spike at age 62 is primarily low-wealth people, which is consistent with his liquidity-constraint story.

Early econometric work suggested that economic incentives can influence individual retirement decisions and that the nature of the incentives and their impact is complex. But this work had many flaws. Boskin and Hurd's analysis ignored pensions and the effect of additional work on Social Security wealth. Quinn studied the importance of pension and Social Security eligibility, but not the size of the benefits. Burkhauser introduced the concept of retirement income wealth to the microeconomic literature, but was not able to analyze Social Security and pension plans simultaneously. Gordon and Blinder's behavioral work assumed that Social Security did not affect the retirement decision and their data set was not amenable to easy extraction of pension benefit amounts. Work in the 1980s, to which we now turn, would address all of these early deficiencies.

NOTES

1. According to Packard and Reno (1989), 43 percent of American men claimed Social Security benefits at age 62 in 1985, including about 11 percent who were disabled. By age 64, nearly two-thirds of all men were receiving benefits. For women, including those receiving benefits as wives and widows, the percentages are even higher—well over half at age 62 and three-quarters by age 64.

2. An excellent review of this earlier literature can be found in Campbell and Campbell (1976). They discuss the literature through 1975—just about the time that modern microeconomists began to research the retirement decision. Boskin (1977) also includes a short overview of these issues.

3. Those who had previously been eligible for disabled-worker benefits were excluded from these calculations. Obviously, health would have been much more important among this group.

4. This categorization shows the difficult in differentiating between voluntary and involuntary retirements. If poor health induces someone to retire, which of the categories is it? The decision may be voluntary; the poor health is not. Packard and Reno list health reasons under involuntary, while Steiner and Dorfman call such retirements voluntary.

5. Research by Ransom and Sutch (1986), mentioned in chapter 1, casts some doubt on the validity of these figures, and suggests that labor force participation rates were approximately constant from the late nineteenth century through 1937. But this only strengthens the point being made, that the development of the Social Security and employer pension plans may have had a significant effect on aggregate retirement patterns.

6. In 1990, workers aged 62 through 64 can earn up to $6840 per year without any loss in Social Security benefits and they lose $1 in benefits for each $2 earned beyond that. For those 65 through 69, the exempt amount is $9360 and the benefit reduction rate is only one-third. At age 70, the earnings test disappears altogether and full benefits are paid regardless of earnings.

7. See, for example, Boskin (1977), Quinn (1977), and Hall and Johnson (1980).

8. See Burkhauser and Warlick (1981) and Moffitt (1984) for discussions of the returns to the Social Security "investment" by cohort.

9. All of the relevant rules and regulations, from the beginning of the program to the present, as well as those already legislated for the future, can be found in the *Annual Statistical Supplement* to the *Social Security Bulletin*.

10. See Kahn (1988) and Burtless and Moffitt (1984) for dramatic illustrations of this circumstantial evidence.

11. A very detailed summary and review of the recent literature, with an emphasis on theoretical issues, can be found in Mitchell and Fields (1982).

12. Boskin attributed the larger Social Security effect to three factors: (1) Social Security benefits are guaranteed until death and fully indexed against inflation; (2) they cannot be bequeathed to heirs; and (3) income from assets includes imputed rent on owner-occupied housing, an asset against which Boskin argues, the elderly are reluctant to borrow.

13. Respondents who were either bedridden or housebound were excluded from the sample. The health variable was based on the answer to the question, "Does your health limit the kind or amount of work or housework you can do?" Although this is a subjective assessment of health, the question was not asked in conjunction with reasons for retirement.

14. It now seems clear that this result is due to the exclusion of an important variable—some measure of the *size* of the retirement benefits for which the respondent is eligible. Higher benefits should induce retirement if we hold all other factors constant. But benefit levels are positively correlated with earnings, since Social Security and many pensions base benefits, even if loosely, on earnings history. The wage rate variable, then, was probably picking up its own positive effect on the probability of remaining at work *and* the negative effect of the higher pension benefits. The two effects approximately cancelled. As we will see below, when some measure of the benefit magnitudes is included, the wage or earnings coefficients are generally significant and of the expected sign.

– 3 –

Retirement Incentives
and the
Retirement Decision

The Current Literature

During the 1980s, there was a dramatic increase in economic research on retirement issues. As we discussed in chapter 1, there are several reasons for this. The nation is aging. The proportion of the population aged 65 and over will continue to grow well into the next century, rising from near 12 percent today to about 20 percent by the year 2030. The ratio of those aged 18 to 64 to those over 64 will decrease from five to three. This change in the basic age structure, combined with the trend toward earlier retirement, has threatened the financial well-being of the Social Security system. The hearings, recommendations, and subsequent legislation prompted by the National Commission on Social Security Reform (the Greenspan Commission) put Social Security on the front page, and concern about demographic trends and the federal budget deficit has kept it there.

The confluence of public interest and the availability of extraordinarily rich data sets have led to a significant increase in retirement research. In this chapter, we will review this modern research and summarize where we now stand. We will try to describe the general framework, the unique contributions, and the qualitative conclusions of some of the major figures in the field.

The research strategies fall into two general classes. Most authors have chosen to utilize the strengths of two large microeconomic data sets—the Social Security Administration's Retirement History Study (RHS) and the National Longitudinal Surveys (NLS), developed by the U. S. Department of Labor and the Center for Human Resource Research at The Ohio State University. These sources provide large representative samples of older Americans and a wealth of demographic, social, economic, and financial data on each respondent. A major drawback of both, however, is the paucity of private pension details. Employer pensions are complicated agreements, and these data sets do not begin to capture the complexities of the individual plans.

This problem suggests an alternative research strategy—to dig much deeper into the details of a small number of specific plans and analyze the impact of particular plan features. Much of this work is based on the Benefit Amounts Survey, a data set developed by the Department of Labor from summary descriptions submitted by individual pension plans. These data include the specific benefit calculation rules missing from the micro data sets above. Their disadvantages are the smaller, nonrepresentative samples of recipients and the lack of much other information on the individuals involved.[1] With this research strategy, we learn much more about pensions and much less about everything else.

In a recent paper, Alan Gustman and Thomas Steinmeier (1989b) report on a data set that combines some of the advantages of both approaches above. They use the 1983 Survey of Consumer Finances, which includes a national random sample of over 4,200 households and information on pension plan details supplied by the providers. Unfortunately, the demographic information is not as complete as in the RHS or the NLS. In addition, since the data set is not specifically designed to study the retirement process, there are fewer older workers than in the two other sources. The survey is well-designed for studying pension incentives, but less applicable for studying their impact on retirement behavior.

Retirement Incentives and Mandatory Retirement

In several 1983 articles, Richard Burkhauser and Joseph Quinn (1983a,b; Quinn and Burkhauser 1983) described the Social Security and pension incentives facing a sample of older Americans and estimated their impact on individual retirement behavior. The initial focus of this research was mandatory retirement. The 1978 amendments to the Age Discrimination in Employment Act (ADEA) raised from 65 to 70 the earliest age at which most Americans could be forced to retire solely because of age. Subsequent legislation has virtually eliminated mandatory retirement altogether.[2] The research question was whether the 1978 change would dramatically alter the trend towards earlier retirement. Casual empiricism suggested that it would, but more careful analysis indicated that it would not. Although mandatory retirement provisions severely constrained the options of certain individuals, the rules were relatively unimportant in the aggregate.

The crux of the issue is that mandatory retirement, Social Security and employer pensions are all closely intertwined. Since they all can influence the retirement decision, it is essential to isolate their individual effects. When this is done, much of what looks like a mandatory retirement effect is, in fact, due to the incentives embedded in the retirement income programs. Financial incentives and mandatory retirement turn out to be a carrot and a stick—alternative means to the same end.

Mandatory Retirement, Social Security and Pensions

Mandatory retirement rules were widespread prior to the 1978 ADEA amendments. They applied to between one-third and one-half of American workers approaching retirement age. For example, of the men and nonmarried women in the Retirement History Study who were aged 58 to 61 and employed in 1969 (the year of the initial survey), 43 percent faced a mandatory retirement age on the job they held. Using three other data sources gathered at about the same time, Janice Halpern (1978) estimated that between 30 and 46 percent of older workers had jobs with compulsory retirement

A simple comparison of the behavior of those with and without mandatory retirement suggested a large impact. Using later waves of the RHS, Burkhauser and Quinn (1983b) followed a sample of men aged 62 to 64 and employed in 1973. Some faced mandatory retirement over the next two years and others did not. Of those who did not, 57 percent were still working in 1975—the remaining 43 percent had withdrawn from the labor force. But of those who *did* face mandatory retirement, 83 percent had left the labor force, and only 17 percent remained at work. The contrast between 17 and 57 percent indicates a large potential retirement effect.

But coincidence does not imply causation. Those with and without mandatory retirement had very different probabilities of pension coverage on that job. Of the RHS respondents who faced mandatory retirement during the subsequent two years, 94 percent were also eligible to collect pension benefits, and most during those same two years. Of those facing mandatory retirement after that two-year period, nearly 90 percent enjoyed pension eligibility. In contrast, fewer than half of those without mandatory retirement would ever collect employer pension benefits from their current jobs. Pensions and mandatory retirement went hand-in-hand. Although there were many individuals with a pension and without mandatory retirement, the converse was very rare.

The relationship between mandatory retirement and Social Security was also very close. Sixty-five was the most popular age for compulsory retirement, and that is precisely the age at which workers became eligible for full Social Security benefits. Sixty-five is also the age at which the delayed retirement credit drops dramatically, from about 7 percent per year of delay between ages 62 and 64 to only 3 percent (and this was only 1 percent prior to 1982).

To disaggregate the effects of Social Security, pensions, and mandatory retirement, as well as all the other determinants of the individual retirement decision, one must first describe and quantify the retirement incentives and then estimate their effects in a behavioral model. The first part of this is difficult for several reasons. Retirement income plans are usually complex. They differ in coverage criteria, ages of eligibility, benefit calculation rules, delayed retirement credits, and inflation protection after retirement. Even if we knew all these details, which we usually do not, we would have to decide how to utilize them in empirical research—which are important and should be included in a summary measure of retirement incentives and which should be ignored.

Fortunately, the RHS has appended to its own data the entire Social Security Administration earnings record (through 1975) for each of the respondents. (This creates the odd situation in which the researcher probably knows more about the individual's Social Security incentives than the individual making the decision does!) With respect to employer pensions, however, we are much less fortunate. The RHS does include questions about the extent and age of eligibility and the size of the annual benefit, but other key details are unknown. In addition, answers to the pension questions are sometimes incomplete, and, in the case of expected pension amounts, frequently so.

Problems with the RHS pension data have discouraged many researchers from utilizing these benefits estimates. A major contribution of the Burkhauser and Quinn research was an attempt to squeeze pension benefit information from every possible source in the longitudinal questionnaires.

Social Security and Pension Incentives

We argued in chapter 2 that the best measure of the value of retirement income rights is the present discounted value of the stream of future benefits—the asset or wealth equivalent. Unlike the annual benefit or the replacement rate, the present value incorporates into one number the age of eligibility, the size of the annual flow, life expectancy and, via the discount rate, the amount of inflation protection after retirement.[3] The value is positive prior to the age of eligibility, which is consistent with a life-cycle view of decisionmaking.

In their empirical work, Burkhauser and Quinn calculated, for Social Security and employer pensions separately, two measures of retirement income incentives—WEALTH and DELTA. WEALTH was merely the present discounted value mentioned above; i.e.,

$$\text{WEALTH}(s) = \sum_{i=s}^{T} (p_i B_i(s)) / (1+r)^i,$$

where p_i is the probability of living through period i, r is the discount rate, T is the age (assumed to be 100) at which the probability of survival drops to zero, and $B_i(s)$ is the annual benefit associated with a pension accepted in period s.[4] The (s) in the expression WEALTH(s) is a reminder that the value of the pension depends on when it is first claimed. This leads directly to the other retirement income incentive, DELTA.

DELTA is the *change* in retirement income wealth that accompanies an additional year of work. When an individual works another year, there is bad news and good news with respect to pensions. The bad news is that a year's worth of pension benefits is foregone. The good news is that future annual benefits may be higher. Whether the asset value of the stream rises or falls depends on whether the increments tomorrow are sufficient to offset the losses today.

DELTA is the change in wealth from one period (s) to the next (s + 1) following an additional year of work; i.e.,

$$DELTA(s) = WEALTH(s + 1) - WEALTH(s) - C(s)$$

where C(s) is the worker's contribution to the plan during the year of work (and equals zero in noncontributing plans). A positive DELTA denotes an increase in Social Security or pension wealth, and, in essence, a wage subsidy. A negative DELTA is a wealth loss—the equivalent of a wage decrease.

For Social Security, WEALTH and DELTA estimates were relatively easy to obtain because the RHS includes actual Social Security records and the exact benefit calculation rules are known.[5] In the derivation of WEALTH(s + 1), workers were assumed to earn the same real wages in year (s + 1) as in year (s). These were added to the earnings records, and the streams of benefits and their present discounted values were then recalculated.

Pension derivations were much more difficult. The first problem was to find the annual amount for which a respondent was or would be eligible.[6] Even with these figures, Burkhauser and Quinn (1983a) still did not know the details of the individuals' pension plans. In order to estimate how annual benefits would change if the respondent worked another year, they assumed

    (a)   the pension plans did not include a joint-and-survivor provision,

    (b)   the benefit amount was based on years of service, so that it increased by [1/n], where n is years of tenure with the current firm, and

(c)   for those eligible for reduced but not full benefits, the benefit amount also increased by an actuarial adjustment.

In the absence of plan-specific information, one-digit industry averages for these adjustments were used, from data in the Bureau of Labor Statistic's Level of Benefits Study. For those respondents who stated that they were already eligible for full benefits, no additional actuarial adjustment was assumed.

With these assumptions, the authors calculated the asset values of Social Security and employer pension claims (and changes in these values with continued work) for the Retirement History Study sample. These assets, though ignored in traditional definitions of wealth, turn out to dominate the portfolios of older Americans. For three-quarters of a sample of RHS men aged 62 to 67 in 1973 (just after several large increases in real Social Security benefits), Quinn (1985) found that retirement income wealth exceeded all other forms of wealth, including equity in the home.[7] Wolff (1987) has confirmed these qualitative results. With slightly earlier data, he estimated that Social Security and pension wealth constituted about 30 percent of total wealth for those aged 65 and over in 1969.

For the mandatory retirement study, Burkhauser and Quinn (1983b) drew a sample of full-time, private-sector men (not self-employed) aged 63 to 65 in 1974. About two-thirds of them had employer pension wealth from a current or previous job. The median value for those with positive pension wealth (using a 5 percent discount rate) was about $21,000 (all figures in 1974 dollars)—slightly more than twice the median annual wage earnings at the time.

For workers aged 63, the pension DELTAs were almost equally split between positive (gains) and negative (losses) values; the median value, therefore, was close to zero. But by age 64, the losers outnumbered the gainers, and the median pension wealth loss accompanying another year of work was over $1,100. At age 65, there were almost no gainers, and the median loss had risen to over $2,000. Six percent of those aged 65 would have lost over $5,000 in pension wealth from an additional year of work and another 8 percent, between $3,000 and $5,000.

The WEALTH and DELTA figures for Social Security were much more dramatic. Coverage was nearly universal, and the value of most people's Social Security rights far exceeded their pension wealth. At a 5 percent discount rate, 70 percent of the sample had Social Security wealth over $50,000.

The change in this wealth following an incremental year of work depends crucially on an individual's age, because the Social Security delayed retirement credit drops at age 65. For respondents aged 63 and 64, the Social Security rules generally provided a net subsidy to work. Those who remained employed received a paycheck *and* an increase in retirement wealth. The median annual gains were about $1,850 at age 63 and $850 at 64. But at age 65, nearly everyone lost because of the inadequate actuarial adjustment—only 1 percent prior to 1982. The median loss was over $3,000.

Are these wealth changes large or small? Since they are part of compensation—a pay raise or a pay cut—they should be compared to annual earnings. For those eligible for Social Security alone, the results mirrored the story above—on average, modest gains occurred at ages 63 and 64, and dramatic losses at 65. The estimates suggested a median loss at age 65 of about a third of gross earnings. When the pension DELTAs are added for those eligible for both, the median loss at age 65 rose to almost half of gross pay—a hefty pay cut indeed.

These are only rough estimates, because they ignore taxes and implicitly assume that full-time workers lose all of their Social Security benefits. (In fact, some low-wage workers may be able to work full time and still collect all or part of their Social Security benefits.) Nonetheless, they indicate that the financial incentives embedded in retirement income programs can be large. Older workers can suffer severe wage cuts, not because the paycheck is reduced but because Social Security and pension wealth decrease with continued work. Economic theory suggests that workers should respond to this abrupt change in compensation and that some who found work worthwhile at the previous rate of pay will not after the decrease. These workers will leave the job and retire.

But do they? Do older Americans understand and respond to these incentives? Although the concepts are not difficult, the actual calculations are. Is there evidence that those facing large wealth losses (DELTAs) are more likely to retire than those who are not?

Retirement Behavior

Burkhauser and Quinn (1983b) found that there is evidence for this effect. They attempted to explain job transitions over time—who did and who did not leave the labor force over a two-year period (1973 to 1975). Their explanatory variables included the retirement incentives discussed above, as well as changes in health status, earnings potential on the job, and marital status. The empirical results indicated that health deterioration during the two-year period increased the probability of retirement, but that marital status and mandatory retirement in the future (after 1975) were relatively unimportant. The financial variables all had the correct signs, and all but one were statistically significant. Higher earnings, *ceteris paribus,* discouraged retirement. Pension wealth and both Social Security and pension DELTAs encouraged it.[8] The higher the wealth loss associated with continued work (the higher the implicit pay cut), the higher the probability that the individual left the labor force and retired.

Mandatory Retirement

As was mentioned above, those with and without mandatory retirement during the two-year period under study behaved very differently. Those with this constraint were much more likely to leave the labor force. But they were also more likely to have employer pensions and therefore to face pension wealth losses if they continued to work. In addition, nearly all faced negative work incentives from the decrease in the Social Security delayed retirement credit at age 65. To what extent were the differences in behavior due to the existence of the mandatory retirement provision and to what extent were they due to the coincident financial incentives?

To tackle this question, Burkhauser and Quinn (1983b) used a job-exit equation, estimated on those who were *not* subject to mandatory retirement over the two-year period, to predict the retirement behavior of those who were. They intentionally ignored that fact that the latter *did* in fact face mandatory retirement and asked what proportion would have retired anyway, because of their health and the financial incentives they faced. The estimate was that 63 percent would have retired. In fact, 83 percent did, compared to only 43 percent of those without mandatory retirement. In other words, about half of the total difference in behavior (43 to 83 percent) could be explained by factors other than mandatory retirement.[9] The remaining half was due to mandatory retirement and to other factors that they were not able to include.[10]

As a final point, the authors estimated the total number of persons aged 63–65 whose retirement behavior would have changed if mandatory retirement at age 65 had been outlawed in 1973, as it was five years later. The estimate was small—about 50,000 men.[11] This would have created a modest increase in the labor force participation rate of that cohort, and an almost imperceptible increase in the labor supply as a whole. Mandatory retirement was much less important than it appeared.[12]

Conclusion

This research suggests that the concepts of retirement income wealth and changes in this wealth are very useful. An individual with high pension benefits may feel induced to retire or to continue working, depending on how the future benefit stream varies with the decision. Neither the current annual benefit nor the replacement rate can capture these important incentives. Only by describing these retirement rights as assets—present discounted values—can one describe and quantify these factors and estimate the magnitude of their effects.

Social Security and many employer pension plans eventually create large financial incentives for a worker to leave a job. Empirical evidence on the actual behavior of a large sample of older American men indicates that they behave as though they understand and respond to these factors. By no means do these factors (or any of the factors that researchers have been able to measure) explain all of the behavior. But they do explain some of it.

This is important for several reasons. First, it appears that one variable that looked very significant—mandatory retirement—is really not so.[13] The elimination of these rules will be important to certain individuals who would have been forced to leave their jobs at some arbitrary age, but should have little impact in the aggregate.[14] Second, we now see that there are alternative means to the same end. Employers can influence retirement patterns with the carrot (financial incentives) as well as with the stick (a compulsory retirement age).[15] A major advantage of the carrot is that those who really want to continue to work are able to. And finally, these findings suggest that retirement trends are not exogenous. They depend on the incentives built into our Social Security and pension systems—incentives that discourage work at age 65, if not sooner. It is no wonder that so few Americans work beyond age 65. Those who do pay dearly for their choice.

Optimal Retirement Age

In a series of recent articles, Gary Burtless (1986, 1987), Robert Moffitt (1984, 1987), and Burtless and Moffitt (1984, 1985, 1986) have made significant advances in the theoretical and econometric analysis of the retirement decision. The major focus of their work is the determination of the optimal age of retirement and the optimal labor supply afterwards. They adopt a life-cycle model of work and consumption and emphasize the nonlinear nature of the budget constraints faced by older Americans.

Retirement Age and Hours of Work

Workers contemplating retirement face budget constraint kinks (nonlinearities) along two dimensions. These dimensions correspond to the major decision variables that Burtless and Moffitt study—retirement age and post-retirement hours of work. As all modern analysts of these issues agree, the choice of the optimal retirement age is complicated by Social Security and private pension incentives. If leisure is a good, then the loss of leisure during an additional year of work lowers an individual's utility. But the increased income earned makes additional consumption possible, which increases utility. In their words, an individual stops working "when the marginal disutility of another year of work is just equal to the marginal utility arising from the consumption that can be financed by the added work" (Burtless and Moffitt 1985).

Their work emphasizes the impact of Social Security on the retirement decision and they delve in great detail into benefit calculation rules. When considering the budget constraint over potential retirement ages, they find nonlinearities at ages 62, 65, and 72 (now 70, when the earnings test disappears), all created by the impact of additional work on the asset value of future Social Security benefits. Because of these kinks, they expect a clustering of retirements at age 65, and depending on the actuarial fairness of the adjustment between 62 and 65, perhaps at age 62 as well.

Burtless and Moffitt have defined retirement as a sudden and discontinuous drop in hours worked, not as complete labor force withdrawal.[16] Under this definition, retired workers can continue to work, and this decision is part of their analysis.[17] When one considers the budget constraint over the number of hours in a given year, another nonlinearity appears. Social Security rules allow a certain exempt amount of earnings—in 1990, $6,840 for those 62 to 64 years old; $9,360 for those 65 to 69—before benefits are reduced by the earnings test. After that amount, benefits are reduced by 50 percent (for those 62 to 64) or 33 percent (for those 65 to 69) of all incremental earnings until they are reduced to zero.[18] In essence, the net hourly wage drops after the exempt amount is earned, and a kink appears (see point C in figure 2.2). (The point at which this happens is different for each individual since it depends on the wage rate.) If potential retirees do not fully understand the impact of benefit recalculation on their Social Security wealth and view the earnings test as a real tax, then Burtless and Moffitt would expect to find earnings of the retired clustered around the exempt amount.

Using a sample of men from the Retirement History Study, the authors found clear evidence of both types of clustering. As seen in figure 3.1, men were most likely to retire at ages 65 and 62. Over a quarter retired

Figure 3.1
Frequency Distribution of Retirement Ages

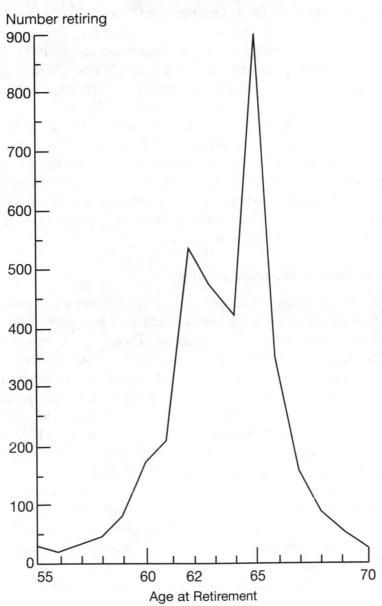

SOURCE: Burtless and Moffitt (1984), p. 154.

at 65, the age at which the delayed retirement credit drops and a significant kink occurs. This is ''consistent with the pronounced incentive to retire at that age in the Social Security benefit formula'' (Burtless and Moffitt 1985). The clustering at 62 is more difficult to explain, since the convexity in the budget constraint is much less severe, if it exists at all. This clustering could be due to ignorance of the benefit recalculation rules or to liquidity constraints—the inability to borrow against future income in order to consume (or retire) today.[19]

Figure 3.2 provides evidence of clustering around the exempt earnings amount. Of the retirees still working, over a quarter were found to be earning between 90 and 110 percent of the exempt amount, and many more were just below the 90 than are just above the 110.[20] Burtless and Moffitt found these results to be strong confirmation of their model's predictions. They then proceeded to estimate the parameters of their comprehensive life-cycle model.

Determinants of Retirement Behavior

The Burtless and Moffitt model contains two other distinctive features. Their specification allows the influence of Social Security benefits to differ from that of other unearned income. There are two reasons for this. Social Security wealth is less liquid than other assets, especially before retirement. For example, one cannot pledge future Social Security receipts as loan collateral. This may make Social Security less valuable than an equivalent amount of other wealth. On the other hand, Social Security benefits are fully indexed for inflation, by law since 1972 and by custom before then. Unlike other assets, they are not subject to the uncertainties of inflation, housing, bond or equity markets, or the state of the economy in general. For this reason, Social Security wealth may have a larger impact on behavior. Burtless and Moffitt permitted the effects to differ and the relative importance to vary over the age of the respondent. In addition, the authors allowed the propensity to retire to vary directly with age, independent of age's effect on the budget constraint. They expected retirement probabilities to increase with age, other factors held constant.

Figure 3.2
Distribution of Retirement Earnings Among Working Retirees

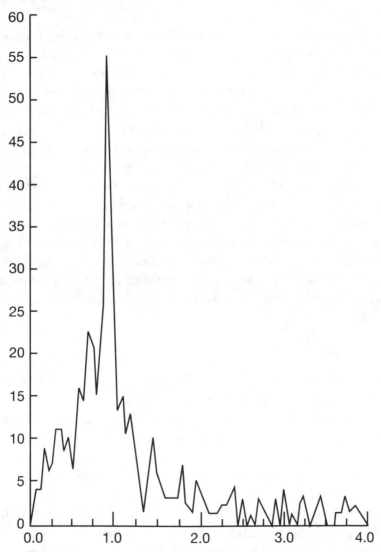

Number of observations

Earnings as a fraction of Social Security exempt amount

SOURCE: Burtless and Moffitt (1984), p. 156.

The parameters of the retirement age and retirement hours equations were generally consistent with economic theory. Respondents in poor health tended to retire earlier, as did nonwhites and those with poor educational backgrounds.[21] As expected, retirement probabilities did increase with age.

The financial results were reasonable. Workers with higher preretirement wages were found to retire slightly earlier, suggesting an income effect stronger than the substitution effect. Postretirement wages were positively associated with postretirement hours of work, but the elasticity was very small. Workers vested in a pension plan were found to delay retirement. This somewhat puzzling result may reflect pension benefit rules that encourage delayed retirement. Workers were found to retire earlier the higher the level of potential retirement income.

The results on the relative Social Security impact were very interesting. The relative effect of Social Security wealth compared to that of other assets went from zero prior to age 57 (perhaps due to high personal discount rates or the low liquidity of this asset) to 1.0 by age 59, 3.8 at 62, and 5.0 by age 65 (Burtless and Moffitt 1984). These final ratios seem unbelievably high, but the evidence does suggest that the impact does change, with Social Security becoming more and more important over time.

Conclusions

This research, as all research, has its shortcomings. The Burtless and Moffitt treatment of pensions is inadequate. They were unable to model how pension benefits changed with delayed retirement—an issue that is central to the life-cycle framework. In addition, the sophisticated econometric techniques have both advantages and disadvantages. The parameter estimates have desirable statistical properties, but are difficult to interpret.

Nonetheless, these papers represent a very important contribution to the field. Burtless and Moffitt have integrated the analysis of both the retirement age and the retirement hours decisions. Their model is consistent with the observed clustering of retirement ages at 62 and 65, as well as the clustering of postretirement earnings near the Social Security exempt amount. And they find evidence of statistically significant, though small, Social Security effects on both retirement age and subsequent labor supply.[22]

The Incentives of Specific Pension Plans

In a book and a series of related articles, Gary Fields and Olivia Mitchell (1984a, 1984b, 1984c), and Mitchell and Fields (1984, 1985) have made major contributions to understanding the retirement decision. Their work differs from most of the literature in two important ways. They are among a small number of researchers who have chosen to delve deeply into the details of a number of specific pension plans. By doing so, they have been able to document the wide variety of retirement incentives that American workers actually face. The precision of their estimates far surpasses what anyone using the limited pension information available in the Retirement History Study or the National Longitudinal Survey could hope to achieve. In addition, they have attempted to calculate the retirement incentives facing a worker in each and every possible retirement year in a planning horizon, rather than in just a specific year or two.

Mitchell and Fields are interested in explaining the age of retirement, and they have generally ignored the issue of labor supply afterwards. Their model "assumes that the optimal pattern is to work full time and then retire" (Fields and Mitchell 1984c). When using the Retirement History Study sample, they defined retirement as departure from a primary job, and assumed that the job held in 1969 (the first year of the RHS) was the primary job. When using the specific pension plan data described below, they defined the age of retirement as the age of pension receipt.

The authors' theoretical model is very much in the life-cycle tradition. The worker looks ahead over a planning horizon and chooses when to retire. The individual's goal is to maximize personal utility, which depends on the consumption of goods and leisure. There is a tradeoff between goods and leisure, because continued work increases lifetime income (and therefore goods), but decreases lifetime leisure.

Earnings, Social Security, and Pensions

The choice of retirement age is affected by three key variables in the Fields and Mitchell model: future earnings, future Social Security receipts, and future pension benefits. Lifetime earnings obviously rise with delayed retirement. Social Security and pensions are more complicated, since each year of continued work means a loss of retirement benefits during that year, but (usually) higher annual benefits in the future.

Mitchell and Fields' strategy is to calculate the present discounted value of the earnings (net of Social Security and income taxes), Social Security and pension streams that would accrue with each possible retirement date over a nine-year planning horizon—from age 60 to 68. They then sum these three values to obtain the present discounted value of the total income stream (PDVY) for each potential retirement age. A major contribution is the method by which the pension data were obtained.

Rather than rely on the limited pension benefit data in the RHS or the NLS, Fields and Mitchell drew a sample of workers from 14 actual defined benefit plans from the Labor Department's 1978 Benefit Amounts Survey (BAS).[23] In addition to having some basic demographic data and the entire Social Security earnings records of the workers in the sample, they had the exact formulas used to calculate pension benefits. They ended up with a sample of nearly 9,000 workers who retired between the ages of 60 and 68 and who had complete data on retirement age, tenure with the firm, and Social Security covered earnings.

The authors' research strategy required them to forecast what workers aged 60 around 1970 thought their earnings, Social Security, and pension benefits would have been had they decided to retire at each age from then to age 68.[24] Future real earnings were estimated on the basis of individual-specific earnings equations. Future Social Security benefits were based on the 1972 Social Security rules, which had already been legislated in 1970. The authors assumed that workers would have expected continued annual real increases of the magnitude that had occurred during the 1960s—about 3 percent per year.

Initial pension amounts were based on the individual plans' benefit calculation rules in effect in 1970, and were then assumed to increase in real terms, prior to retirement, at whatever annual real rate of increase the plan had experienced during the 1960s. In five of the plans, benefits were held constant in nominal terms after retirement. In the others, postretirement increases had occurred in the past and were assumed to continue in the future. The earnings, Social Security, and pension streams were then multiplied by the appropriate survival probabilities and discounted at a 2 percent real rate of interest.

The present values of the pension streams for an identical illustrative worker in each of the 14 plans appear in table 3.1. In all cases, the PDV of the pension stream began to decrease at some age. But there was considerable variety in the asset profiles over time.[25]

Mitchell and Fields differentiated between pattern and conventional pension plans. In pattern plans, common in union agreements, the annual benefit is almost exclusively a function of the years of service with the firm. Conventional plans use both years of service and final salary (often over the last few years on the job) in determining initial benefits.

As seen in table 3.1, the pattern plans were generally structured to encourage early retirement. Four of the six plans peaked in the initial year of eligibility (age 60), one peaked at age 62, and one peaked at 65. After the maximum, an individual lost pension wealth with every single year of delayed retirement. In one case (Plan E), the losses were extreme; the value of the pension at age 68 was only 42 percent of its value at age 60. Conventional plans, with their emphasis on final earnings, were more likely to encourage work after age 60. Only one plan peaked at age 60. Far more common was growth through age 65 and decline thereafter.

Olivia Mitchell and Rebecca Luzadis (1988) traced changes in the retirement incentives in these 14 defined benefit plans between 1960 and 1980. They found that the incentives in the four United Auto Worker plans had changed dramatically. In 1960, the present discounted value

Table 3.1
Present Values of Net Private Pension Benefits for Alternative Retirement Ages: Plan-Level Data

| | | | | If retirement age occurs at age | | | | | |
	60	61	62	63	64	65	66	67	68
				A. Pattern Plans					
UAW plans									
Plan A	$28,181	$27,586	$27,189	$25,455	$23,787	$22,195	$21,706	$21,140	$20,500
Plan B	36,030	36,146	36,599	36,341	35,730	34,987	34,081	--	--
Plan C	28,176	27,571	27,189	25,455	23,787	22,195	--	--	--
Plan D	28,176	27,571	27,189	25,455	23,787	22,195	21,706	21,140	20,500
Non-UAW plans									
Plan E	21,858	19,814	17,912	16,147	14,512	13,001	11,608	10,328	9,153
Plan F	6,351	6,464	6,641	6,850	6,986	7,079	6,620	6,156	5,692
				B. Conventional Plans					
Plan G	0	0	9,300	10,027	10,087	10,497	9,461	8,891	7,951
Plan H	13,527	14,176	20,471	19,364	18,173	16,869	--	--	--
Plan I	16,410	16,709	16,841	16,977	17,028	16,893	--	--	--
Plan J	20,012	20,256	20,270	19,335	18,359	17,246	16,190	15,081	13,841
Plan K	14,851	15,079	15,290	15,504	16,318	17,174	16,563	15,866	15,109
Plan L	17,671	19,669	21,594	23,468	25,295	26,981	--	--	--
Plan M	16,526	17,042	17,668	18,291	18,810	19,084	--	--	--
Plan N	19,491	17,254	15,193	14,230	13,742	13,198	12,605	11,592	10,950

SOURCE: Mitchell and Fields (1985), p. 283.
NOTE: This table is based on pension algorithms as applied to illustrative worker; see source text. Underlined numbers are row maxima. Dashes indicate retirement is mandatory in that plan at that age.

of the benefit stream increased with delayed retirement up through age 65, thereby discouraging early retirement. In both 1970 and 1980, however, pension wealth peaked at age 60, and declined with each year of additional work after that.

In four other union plans, the peak in pension wealth occurred at age 65 in 1960 and 1970, but had moved to 62 by 1980. In six nonunion plans, the peak was at age 65 in all three years. In this small sample of union plans, then, the incentives changed significantly, from discouraging early retirement in 1960 to actively encouraging it two decades later. In later work with 83 defined benefit plans, Luzadis and Mitchell (1989) presented preliminary evidence that employer pensions did indeed respond to changes in the retirement environment—in particular, to changes in mandatory retirement legislation, Employee Retirement Income Security Act (ERISA) regulation, and Social Security benefit calculation rules. The carrot replaced the stick.

Richard Ippolito (1990) demonstrates the same trends. He documents the dramatic increase over the last several decades in the number of pension plans that offered reduced (and usually actuarially subsidized) benefits at age 55 or full benefits prior to age 65. Using data from several sources, he estimates that the percentage of male workers eligible for full benefits prior to age 65 increased from almost none in 1965 to 15 percent in 1985.

Alan Gustman and Thomas Steinmeier (1989a) have shown that, because of the service requirements in many defined benefit plans, the age at which pension wealth peaks depends on when the worker joined the firm. The later one has joined, the later the wealth peaks. In other words, plans often provide less incentive for long-term employees to keep working than they do for more recent hires of the same age. Their work confirms the view that there is an extremely wide variety of work incentives embedded in pension plans and suggests that, because of service requirements, knowing just the worker's age and the dates of early and normal retirement may not be enough to calculate true compensation accurately.

Work Incentives

These pension values are only one-third of the financial story. Workers must also consider earnings on the job and the asset value of their Social Security benefits. Social Security may be close to actuarially fair between 62 and 65, but is definitely less than fair after that. The Social Security wealth losses after age 65 compound the pension losses documented above and offset some of the earnings from continued work.

Fields and Mitchell (1984a) have analyzed the incentive structure, by year of retirement, facing 390 men in one of their plans (Plan A).[26] As seen in the averages in table 3.2, the present value of earnings rose with each year of delayed retirement. The asset value of the pension rights declined monotonically and lost about one-quarter of their value by age 68. Social Security rights rose in value through age 65, and then declined. The net result of all three of these factors is seen in row 7. Several conclusions are apparent. The present discounted value of lifetime income always rises with delayed retirement because earnings exceed the losses in retirement wealth. An income or wealth maximizer would never retire for financial reasons. But a utility maximizer might. The true net annual compensation (the *change* in lifetime income) declined steadily, from about $7,500 (1970 dollars) at age 60 to less than $3,000 at age 68. This was not due to declines in the paycheck, but rather to losses of Social Security and pension wealth.[27]

In another paper (1984b), the authors did an analogous experiment, using the 1982 Social Security laws and a sample drawn from the RHS. Their pension figures were much less reliable here. In fact, they were not based on the pension data available in the RHS, but rather on industrywide averages of benefit amounts. The same qualitative conclusions appeared. Lifetime income rose with continued work, but by smaller and smaller amounts. The true earnings of an illustrative worker at age 61 were over $17,500 (1982 dollars). This decreased to less than $10,000 at age 65 (when Social Security wealth declines begin), and dropped further to nearly $6,000 at age 67. The worker's true compensation declined with each additional year of work, with a particularly severe cut at age 65.

Table 3.2
Expected Future Income Opportunities as Viewed From Age 60
(in 1970 dollars)

	If retirement occurred at age								
	60	61	62	63	64	65	66	67	68
Annual amounts									
(1) Net earnings	0	7,302	7,503	7,549	7,450	7,430	7,399	8,471	7,295
(2) First year's net private pension	3,140	3,157	3,513	3,487	3,451	2,449	2,608	2,775	2,953
(3) First year's Social Security benefit[a]	1,904	1,901	1,894	2,172	2,480	2,807	2,991	3,181	3,376
Present values									
(4) PDV net earnings	0	7,022	13,950	20,625	26,920	32,905	38,571	43,900	48,904
(5) PDV net private pension	28,879	28,425	28,008	26,290	24,699	23,355	22,811	22,181	21,503
(6) PDV Social Security	28,589	29,529	30,412	31,930	33,305	34,332	33,203	31,947	30,561
(7) PDV net lifetime income (=(4)+(5)+(6))	57,468	64,977	72,370	78,846	84,923	90,592	94,586	98,028	100,968

SOURCE: Fields and Mitchel (1984a), p. 255.

a. Social Security benefits are computed as of the year of first eligibility. Thus, an individual retiring at age 60 would not begin receiving benefits until attaining age 62.

Retirement Behavior

Mitchell and Fields proceeded to test whether work or retirement incentives actually did influence the behavior of the men in their Benefit Amounts Survey sample. This involved reducing the eight years of incentives facing each worker (corresponding to retirement at ages 60 through 68) to simpler summary parameters. The authors chose two: the present discounted value of future earnings, pensions, and Social Security associated with retirement at age 60 (YBASE), and the *change* in this figure between ages 60 and 65 (YSLOPE).[28]

Economic theory suggests that, *ceteris paribus*, retirement age should be an inverse function of YBASE. This is basically a wealth effect—those with more wealth will buy more of all normal goods, including leisure. One way to buy more leisure is to retire earlier. The effect of YSLOPE is theoretically ambiguous because of offsetting income and substitution effects. The authors expect, however, that the substitution effect dominates, and those with the more to gain from continued work will tend to retire later.

Simple regression estimates with retirement age as the dependent variable supported their hypotheses. With a sample of workers from 10 of the BAS pension plans, the YBASE coefficient was significantly negative and the YSLOPE coefficient significantly positive (Fields and Mitchell 1984c). Each additional $1,000 of Social Security and pension wealth at age 60 was associated with retirement about one-half to one month earlier. Each $1,000 in potential wealth gain between ages 60 and 65 delayed the average retirement age by one-third to two-thirds of a month.[29]

Silvana Pozzebon and Olivia Mitchell (1989) analyzed the retirement behavior of a small sample of working wives in the RHS. In contrast to the men, the wives' economic opportunities did not seem to be significant determinants of their retirement behavior. Neither the base level of Social Security and pension wealth nor changes in lifetime wealth, if retirement were delayed from age 60 to 65, was statistically significant. The wives' decisions were affected by their husbands' health, their husbands' incomes and the age differences between their husbands and themselves, but not by the financial incentives they themselves faced.

Since there is little literature on the retirement behavior of wives, and since this research was done with a very small sample, it is impossible to draw strong conclusions. But the suggestion is that working husbands and wives may respond differently to their economic circumstances.

Finally, Laurence Kotlikoff and David Wise (1989) estimated the impact of the pension plan of a specific Fortune 500 company on the behavior of its workers. As did Fields and Mitchell, they knew all the details of the benefit calculation rules. In this plan, there was a very large reward for remaining on the job until age 55. Pension accruals after that were either small or negative, depending on the worker's age and service. At age 65, Social Security accruals also turned negative, compounding the pension effect, and resulting in wealth losses equal to about one-third of annual pay.

Kotlikoff and Wise compared the pension accrual patterns with observed retirement behavior. They found large increases in retirement rates at ages 55, 60, and 62 (the age of first Social Security eligibility) for those vested in the pension plan (10 years of service), but no such jumps for those not yet vested. At age 65, there was a large increase in the probability of retirement for those few still working. This pattern is consistent with response to the financial incentives embedded in the pension and Social Security plans. The authors concluded that

> It is clear . . . that the inducements in the plan provisions
> to retire early have had a very substantial effect on depar-
> ture rates from the firm . . . The jumps in departure rates
> at specific ages coincide precisely with the discontinuities
> and kink points in the worker compensation profiles that result
> from the pension plan provisions together with wage earn-
> ings profiles and social security accrual.

Conclusions

A major contribution of this line of research is the detail provided about specific retirement plans—detail that is simply nonexistent in the large microeconomic data sets. The price paid is considerably less information about most other aspects of the individuals under study.

Another contribution is the specific detail on how retirement incentives change, year-by-year, as workers age beyond 60. The authors found that retirement income programs are seldom actuarially fair.[30] The present discounted value of the income streams depends critically on when the benefits are first claimed.

For workers in the Labor Department's Benefit Amounts Survey, Social Security wealth generally increased with work up to age 65 and declined thereafter. Defined benefit pension plans displayed greater variety. Pattern plans tended to encourage early retirement (prior to 65), while conventional plans (which include earnings in the benefit calculation rules) generally discouraged it. Delaying retirement always increases lifetime income, but by smaller and smaller amounts as one ages. The true compensation for work at age 68 can be less than half of what it was at age 60.

Work incentives change dramatically over time. Mitchell and Fields' and Kotlikoff and Wise's research on the retirement behavior in specific firms suggests strongly that workers do respond to these incentives, and therefore that individual retirement behavior and aggregate retirement trends can be influenced by changes in public policy.

Uncertainty

Most retirement models have assumed a world of certainty in which people make decisions on the basis of their current situations and their best estimates of the future. In fact, however, the future is very uncertain. There are probability distributions around these best estimates and many predictions turn out to be wrong. Health and living arrangements change and unexpected layoffs occur. Labor market conditions improve or deteriorate. And retirement benefits can turn out to be very different from earlier expectations, either because individuals did not understand the benefit calculation rules completely or because the rules changed after their initial expectations were formed.

The latter is particularly likely for Social Security. Prior to the 1972 amendments, which indexed benefits to the cost of living, Congress periodically increased nominal and, sometimes, real benefits. Between

1968 and 1975, for example, real benefits increased dramatically—on the order of 45 percent (Anderson, Burkhauser, and Quinn 1986). This occurred after a 15-year period in which real benefits were essentially constant. In 1983, amendments were passed that altered benefits by delaying a cost-of-living adjustment for six months, taxing half the benefits of high-income recipients, and legislating an increase in the age of eligibility for full benefits to age 67 (by the year 2027). Pension benefits are also subject to change, particularly for workers still on the job. Steven Allen, Robert Clark, and Daniel Sumner (1986) have argued that postretirement inflation adjustments are made much more frequently than commonly believed, even when employers have no contractual obligation to do so.

A few researchers have studied the effect of unanticipated changes on retirement plans, and a major effort in that direction is currently underway. Much of this research has focused on the extent to which the large—and presumably unanticipated—increases in real Social Security benefits during the early 1970s were responsible for the dramatic declines in the labor supply of older men that followed.[31] We will see below that there is wide disagreement on the answer. Others have asked whether changes in retirement plans are correlated with observed changes in the respondent's circumstances.

Social Security Increases and the Decline in Participation Rates

Jerry Hausman and David Wise (1985) analyzed the labor force behavior of the wage and salary men in all six waves of the Retirement History Study. They used a subjective definition of retirement—a respondent is retired when he says he is; that is, when he calls himself fully or partially retired. This definition corresponds more closely to exit from a career job than it does to withdrawal from the labor force. The authors estimated the effects of a number of explanatory variables in a hazard model of retirement. The observations were retirement transitions over two-year RHS interview periods.

The model included standard variables such as health status, annual earnings, assets, age, dependents, and pension eligibility, but the focus was on Social Security.[32] Its influence was measured by both flows (annual benefits) and stocks (the present discounted value of future benefits), and by both the current value of these two measures and the *changes* in these values following an incremental year of work. It is interesting to note that the asset or wealth specification fit the data better than the annual benefits version. As expected, high Social Security wealth increased the probability of retirement (and more so at age 65 than earlier) and wealth losses associated with additional work decreased it.

With their empirical results, Hausman and Wise were able to simulate retirement patterns with and without the increases in Social Security primary insurance benefits that occurred between 1969 and 1975. They compared the differences in their estimates with the actual declines in labor force participation rates, and concluded that "the increases in social security benefits over this period may account for possibly one-third of the decrease." Although their comparison of subjective self-defined retirement status to objective participation rates makes the precise numerical estimates suspect, the qualitative finding that the impact of these Social Security benefit changes was large is interesting.

In contrast, Gary Burtless (1986) attributed "only a small role in the decline in the average male retirement age" to the benefit increases. He defined retirement as a discontinuous drop in annual labor supply and his dependent variable was retirement age. Lifetime Social Security benefits were calculated under three different sets of benefit rules: those in effect prior to 1970, those that applied during the period from 1970 to 1972, and those applicable after 1972. These benefits were included in a lifetime budget constraint and the effects of the parameters of this constraint on the retirement age were estimated.

Burtless found statistically significant, but modest, effects of Social Security increases on retirement behavior. In particular, he estimated that the increases legislated in 1970 and 1972 reduced the average retirement age by only one month. The long-run effect, had the changes occurred much earlier so that respondents could have had longer to adjust to the change, would have been about two months. Although these changes are not inconsequential in the aggregate, they represented, according to Burtless, only a small portion of the participation decline that actually took place. He viewed rising personal wealth levels, increases in unemployment after 1969, and changing attitudes toward retirement as alternative explanations.

Robert Moffitt (1987) and Alan Krueger and Jorn-Steffen Pischke (1989) are skeptical of even this small role for Social Security. Moffitt's approach to the problem was very different and relied on aggregate time series data on labor supply and Social Security wealth. He pointed out that the Social Security wealth of a cohort can rise for at least two reasons: increases in benefits for individuals already in the system, as is studied above, but also extensions of coverage to include those previously excluded.

With various assumptions about how people form expectations about the future, Moffitt presented evidence that the unanticipated increases in aggregate Social Security wealth were actually larger in the 1950s, when coverage was expanding rapidly, than they were in the early 1970s. But the decreases in labor force participation in the early 1950s were much more modest. In addition, Moffitt argued that there were large negative unanticipated wealth shocks in the mid- and late-1970s, when actual Social Security increases failed to keep pace with what recipients may have expected based on the early 1970s experience. Despite these negative shocks, participation rates continued to decline.

Krueger and Pischke (1989) analyzed the behavior of the so-called "notch babies"—workers born between 1917 and 1921—who, due to a 1977 Social Security Act amendment, suffered an abrupt and unexpected decrease in their future Social Security benefits. They found little evidence that this affected the labor supply behavior of these individuals and conclude that there is probably little hope for reversing the trend toward early retirement by reducing Social Security benefits.[33]

Microeconomic cross-section findings are difficult to compare with aggregate time series results. Each approach has its own advantages and disadvantages and these are nicely summarized in the Moffitt article. But he and Krueger and Pischke have pointed out a potential inconsistency between the long-run trends in aggregate Social Security wealth and participation rates and prompted at least a temporary pause among those deducing causation from recent patterns of Social Security growth and elderly labor force decline.

Changes in Circumstances and Changes in Plans

With a sample from the National Longitudinal Surveys, Gilbert Nestel (1985) compared the retirement plans of respondents at age 59 with their subsequent behavior. He noted a significant shift in expectations over time. Between the middle 1960s and the middle 1970s, the proportion of respondents planning to retire prior to age 65 increased from about 30 to about 40 percent.

The predictions turned out to be relatively inaccurate. By 1981, only 31 percent of the whites interviewed, and 26 percent of the blacks, had actually retired in the age interval in which they had said they would.[34] The predictions were more accurate the nearer the planned retirement age was to age 59. Those who did not predict accurately were much more likely to retire earlier than planned than later. These findings suggest that something happened between the date of prediction and the date of planned retirement, but give no insight into what might have occurred.

Kathryn Anderson, Richard Burkhauser, and Joseph Quinn (1986) compared the planned and actual retirement dates of a sample of nearly 1,600 men from the Retirement History Study and found that about 60 percent left work within a year of their predicted dates.[35] More retired before than after they had planned, and the proportion of "on-time" retirements increased with the age at the time of the prediction.

More important, the authors found that changes in plans were correlated with what they assumed were unanticipated changes in the environment. They studied three such changes: the dramatic increases in Social Security benefits mentioned above, changes in individual health status, and changes in local labor market conditions.

The Social Security variable was measured as the unexpected increase in Social Security wealth caused by the changes in the benefit rules. The authors calculated the asset value of the benefit stream in the year of predicted retirement (R^*) using two sets of rules—those in effect in 1969, the year when the prediction was made, and those eventually in effect in year R^*. The difference between the two asset values was the unexpected increase in wealth, and it was expected to induce earlier retirement. The authors also included dummy variables, indicating health status improvement or deterioration and differences in the local unemployment rate between 1969 and the earlier of R* and the actual retirement date.

The empirical results were reasonable. As expected, increases in Social Security wealth increased the probability of retiring earlier than planned and decreased the likelihood of retiring later. Self-defined health deterioration had the same effects. A loosening of the local labor market did just the opposite. The greater the increase in local unemployment rates, the less likely the workers were to retire early and the more likely they were to stay in the labor force longer than planned. This preliminary evidence contradicts the view that older workers, often protected by seniority, are likely to be forced out of employment during economic downturns (although some individuals certainly are), and suggests that they may want to and may be able to remain employed longer when economic conditions decline.

This research demonstrates that plans do change and, therefore, that models based on assumptions of certainty will miss an important part of the story. But it is reassuring to find that the changes in plans are not entirely random. In fact, they turn out to be correlated with observable and often unforeseeable changes in circumstances. When expectations prove inaccurate, so do the plans based on them.

Dynamic Programming Models

Much of the most current and sophisticated retirement research focuses specifically on issues of uncertainty. John Rust (1987), James Berkovec and Steven Stern (forthcoming), and James Stock and David Wise (1990) have used dynamic programming models to describe individuals who recalculate their optimal behavior each time period, using new information about the present and their best predictions about the future. The computational requirements are so burdensome that these models are usually streamlined along other dimensions and are quite limited in the options they allow. The results thus far are generally consistent with the previous literature—retirement decisions are influenced by Social Security and pension provisions, age and health status.

What makes these models particularly interesting is that they do not assume that workers know their future wage rates and retirement income flows with certainty. Stock and Wise, for example, argue that workers decide whether to retire today by making best guesses about future wages and Social Security and pension rules. If any time in the future looks better, the individual continues to work. After another year, the worker has more information about the future, based on actual earnings during that year and any other relevant knowledge acquired, and must then make another retirement decision, again comparing immediate retirement with retirement in all subsequent years.

The key is that forecasts of future conditions will be different from what they were a year ago. What becomes critical in these models are assumptions about how expectations are formed and how sensitive they are to new information. This is obviously difficult to model. And some of what is gained in the theoretical sophistication is lost when one is forced to operationalize the concepts for empirical estimation.

Social Security Reform

Gary Fields and Olivia Mitchell (1984b,c), Gary Burtless and Robert Moffitt (1984), Stephan Gohmann and Robert Clark (1989) and Alan Gustman and Thomas Steinmeier (1985b, 1989d), whose work we will discuss more fully in chapter 5, have all utilized retirement models to estimate the effects of Social Security reforms similar to those enacted in 1983.[36] They all conclude that these policy changes would indeed alter aggregate retirement patterns but suggest that the magnitude of the change would be small.

Mitchell and Fields studied the impact of four changes in Social Security regulations on the retirement ages and retirement incomes of a sample of older Americans drawn from the Retirement History Study. They defined retirement as the departure from the job held in 1969, the year of the initial RHS survey. They calculated the impact of specific reforms on the budget sets of the respondents and estimated the effect of these changes on labor supply behavior. The four reforms were

(1) an increase in the age of full Social Security benefits from 65 to 68, with benefits reduced by 6.67 percent for each year of receipt before age 68,[37]

(2) a one-time six-month delay in the Social Security cost-of-living adjustment,

(3) an increase in the delayed retirement credit after age 65 from 3 percent per year of delay to 6.67 percent—the factor currently applied between ages 62 and 65[38] and

(4) an increase in the early retirement penalty from 6.67 to 15 percent for each year of Social Security receipt prior to age 65.

Three of the four proposals would lower benefits. The third leaves benefits prior to age 65 unchanged and increases them for those who retire thereafter.

The last proposal, a severe penalty for early retirement or, alternatively, a large reward for continued work, had the largest predicted effect on behavior. Fields and Mitchell (1984b) predicted that average retirement would be delayed about three months. The first proposal, which combines a decrease in Social Security benefits with a larger delayed retirement credit for work after 65, had about half that effect—an average delay of 1.6 months. The other two reforms—the one-time delay in the cost-of-living adjustment and the increased delayed retirement credit— had almost no effect, the former because the impact on lifetime wealth is so small and the latter because it only changes incentives after age 65, when most people have already retired. These results predict that workers will respond to Social Security cuts with very modest increases in their work lives. They will choose to take the cut in income, not in leisure.

Burtless and Moffitt (1984) used their empirical results to simulate the impacts on retirement ages and Social Security outlays of three possible Social Security amendments:[39]

(1) a delay in the normal retirement age from 65 to 68 (the same as the Fields and Mitchell proposal [1] above),

(2) a 20 percent reduction in Social Security benefits at every age, and

(3) an actuarially-fair delayed retirement credit at all ages.[40]

The first two proposals would lower benefits and the last would increase them after age 65, when the current delayed retirement credit drops from near 7 percent to 3 percent. These amendments were imposed on the budget constraints of three hypothetical recipients—married males with and without a working spouse, and an unmarried male.

All three proposals were predicted to delay retirement, but the changes in behavior are modest. The increase in the normal retirement age to 68 delays the retirement of the married men by about 4.5 months and that of the unmarried man by 2.5 months. These estimates are qualitatively similar to those of Fields and Mitchell. The third proposal (an actuarially fair adjustment at all ages) has similar effects and the across-the-board 20 percent benefit reduction has about half that impact. Since the behavior responses are small, these reforms would substantially alter Social Security outlays, decreasing them under the first two proposals and increasing them in the third.

It is difficult to compare the Gustman and Steinmeier findings to those above because they calculated changes in the percentage working full time and part time rather than changes in the average age at retirement. They simulated the effects of four actual Social Security changes:

(1) A delay in the age of normal retirement to 67, with the penalty for receipt at age 62 at 30 percent,

(2) An increase in the delayed retirement credit after age 65 to 8 percent per year,

(3) A reduction in the benefit reduction rate applied to earnings over the exempt amount (for those aged 65 to 69 only) from 50 to 33 percent, and

(4) A one-time six-month delay in the cost-of-living adjustment.

The first two proposals have been legislated for the future; the others have already taken place.

Gustman and Steinmeier (1985b) estimated that the entire reform package will have little long-term effect on the retirement probabilities of those younger than 65—the percentage fully retired (not working) falls by less than 1 percentage point. But between ages 65 and 68, the proportion retired falls by about four points. This is the net result of a six-point increase in the percentage working full time and a 2 percent drop in those employed part time. The retirement bulge at age 65 disappears. The component responsible for most of the change is the increase in the delayed retirement credit. There is some effect of the decrease in the benefit reduction rate and almost none from the delayed cost-of-living adjustment. The authors pointed out that with actuarially fair adjustments, the designation of the "normal retirement age" is irrelevant, since the incentives for delayed retirement are the same before and after this arbitrary age.

Gohmann and Clark (1989) have developed a model in which the decision to claim Social Security benefits and the decision to retire (leave the labor force) are treated separately and therefore allowed to move in separate directions in response to a policy change. They used a sample of married, wage and salary men from the Retirement History Study to estimate behavioral equations for both decisions, and found that they are simultaneously determined. When they altered the parameters of the model to reflect the eventual outcome of the 1983 Social Security amendments, their simulations suggested only slight changes in the age-specific probabilities of enefit acceptance and retirement.

These researchers all predict that changes in Social Security incentives like those legislated in 1983 will alter retirement patterns, but only modestly.[41] But all of these estimates are only partial equilibrium predictions, since they assume that the other parameters in the decisionmaking process, in particular, the structure of employer pension benefits, will remain the same.[42] If these are also endogenous to the system, as we expect they are, then the final results could differ substantially from the simulations above.

Involuntary Retirement

Although economists have focused primarily on retirement as a voluntary choice (the rational response to the set of options available), there has been a resurgence of interest in factors that limit or eliminate this choice. This is very much in the older tradition—the view that retirements are often involuntary, the result of circumstances beyond the worker's control. The two most important such factors are health and labor market obstacles late in life.

Health

Interest in the interaction between health and retirement has grown in recent years because of the 1983 amendments to the Social Security

Act, which will increase the age of normal retirement to age 67 by the year 2027 and raise the penalty for claiming Social Security at age 62 from 20 to 30 percent of the full benefit amount. Part of the justification for this change is the recent increase in the life expectancy of the elderly. This puts financial strains on the resources of the Social Security system, but also suggests that workers may well be able to work longer than they do now.

Recent reviews by Steven Chapman, Mitchell LaPlante, and Gail Wilenski (1986) and by Martynas Ycas (1987), however, have cast some doubt on the popular presumption that life expectancy and health go hand-in-hand. The trends on longevity are clear—older Americans are living longer now than they did two decades ago. The increases in life expectancy at ages 60 or 65 are well-documented and are significant for males and females, for whites and nonwhites. What is surprising is that they do not seem to be accompanied by increases in health status. Chapman *et al.*, reporting on a variety of studies and data sources, concluded that morbidity and the prevalence of disability have actually increased. Ycas used a number of measures of health status and found that they produced very similar patterns over time, suggesting increasing health problems at least through the late 1970s.[43]

One explanation for the declining health of the elderly is the "failure of success"—that medical advances keep people alive today who would have died in the past (Berkowitz 1988). The additional years may be ones of chronic illness, not good health. Regardless of the explanation, an implication is that the impact of health on the retirement decision is likely to remain at least as important in the future as it is now.

Many economists are skeptical about the usefulness of subjective health evaluations, especially when given as a reason for retirement or as part of an application for health-related benefits. One concern is that respondents may view health as a socially legitimate reason for stopping work and therefore mention it even when it is not the primary reason for retirement. Joseph Quinn (1977) found that among retired RHS respondents who claimed that they had *no* health limitations and had health *better* than that of their peers, 10 percent still claimed health as the primary motivation for retirement, as did 13 percent of those with *no* health limitation and health the *same* as their peers.

On the other hand, Frank Sammartino (1987) and Gary Burtless (1987) have argued that self-evaluations of health may be a better measure than objective standards because they implicitly include information about the quality of health required on the individual's actual job. Sammartino has pointed out that several studies report a high correlation between medically determined health status and subjective descriptions. Despite this, there is a great deal of interest in alternative measures of health and in estimating how sensitive empirical results are to the definition used.

In a very thorough recent review of the health and retirement literature, Sammartino described three causational links. Poor health can make work more arduous and therefore increase preferences for leisure; it can lower an individual's market wage rate; and it can decrease life expectancy. All three can induce earlier retirement.

In empirical work, poor health is almost always associated with earlier retirement (see Sammartino [1987] for a list of recent references). The effects are large and significant. Exact comparisons are impossible because of the variety of definitions of both health and retirement. Sammartino reported on several studies that conclude that poor health raises the probability of retirement for workers aged 60 to 67 by 14 to 18 percentage points and lowers the expected age of retirement by one to three years.

Some recent studies have focused on health measures other than self-defined status at the time of retirement. Donald Parsons (1982), Eric Kingson (1982), and Kathryn Anderson and Richard Burkhauser (1985) utilized subsequent mortality. Gloria Bazzoli (1985) and Herbert Parnes and Lawrence Less (1985a) used self-reported health, but from a survey wave prior to retirement. The hope here is that prior health is more likely to be an accurate representation, and less likely to be used as a social justification for retirement.

Thomas Chirikos and Gilbert Nestel (1981) and Gloria Bazzoli (1985) created an index from a series of impairments. J. S. Butler, Richard Burkhauser, Jean Mitchell, and Theodore Pincus (1987) compared self-reports on a specific condition—arthritis—with a clinical measure. Gary Burtless (1987) compared three commonly used subjective measures with subsequent mortality and found them to be highly correlated.

These and other studies continue to confirm that health, however measured, is an important determinant of the individual retirement decision. But they suggest that the use of self-defined health status at retirement exaggerates its importance and may reduce the measured effects of other factors. For example, Parsons (1982), using a sample from the NLS, found that older men were more likely to declare themselves in poor health the larger the Social Security benefits for which they were eligible. This suggests that retirement status and declared health status may be jointly determined. If so, then the coefficient of subjective health status in a retirement equation might reflect both the legitimate impact of health and the financial incentives in retirement income programs. Parsons found a stronger and cleaner Social Security effect when an objective measure of health—subsequent mortality—was used.

Anderson and Burkhauser (1985) reached similar conclusions with respect to the wage rate. They used both a subjective measure based on the (RHS) respondent's self-assessment and an objective one based on subsequent mortality. Although they found significant wage effects in their retirement equations in both cases, the elasticities were about five times larger when the mortality measure was used. Finally, Burtless (1987) compared a subjective measure of impairment with an index based on predetermined conditions. He found that both variables were significant determinants in retirement equations, but that the measured effects of economic variables (Social Security benefits, pension entitlement, and potential earnings) were much larger when the more objective index was used.

These authors have suggested that self-declared health status may really be an endogenous variable, jointly determined with retirement status. If so, it is not a legitimate explanatory variable in a single-equation labor supply equation. Steven Stern (1989) has tested this hypothesis explicitly, although not with a sample of older workers. He considered reported disability and labor force participation as a system of simultaneous equations, and used symptoms and diseases as the underlying index of true health status. In contrast with the suggestions in much of the literature, Stern found very little evidence of endogeneity when using standard subjective health questions and very little bias on other coefficients in the equations. Although he admits that his evidence is not conclusive, he finds that the traditional disability measures are useful and reasonably exogenous predictors of labor force participation. The last word has certainly not been spoken on this issue.

Several authors (Sickles and Taubman [1986] and Butler, Anderson, and Burkhauser [1989]) have gone a step further and presented models in which actual (not just reported) health is endogenous, since medical care over the lifetime is a matter of choice. If medical care depends on income, then financial resources have two effects on the retirement decision: a direct one as in all the modern models, and also an indirect one via their impact on health status. If this story is correct, then use of health status, even if perfectly measured, in a single equation model will yield biased coefficients for the explanatory variables.

This current literature on health and retirement yields several conclusions. The most obvious is additional confirmation that health is a key determinant of labor force status, even in sophisticated models that focus on choice and the role of financial incentives. But there is considerable debate on the magnitude and exact nature of its influence. The size of the estimated effects of health and economic factors depends on the nature of the model (whether health is viewed as exogenous or endogenous) and on the precise measure of health status used.

Labor Market Obstacles

Even in an era when an increasing number of retirements appear to be voluntary, there is widespread interest in the special labor market problems of middle-aged and older workers. This interest was accentuated by the job losses caused by two recessions in the early 1980s and by recent and current corporate restructuring, often in conjunction with mergers and acquisitions. The special problems of the elderly include the difficulty of finding new full-time work late in life, the shortage of well-paying part-time job opportunities, and age discrimination.

The official unemployment rates of older workers are lower than those of the labor force as a whole.[44] These official statistics, however, conceal part of the story. Older Americans are more likely than others to be discouraged workers—out of work but no longer looking, and therefore not counted among the unemployed. Diane Herz and Philip Rones (1989) showed that the inclusion of discouraged workers adds over a third to the unemployment rate of men aged 55 and over and adds over 70 percent for analogous women, but has only a very small effect on the unemployment rate overall.[45] Although workers aged 55 and over were about as likely to be laid off in the mid-1980s as those who were younger, the older workers who were laid off were much more likely to leave the labor force—one-third of those aged 55 to 64 did, as did three-quarters of those 65 and over, compared to less than 10 percent of those aged 20 through 54 (Herz and Rones 1989).

David Shapiro and Steven Sandell (1987) have specifically studied older displaced workers in the NLS surveys—those men who were permanently laid off or fired between 1966 and 1978. They found that older job-losers faced special difficulties. They were more likely to suffer long spells of unemployment and greater earnings reductions when they did find work. Layoffs were also highly correlated with retirement. Almost 30 percent of male job-losers aged 60 retired, compared to only 10 percent of those still employed.

Robert Hutchens (1986, 1988) has argued that job opportunities decline with age because older workers have fewer years to offer a prospective employer. Therefore, firms have less time to recoup the fixed costs of employment (such as the costs of firm-specific on-the-job training) and are less able to utilize compensation schemes that delay part of the pay until the end of the contract. In addition, the physical requirements of some jobs may put older workers at a disadvantage. Using data from the 1983 Current Population Survey, Hutchens (1988) showed that recently hired older workers were found in a narrower band of industries and occupations than were either recently hired young workers or all old workers. Although this could occur because older job-changers voluntarily choose this limited range of jobs, it is also consistent with the hypothesis that the breadth of opportunity declines.

According to Jim Jondrow, Frank Brechling, and Alan Marcus (1987), many workers would like to retire gradually. In one survey, 80 percent of respondents over age 55 preferred part-time work to complete retirement. In another, 60 percent of a sample of managers preferred phased retirement. Two-thirds of another group said they would consider a transitional step of part-time employment. Many of these individuals would have liked part-time work with their full-time employer. Despite these preferences, as we will see in chapter 5, the modal pattern of retirement still involves an abrupt transition from full-time work to complete labor force withdrawal. Most wage and salary workers who are able to reduce the number of hours they work must switch jobs to do so. Why do the desires and opportunities for part-time work not match?

A primary reason is that part-time pay is lower than full-time compensation. According to Alan Gustman and Thomas Steinmeier (1985a), older workers in the RHS who reported themselves partially retired suffered an hourly wage loss of 10 percent if they remained with their previous full-time employer, and 30 percent if they did not. In chapter 6 below, with the RHS sample, we report similar findings—significant wage losses associated with movement to part-time work, especially if accompanied by a change in employer.

Jondrow, Brechling, and Marcus (1987) suggest that these wage declines are due to the lower productivity and higher fixed administrative and training costs of part-time work. They hypothesize that employers have to pay less to make part-time employment profitable. This is especially true when a worker has changed employers, lost specific human capital, and has to be retrained on the new job.

Why then do workers not reduce hours on their career jobs, and thereby maintain their specific human capital and wage rates? According to Gustman and Steinmeier (1983, 1985a), they do not because they cannot. Only 15 percent of firms responding to a 1979 survey permitted some employees to reduce hours as they approached retirement. Only 7 percent offered this option to all employees. A survey of individuals suggested that two-thirds to three-quarters of older wage and salary workers were unable to work fewer hours. Shirley Rhine (1984) reported that only 3 percent of a sample of over 350 large firms permitted phased retirement. The self-employed, on the other hand, who have more control over their hours, are much more likely to utilize a transitional period of partial retirement.

What many workers want, but cannot find, is part-time employment at their old wage rates. What some find, but do not want, are jobs at lower pay.[46] Many older workers, therefore, face unattractive alternatives as they age. Continued full-time employment on a career job eventually results in significant losses of retirement income wealth—in essence, a pay cut. Part-time work on this job is rarely available for the wage and salary population. A new job usually means a substantially lower wage rate.

Faced with these unattractive alternatives, many older Americans stop working. Is this decision voluntary? In one sense it is, because individuals choose to do it under the circumstances. But in another sense it is not, because the circumstances change dramatically as they age. Older workers face special problems in the labor market, and the interaction between supply and demand, choice and coercion, is a complex one.

The National Longitudinal Surveys

Herbert Parnes and his colleagues at the Center for Human Resource Research at the Ohio State University are responsible for the development, collection, and much of the analysis of the data collected in the National Longitudinal Surveys of Labor Market Experience (NLS). Four demographic groups were surveyed, including a sample of approximately 5,000 men aged 45 to 59, in 1966. Although the study was initially scheduled to last only five years, concentrating on the preretirement experience, it was later extended to 10, and then to 17 years. Respondents were interviewed a total of 10 times, by telephone, mail, and in person. Since this group was 62 to 76 years of age by the time the surveys ceased in 1983, most of them were followed through their retirement and well into their postretirement years.[47]

The NLS data on older workers have generated a remarkable amount of research—six volumes of papers by members of the Center for Human Resource Research (all referenced in Parnes et al. [1985])—and hundreds of papers by these and other researchers throughout the country. Their last monograph includes research by economists, psychologists, sociologists and statisticians. We include only a cursory review of this literature here, and highlight some of the findings that bear most directly on our research below.

Definitions of Retirement

Using 15 years of longitudinal data, Herbert Parnes and Lawrence Less (1985a) analyzed the volume and patterns of retirement over this period and documented the importance of the definition chosen. They experimented with three. The first is subjective—individuals are labeled retired whenever they state that they have stopped working at a regular job. The other two are objective. One is based on the receipt of pension or disability income (from Social Security or an employer pension), and the other on annual labor supply. In the latter, the authors defined as retired anyone working fewer than 1,000 hours per year—approximately half-time or less.

There are several other choices that the researchers must also make in calculating how many people retired during a given time period. One is whether to treat retirement as a one-time event (once retired, always retired) or as a function of current labor force status and, therefore, reversible. Another issue is which samples to use—those available at the beginning of the period or the smaller group left at the end.

Parnes and Less demonstrated that these definitional issues are very important. If one requires only that the individual meet *one* of the three criteria *at some point* during the 15 years, then 86 percent of the men in the sample (aged 60 to 74) were retired in 1981. At the other extreme, if *all three* criteria have to be met and the definition is based on *current* status, only 59 percent of this same sample were retired.[48] In proportional terms, the differences were even greater earlier in the surveys, when the absolute number of retired was much smaller. Parnes and Less concluded that there is no best definition of retirement, but that the appropriate definition varies with the purpose of the research. In their volume (Parnes *et al* 1985), the authors all used the subjective criterion (stopped working at a regular job) and treated retirement as irreversible. With this definition, they found a considerable amount of work after retirement.

Reasons for Retirement

Parnes and Less attempted to determine why those who had retired had done so. They did not rely on retrospective answers to direct questions about motivations, but rather relied on the longitudinal record *prior to* the retirement decision.[49] They categorized the reasons into four groups: (1) involuntary retirement under mandatory retirement plans, (2) retirement dictated by poor health, (3) retirement because of labor market adversities, and (4) voluntary retirement. Individuals were included in the first category only if they retired at the mandatory retirement age and had reported in earlier interviews that they preferred to work longer.[50]

When all the retirements during the 15 years were analyzed, the first and third categories turned out to be relatively unimportant. Only 3 percent of the men retired because of mandatory retirement, and only 5 percent because of adverse labor market conditions.[51] About a third seemed to be "forced" into retirement because of poor health, and the majority—nearly 60 percent—appeared to have retired voluntarily.

There were some interesting differences among subgroups. Blacks were significantly more likely to have retired for health reasons (47 versus 34 percent) and, therefore, less likely to have made an unconstrained voluntary decision. Those who stopped working at their regular jobs before age 62 were much more likely to have had a prior health problem. This finding is consistent with the research of Eric Kingson (1982), mentioned in chapter 2, who studied the NLS men who permanently withdrew from the labor force before age 62. Kingson found that among these "very early retirees," 85 percent of the white men and 91 percent of the black men had health problems—they either reported that health limited their work or they had medically certified disabilities that enabled them to receive Social Security disability benefits.

These NLS results—at least those for respondents retiring at age 62 or later—are consistent with most of the modern research and at variance with the early Social Security questionnaires discussed in chapter 2. There is considerable evidence that today many of the labor market transitions in the later years are voluntary, made by individuals choosing among alternative lifestyles and income streams. Many of these transitions take place before the age of 65. Of course, health and labor market obstacles remain important constraints for certain individuals, especially for very early retirees. They preclude continued work for some and change the terms of the tradeoff for others. But they are by no means the dominant factors that they once appeared to be.

Postretirement Work Experience

When the definition of retirement is based on something other than current labor force status, it is possible for individuals to work while retired. In another paper, Parnes and Less (1985b) studied the labor market activities of the men who had retired between 1967 and 1979. At the time of the 1981 survey, nearly 20 percent of them were either employed or looking for work.

This percentage differed dramatically by other characteristics. Retired whites were more likely to be in the labor force than were blacks (18 percent versus 13 percent), and the white labor force participants were much less likely to be unemployed. More than a quarter of the individuals from professional and managerial occupations remained in the labor force, compared to only 15 percent of the others. Those who retired voluntarily were only slightly less likely to keep working than those driven out by mandatory retirement or labor market adversities (23 percent versus 27 and 24 percent), but people in all of these categories were much more likely to be at or looking for work than those driven out by poor health. Only 11 percent of the latter group remained in the labor force.

Parnes and Less also found that the likelihood of being in the labor force was highest right after retirement, and declined thereafter. It was higher for younger retirees, for the self-employed, for those with working wives, and for those with high levels of wealth. This last result suggests that postretirement employment may be for reasons other than financial.

Of the retirees who worked during 1981, half of them had full-year jobs, but 60 percent worked part time during the weeks they worked. Altogether, 20 percent of those employed worked more than 2,000 hours per year, and 30 percent worked less than 500. Three-quarters of the working retired were in new occupations (defined by Census 1-digit categories), two-thirds in new industries, and most were in jobs lower on the economic scale than the ones they had left. In real terms, median average hourly earnings were less than half what they had been on the preretirement job.

Conclusions

Parnes and Less found a wide variety of labor market experiences among the older workers in their NLS sample. By various definitions, they found between 60 and 85 percent were retired by 1981, when the age range was 60 to 74 years. The term "retired" covered individuals in very different states of labor market activity—from those continuing to work full time to those who had completely withdrawn from the labor force.

Our focus differs from that of Parnes *et al.* We are interested in departures from what we define as a career job—full-time work on a job held for at least 10 years. Nonetheless, the Parnes results are very similar to those which we find with the Retirement History Study data, and discuss in chapters 5 and 6 below. After exit from full-time work on a career job, many people continue to work, sometimes part time on the same job, but more often with a new employer at substantially lower wages. Whether these individuals define themselves as retired or not is of secondary concern to us. We are more interested in what they do than in what they call it.

Summary

The retirement literature has come a long way since the mid-1940s. Research methodologies and conclusions have changed. The early work relied primarily on cross-sectional questionnaires in which retirees were simply asked why they retired when they did. Much of the modern work is based on large longitudinal data sets with detailed demographic, economic, and social data on thousands of individuals. This permits researchers to study the objective circumstances that existed prior to the behavior under study and, thereby, to supplement the explanations given by the respondents themselves.

Over these past four decades, our understanding of the retirement decision has grown significantly. Early evidence suggested that the overwhelming reasons for retirement were health and labor market constraints, and that very few people retired voluntarily. Modern research suggests the opposite—that many older Americans do leave their career jobs voluntarily. Although some are still forced out by bad health and layoffs, many others are induced out by the financial incentives embedded in our retirement income systems.

Most of the recent work by economists in this field has concentrated on the details of these financial incentives. A major breakthrough was the treatment of retirement rights as *stocks of wealth* rather than as annual flows. It soon became clear that the asset value of these rights could either rise or fall with continued work, depending on the details of the benefit calculation formulas, and that these changes in wealth are really a component of compensation. Therefore, an individual's true earnings could rise or fall over time without any change in the size of the paycheck.

Modern retirement research has taken two tacks. One approach, narrow and deep, is to look very carefully at the mechanics of actual pension plans and deduce whether the rules subsidize or penalize work at various ages. The problem here is that the data sets with considerable pension detail provide little other information about the individuals enrolled in the plans. The other approach, wide and shallow, is to utilize one of the superb longitudinal data sets mentioned above, with excellent information about the individuals in the sample, but relatively little detail about their pension plans. Fortunately, both avenues suggest that retirement incentives do exist and that many people behave as though they understand and respond to them.

While the work on the theory and the explanatory variables has gotten more and more sophisticated, economists have paid considerably less attention to the actual behavior being explained. With the exception of a few analysts who have studied hours of work and a few more who have analyzed partial retirement, most have treated retirement as dichotomous. In fact, as we demonstrate in chapter 5, the labor market behavior of older Americans is anything but dichotomous. A wide variety of withdrawal patterns is observed. Although it is always possible to squeeze them all into two categories, we suspect that insight is lost rather than gained in the process.

Before looking ahead to work after retirement, however, we first look back, to a body of research on the influence of retirement income plans on behavior much earlier in the life cycle—in the prime working years, long before thoughts of retirement.

NOTES

1. The Benefit Amounts Survey includes the birth date and date of retirement for each pension recipient, as well as earnings histories and some very basic demographic information from the Social Security Administration's records. (See Fields and Mitchell 1984c.)

2. Martin Levine (1988) has recently published a book on mandatory retirement. He reviews the literature on mandatory retirement and aging, and concludes that mandatory retirement is an unjustifiable form of age discrimination. Karen Holden and Lee Hansen (1989) have edited a volume on the impact of changing mandatory retirement rules on higher education.

3. The discount rate has two components: the real rate of interest (assumed to be 2 percent), and the expected rate of inflation. In cases where future retirement benefits are fully indexed for inflation (such as Social Security and federal employee pension benefits), the inflation component disappears. When future benefits are only partly indexed) as with many state and local government plans), only the uncovered portion of inflation is included. Future benefits that are fixed in nominal terms at initial receipt (like many private sector pensions) are discounted at the full nominal discount rate.

4. A more detailed description of the derivation of the WEALTH and DELTA terms can be found in Burkhauser and Quinn (1983a).

5. Although the WEALTH formula in the text does not reflect it, the calculations for couples include the expected benefits going to a surviving spouse, at two-thirds the amount that a couple received.

6. Information was available in three parts of the RHS questionnaire: a section on pension plans, a section on retirement income expected in the future, and a section on actual income received. In the first four waves of data, then, there were 12 potential sources of information. Not everyone was asked every question and not every question asked was answered. A decision tree was developed to search all the sources in a specific order, to maximize the probability of obtaining useful information. Whenever possible, the pension data were based on actual pension receipt. If these data were not available, the authors turned next to the details of the pension plan on the current or last job. Finally, if still not successful, they looked at answers about expected retirement income. In the end, they obtained benefit estimates for about 85 percent of the sample.

7. This was most true in the intermediate wealth categories. The poorest were the least likely to have pension and Social Security coverage. The wealthiest tended to have other assets that dominated retirement rights.

8. The Social Security wealth coefficient was insignificant. This is surprising, from a theoretical point of view, but, in fact, weak wealth effects are frequently found in the retirement and other labor supply literature. One hypothesis is that wealth is correlated with an unobserved measure of proclivity for work. Those with a taste for work have accumulated wealth (retirement income wealth, in this case), *and* are likely to continue to work as they approach retirement age—not because one causes the other, but because both are caused by this unmeasured underlying personality characteristic. The correlation between wealth and attitude toward work masks the true relationship between wealth and the probability of retirement.

9. Malcolm Morrison (1988) found similar results with a small sample of women. About a third of the actual differences in behavior between those with and without mandatory retirement could be explained by other factors.

10. Mandatory retirement is probably even less important than it appears here. If workers select jobs in part because of their compulsory retirement provisions, then those who plan to retire at the mandatory age anyway are more likely to end up in jobs with that constraint, because it is not a drawback to them. They will then retire at mandatory retirement age, but not because they had to, but because they wanted to. Those who prefer to stay on the job beyond then will tend to avoid firms with such rules and then work beyond mandatory retirement age. Since these preferences are not measured and are correlated with mandatory retirement status, mandatory retirement will look more important than it really is.

11. Morrison (1988) estimates this number at 200,000, which is still very small in comparison to the national labor supply.

12. Using a very different methodological approach, James Schulz (1974) and Janice Halpern (1978) reached the same conclusion. Schulz found that only 10 percent of a cohort of retired men was subject to mandatory retirement, worked up to that age, and claimed that they were willing and able to work longer. Using several data sets that asked similar questions, Halpern reported that only 4 to 8 percent of the older population was really constrained by these rules.

Data from the first 15 years of the National Longitudinal Survey of older men tell a similar tale. Parnes et al. (1985) report that "of the nearly 8.5 million men aged 60–74 in 1981 who had retired over the preceding 15 years, fewer than 5 percent had been unwillingly removed from jobs by mandatory retirement rules."

13. Steven Sandell (1988) has questioned this conclusion, and pointed out that it is based on research undertaken in an institutional environment different from that today. In particular, the Omnibus Budget Reconciliation Act of 1986 requires continued pension credits and accruals for work after age 65. This was not the case previously. It is certainly possible that this increased incentive to work may encourage some workers to remain on the job and therefore make the elimination of mandatory retirement at age 65 more important, but the magnitude of this effect is unknown.

14. There has been a particular concern in the university community about the elimination of mandatory retirement in an environment with tenured employment and no heavy lifting. Recent research by Holden and Hansen (1989) and Montgomery (1989) suggests that the increase in the mandatory retirement age from 65 to 70 might delay average faculty retirement ages by one to two years, but also that faculty would probably be responsive to early retirement incentives designed to induce them out.

15. Olivia Mitchell and Rebecca Luzadis (1988) presented additional evidence that this is the case. They quantified the retirement incentives in 14 defined benefit pension plans from 1960 to 1980—a period during which mandatory retirement at age 65 was outlawed (in 1978), and the elimination of mandatory retirement altogether was discussed. (It was outlawed for most workers in 1986.) They found that the pension incentives in union agreements changed from discouraging early retirement (in 1960) to encouraging it (in 1980). This paper is discussed below.

16. For those with a decline in hours over time, but without a clear and discontinuous drop, retirement status was based on a combination of self-defined retirement status, labor force status, and Social Security receipt status.

17. About one-fifth of the retirees in the sample continued to work. Their average workweek was about 16 hours (Burtless and Moffitt 1984). In subsequent work, Burtless (1986) considered this partial retirement insignificant enough to ignore it and treated partial retirement as indistinguishable from full retirement.

18. The Burtless and Moffitt analysis ignored the increments to future benefits that occur because of the earnings beyond the exempt amount. Because of these future increments, the true earnings-test tax was less than the 50 percent legislated prior to 1990. (If the increments are actuarially fair, the earnings test disappears, since the benefits foregone are returned in the future. If the adjustments are more than actuarially fair, the earnings-test tax actually becomes a subsidy.) Burtless and Moffitt (1984) ignored this complication because they believe that retirees are generally unaware of its existence.

19. The impact of borrowing constraints and the clustering of retirements at age 62 are discussed in more detail in Burtless and Moffitt (1986). In addition, Kahn (1988) has presented evidence for the liquidity constraint hypothesis. He found that the retirement cluster at age 62 is primarily among low wealth people, who can neither dissave, since they have little wealth, nor borrow against future benefits. Therefore, they have to work until actually eligible for benefits.

20. The authors acknowledged the possibility that these results represent reporting bias, rather than the actual earnings distribution. In other words, respondents may underreport earnings to avoid the reduction in Social Security benefits. But since these figures were reported to Census workers (who actually collected the RHS data), not to the Social Security Administration, this may not be a serious problem.

21. In more recent work, Burtless (1987) has written in detail on the impact of health on retirement. He found that industrial and occupational attachments affect work-related health status, and that both health and industrial and occupational attachments have independent impacts on the employment patterns of older workers.

22. Burtless (1986) used a similar model, estimated with the same data set, to simulate the impact on retirement trends of the large increases in real Social Security benefits between 1969 and 1972. He concluded that "social security is found to have a precisely measured but small overall effect on retirement. If these estimates are approximately accurate, rising social security benefits in the 1970s played only a small role in the decline in the average male retirement age in recent years. The labour force participation rate of older men has declined for various reasons in addition to the increases in social security payments: rising personal wealth levels, sharply higher unemployment levels in the period after 1970, and changing attitudes toward work and retirement."

23. Eight of the plans were union agreements—four in durable manufacturing, negotiated by the United Auto Workers, and four others in transportation, trade, and construction. The other six nonunion plans were in the service and finance industries. (See Mitchell and Luzadis 1988.)

Four of the pension plans had insufficient data on the retirees to use in the behavioral equations. Therefore, all 14 could be used in describing the retirement incentives, but workers in only 10 of them were included in the behavioral equations.

24. See Fields and Mitchell (1984c, chapter 3) for more details on their forecasting techniques.

25. Their qualitative results were similar to those of Kotlikoff and Wise (1989) who studied the accrual patterns of nearly 1,200 plans and also found a wide variety of incentives.

26. The present discounted values of the pension plan in table 3.2 are different from those for plan A in table 3.1, because table 3.1 described the incentives for a single illustrative individual, while table 3.2 averages the values over the 390 men in the plan A sample.

27. In their book, Fields and Mitchell (1984c) calculated the average incentives across 10 of the pension plans (the 10 plans that they used in the behavioral work), but only up through age 65. The average (across people and plans) true compensation peaked at $8,711 (in 1970 dollars) between ages 61 and 62, and then declined to $7,306 between ages 64 and 65. Presumably, the declines continued after age 65, when the Social Security wealth gains became losses.

28. The earnings component in YBASE is zero, because retirement at age 60 implies no future earnings in the Fields and Mitchell model.

29. Similar results were found in an analysis of the 390 workers in pension plan A (Fields and Mitchell [1984a]) and in a regression on workers in the RHS. In the latter case, however, the magnitude of the YSLOPE effect was much smaller and barely significant.

30. An exception to this is the defined-contribution employer pension plan, which is really just a tax-deferred savings plan.

31. Bernheim (1988) presents evidence that respondents in the RHS form generally unbiased estimates of future Social Security benefits, and that this was true even when the predictions were made prior to the large increases legislated in the early 1970s. This suggests that these increases may not have been entirely unanticipated, despite the fact that they followed a decade-and-a-half of roughly constant real benefits.

The literature below, in contrast, assumes that these real increases were not foreseen. See Anderson, Burkhauser, and Quinn (1986) for arguments on why this is a more reasonable assumption.

32. With the exception of the pension eligibility variable, which was statistically insignificant, the other coefficients were of the expected sign, and significant.

33. Krueger and Pischke (1989) admit that there are alternative explanations for their nonfinding. Integrated employer pension plans would have offset part of the wealth loss, and even where they did not, the impact of the loss on lifetime wealth may have just been too small to create a discernible retirement effect. If so, it would be incorrect to conclude that a more substantial and widespread change in Social Security benefits would have little effect.

34. The age intervals were 58–61, 62–64, 65, 66–70, and 71 and older. Since most of these intervals are several years wide, it is all the more surprising that the predictions were so inaccurate.

35. There are several differences in the two studies that might explain the conflicting results on the accuracy of plans. Anderson, Burkhauser, and Quinn's predictions were all made in the year 1969, when the respondents were 58–63 years old. They defined a prediction as accurate whenever retirement occurred within a year on either side of the date. Nestel's predictions were all made by 59-year-olds, who were probably further away, on average, from their predicted retirement age. Nestel also required retirement within the predicted interval (see footnote 34), rather than within a year of the predicted age.

36. See Svahn and Ross (1983) for a detailed description of the 1983 Social Security amendments.

37. This would imply a 20 percent reduction for retirement at age 65 and a 40 percent reduction for those claiming benefits at age 62. The legislation actually passed in 1983 will raise the age of full benefits to 66 by the year 2009, and eventually to 67 in 2027, and will set the maximum reduction for retirement at age 62 at 30 percent.

38. In fact, the 1983 legislation will slowly raise the delayed retirement credit from 3 to 8 percent per year of delay after age 65.

39. Burtless and Moffitt define retirement as a discontinuous drop in labor supply.

40. The actuarial fairness is based on the actuarial life tables for single men. This implies, according to Burtless and Moffitt (1984), very slight reductions in benefits between ages 62 and 64 (since they estimate that the current rules are slightly more than actuarially fair) and dramatic increases after 65. Their delayed retirement credits are not constant per year; for example, their adjustment factors are 1.10 (rather than the current 1.03) at age 66, 1.33 (up from 1.09) at 68, and 2.05 at 72.

41. In a recent paper focusing on disability issues, Haveman, Wolfe, and Warlick (1988) analyzed the impact of a 20 percent decrease in Social Security early retirement benefits. Their simulations suggested that the number of early retirees would decrease by only a small percent and that only about a quarter of those who would leave the early retirement rolls would be able to join

the Social Security disability rolls. In contrast, a 50 percent earnings supplement (up to a maximum of $1,500 per year) for workers aged 62 to 64 was estimated to have a much larger effect on reducing the number of early retirees.

42. Gustman and Steinmeier (1985b) simulated what might happen if the age of normal retirement in an employer pension plan were changed from 65 to 67, to match the Social Security change. They predicted that the percentage working full time would increase by another 3 to 4 percentage points.

43. Ycas (1987) reported some preliminary evidence that this trend may have leveled off or perhaps even reversed during the 1980s.

44. Rones (1983) points out that this was not the case prior to the late 1960s, when the official unemployment rates for men aged 55 to 64 and 65 and over were slightly higher than those for prime aged men.

45. Part of the reason for this difference is that there is a huge pool of older Americans out of the labor force, and, therefore, potentially discouraged workers, and only a relatively small such pool among the younger. Older workers are more likely than the young to have alternative income sources (Social Security and pensions) that permit them to stop searching and leave the labor force.

46. Confusion arises in the literature because the survey instruments usually do not clarify the conditions of the hypothetical part-time job when people are asked, "Would you like to work part time?" This is not a very useful question unless accompanied by details on wages, benefits, and other terms of employment. See Rones (1983) for more elaboration on this point.

47. By 1981, 43 percent of the original sample had been lost due to attrition—26 percent had died and another 17 percent had disappeared for other reasons, usually refusal to participate. See Parnes *et al.* (1985) for an overview of the data set.

48. If all three criteria must be met, but met *at any time* during the 15 years—in other words, if retirement is a once-and-for-all event—then 68 percent of the sample had retired.

49. A comparison of the results based on information given prior to retirement with those based on retrospective reasons given after retirement "reinforced our *a priori* view that retrospectively reported reasons for retirement are suspect" (Parnes and Less 1985a).

50. This may understate the importance of mandatory retirement if some individuals retire prior to the mandatory retirement age but were nonetheless influenced by the fact that they could not have worked beyond it. These people would not end up in Parnes and Less' first category.

51. Even when only those who retired at age 65 or later are considered, only 9 percent seemed to have retired because of a mandatory retirement provision on their regular jobs.

– 4 –

The Importance
of Employer Pensions and Social Security
at Younger Ages

In the previous two chapters, we reviewed the literature on the importance of Social Security and employer pensions on the labor supply decisions of older workers. The characterization of retirement income rights as special forms of wealth, whose value affects and is affected by labor force behavior, is at the core of the modern economic analysis of retirement. Less well understood is the role that Social Security and pensions play at younger ages. Although the actual receipt of retirement benefits occurs near or at the end of the work life, their values are determined by decisions made much earlier.

In this chapter, we consider the effects of pensions on the patterns of wage compensation and on work behavior earlier in an individual's career. Although it is still controversial, there is emerging a life-cycle, implicit-contract view of the relationship between workers and the firms that employ them. Employer pensions play an integral role in this relationship. Chapters 2 and 3 focused on the most obvious aspect of this contract: nonactuarially fair pension plans can penalize workers who stay on career jobs too long. Here, we suggest that pensions can also affect mobility much earlier. In summary, they penalize workers who leave too early as well as those who leave too late.

In the "spot" market view of competitive markets, workers are paid the value of their marginal products in every time period. At the heart of the implicit contract view, and the controversy surrounding it, is the notion that workers are paid their marginal product over their careers with a firm rather than at every moment during that career. They can be overpaid or underpaid at any moment, as long as it averages out in the end. This view of labor market equilibrium turns out to be more than an esoteric point of theory. It is an important distinction that fundamentally alters one's view of who pays for pensions, who loses when a worker leaves a career job "too early," and how the size of a firm's pension liability varies over the career of its workers.

We also discuss the role of the Social Security system earlier in a worker's career. Since a link exists between Social Security taxes and future benefits, one can estimate the net effect of Social Security on the wage of a worker of any age. We argue that changes in Social Security policy could influence work across the entire life cycle.

Pensions

In the last chapter, we discussed how a worker's pension wealth changes if benefit acceptance is delayed. Here the value of pension wealth is shown to change throughout an employee's work career with the firm. Pension accrual (the change in the present discounted value of a pension following an additional year of work) starts not when one is first able to claim benefits, but as soon as one is vested with a firm. If changes in pension wealth affect net compensation and labor supply of older workers, they may do the same at younger ages as well.

Defined Benefit vs. Defined Contribution Pension Plans

Pension plans are generally of two types. Defined contribution plans establish a contribution rule; for example, the employer and employee may each pay 5 percent of current salary into a pension fund. Contributions are invested and the eventual benefit is based on the value of the funds at the time. If workers who leave the firm before retirement have a right to the full current value of the contributions, then the plan should have little effect on mobility. Because defined contribution plans are usually actuarially fair across possible retirement ages, they should play a relatively minor role in the timing of retirement.

Defined contribution plans are really just mandatory saving plans with tax advantages. Their effect on work behavior is not significantly different from that of other forms of wealth. While this is the dominant form of pension for university professors, fewer than 30 percent of covered workers have a defined contribution as their primary plan (table 1.3). But as we saw in chapter 1, these types of pensions have been growing rapidly in recent years. If this continues, it will diminish the importance of the employment penalties late in life that we emphasized in chapter 3, as well as the earlier incentives discussed below.

Defined benefit plans are a more complex form of savings and play a much more important role in work decisions. These plans promise workers a benefit at retirement based on an agreed-upon formula. Employees usually make no explicit contribution to the plan. A typical defined pension plan offers benefits beginning at some stated age to workers of specified tenure, and is usually based on years of service and/or some average of highest nominal earnings. In practice, the latter generally means the earnings in the last few years of employment with the firm.

One method of calculating pension accrual is to estimate, year by year, what the present discounted value of the pension would be if the worker were to leave the firm after that year. This is the "quit value" of the pension—what it would be worth were the worker to quit. Positive accrual (growing pension wealth with continued employment) means that true compensation exceeds the paycheck; negative accrual means the opposite. Tracing the actual quit value for a worker in a given pension plan requires information on the worker's annual earnings, the appropriate interest rate, the life expectancy of the worker, and the often very complex pension plan rules.

Larry Kotlikoff and David Wise (1989) have studied the sensitivity of lifetime accrual patterns to changes in each of these parameters. They used a pension plan with cliff vesting, in which workers lose all benefits unless they stay with the firm for 10 years. Prior to 1987, this was the maximum number of years a firm could require before vesting. The 1986 Tax Reform Act reduced the normal maximum to five years.

Kotlikoff and Wise also assumed that, in addition to a normal retirement age, the plan had an early retirement option subject to an actuarial reduction in annual benefits. This is typical of most defined benefit plans.

For simplicity, benefits were assumed to be some fraction of final year's earnings and service, with no offset for Social Security. Finally, they assumed that the worker would live to early retirement age and had a normal life expectancy thereafter.

The authors calculated the ratio of pension accrual to salary in each year for workers with constant growth in real wages. Under these assumptions, the accrual paths shown in figure 4.1 have two major spikes. This contrasts the accrual path for the defined contribution plan, which would be a constant proportion of the wage.

Figure 4.1
Pension Increments as a Percentage of Salary, by Age,
for a Wage Stream with 6% Inflation Discounted at
Real Interest Rates of 3%, 6%, and 9%

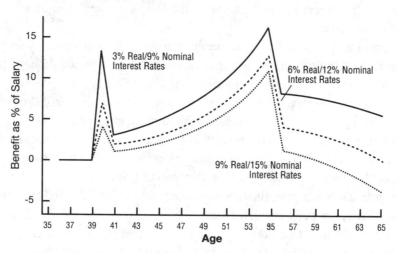

SOURCE: *Kotlikoff and Wise* (1989), p. 21.

For ease of explication, Kotlikoff and Wise assumed that work begins at age 30, early retirement is available at age 55, and normal retirement occurs at 65. Therefore, the first spike appears at age 40, after 10 years of service with the firm, when the worker becomes vested.

A worker who leaves before then loses all pension benefits, so the quit value of the pension is zero up to this point.

Once the worker is vested, pension accrual is found to be a smoothly increasing percentage of salary up to the point of earliest benefit eligibility. This pattern is caused both by the aging of the worker, which moves him closer to the promised benefit stream, and by the increase in years of service with the firm. The second peak in pension accrual occurs at the early retirement age. It is the period after early retirement eligibility that was the focus of much of our discussion in the previous two chapters.

Since pension plans usually did not provide full service credit after normal retirement age, accrual was likely to be negative after that age and pension wealth fell for the majority of workers.[1] (This is not shown on figure 4.1 which stops at age 65.) The accrual rate between the early and normal retirement ages is more varied. The Employee Retirement Income Security Act (ERISA) regulations forbid early benefit reductions larger than necessary to offset the additional years of expected benefit receipt. In other words, the reduced benefits must be at least actuarially fair.

In figure 4.1 all three assumptions about real wage growth and nominal interest rates yield peaks at the earliest retirement age, but only the lowest line shows negative pension accrual immediately thereafter. The top two lines simply show smaller positive accrual. Actual accrual will depend on the size of the actuarial reduction factor and other details of the benefit calculation formula. All that is required for the pension to peak at early retirement is that the early retirement penalty be less than an actuarially fair reduction. If this adjustment factor is tilted strongly enough toward early acceptance, it can even offset the increase in benefits caused by wage growth and another year of tenure. In such a case, the worker is "over-rewarded" for retiring early, "under-rewarded" for staying on, and accrual can be negative after the early retirement age.

Sara Hatch (1981) found that the majority of retirement programs with early retirement options have reduction factors that are smaller than actually fair. They do not sufficiently "punish" early retirement and, therefore, they actually encourage it. For simplicity, Kotlikoff and Wise (1989) assumed that benefits are based on a single year of earnings, real wages grow at a constant rate, and hours worked are constant over all years. Most pension plans use more years in their calculations, and real earnings growth may decline at older ages. These two factors would make negative pension accrual more likely after early retirement age.

Kotlikoff and Wise (1989) also looked at a national sample of pension plans and estimated accrual paths for a typical worker who joined the plans at age 30. Average accruals closely followed the trends in figure 4.1. They peak just before early retirement age, fall during the early retirement window, and then turn negative after normal retirement age. The recent change in pension legislation that required all plans to continue pension credits past age 65 (with the caveat noted in footnote 1) will reduce these negative accruals to some extent and therefore diminish the work disincentives facing older workers.

The Spot vs. Implicit Contract View of Pensions

Despite the fact that most workers make no explicit contributions to their defined benefit pension funds, it is unlikely that pensions are a free gift from a firm to its workers. Rather, both sides recognize that pension promises are costly to the firm. This cost must be offset by the willingness of employees to receive lower current earnings. There is profound disagreement, however, over the nature of this pension promise and the amount of reduced wages workers are willing to accept for it. Two contending theories of competitive labor markets offer significantly different views of how workers value the pension promises of their firms and how the resulting liabilities of these firms should be determined.

We discussed above the quit value of a pension. Annual pension accrual was measured as the difference between the pension's value were the worker to quit at one point in time versus its value following a quit one year later. While this calculation is straightforward, its implications for work behavior and pension liability are not. Neoclassical economic theory posits that in a competitive market, workers are paid the value of their marginal product to the firm. Total compensation includes both wage earnings and the pension accrual associated with that extra work. But how does a worker actually value this accrual? More specifically, what will workers be willing to forego in reduced wages for the promise of future benefits?

Jeremy Bulow (1982) has argued that workers are unlikely to give up anything more than the change in the quit value of the pension. In this "spot" market view of labor contracts, workers do not view their relationship with the firm as a multiperiod one. They demand that total compensation (wages plus pension accrual) equal the value of their productivity in each period. If they leave, they will have been paid in full.[2]

But as Kotlikoff and Wise (1989) point out, estimated accrual patterns and the assumption of spot labor markets imply a very unlikely productivity pattern during a worker's tenure with the firm. As figure 4.1 shows, workers assumed to have constantly increasing real wages will have total compensation spikes at the year of vesting and once again at the first year of early retirement. This seems incompatible with any reasonable assumption about productivity and suggests that a strict spot market model does not adequately explain the reality of pensions. A more complex model of labor market behavior is required to understand the role of pensions at younger ages.

Richard Ippolito (1986, 1987, 1989) has offered an alternative explanation for the pension contract—that it is the enforcing mechanism in an implicit *long-term* contract between the workers and the firm.[3] The firm promises not to terminate the worker (except for cause) or the pension plan (barring unforeseen exigencies), and the worker promises not to quit. The advantages to the firm are a stable workforce and lower turnover and training costs. The advantages to the workers are stability of employment and the opportunity to reap the returns from long tenure with the firm.

To hold workers to their end of the bargain, they are asked to forego wages *in excess of* the quit value of their pensions, despite the fact that firms are only required to turn over this quit value to a worker upon termination. This model relaxes the requirement that marginal product equal compensation each year, and instead requires only that lifetime compensation equal lifetime productivity.[4] But this equality will occur only if workers stay with the firm until the end of the implicit agreement—sometime around retirement age. As we saw in the last chapter, workers who stay beyond this are penalized by a loss in pension wealth. According to Ippolito, the same thing occurs to those who leave too early.

The mechanism for this mobility penalty is found in the mechanics of many defined benefit plans. Benefits are generally based on years of service and on some measure of average earnings, usually over the last few years of employment with the firm. If a vested worker leaves in mid-career, these *nominal earnings* are frozen and become the basis for *nominal benefits* many years later, at the age of receipt eligibility. Pension benefits are tied to a much lower nominal wage base than if the worker had stayed with the firm. Wages that would have been earned in future years with the firm would have been higher because of productivity increases and inflation. It is the employer's promise to pay a pension based on these higher wage years that is forfeited when a worker quits "too soon."

Because of the implicit contract that encourages workers not to quit, Ippolito argues that the current "stay" value of the pension is a better measure of the firms' current obligation to its workers. The stay value is based not on the current nominal wage (as the quit value is), but rather on the nominal wage the worker expects to receive on the eve of retirement. Since this is a higher nominal wage than the current one, the stay value of the pension exceeds the quit value. They become equal only at retirement age. Although the current legal obligation of the firm is only the lower quit value, its actual obligation is higher, Ippolito argues, because the quit value is not likely to be exercised. It is the final stay value that firms expect to pay. Their current liability, therefore, is the present discounted value of that, and it is changes in the stay value that are the appropriate accruals for the workers who remain on the job.

In Ippolito's model, pensions are seen as mechanisms to ensure that workers leave their jobs at the right time. Negative accruals at older ages assure that they do not stay too long. Substantial losses in pension wealth at younger ages assure that they do not leave too soon. The penalty to workers who do leave is the difference between the foregone wages (high enough to finance a stay pension) and the smaller quit pensions they actually receive.

The loss is not likely to be trivial. With some simplifying assumptions and an interest rate of 10 percent, Ippolito shows that a worker who quits a job 10 years from retirement can lose nearly two-thirds of the stay value of the potential pension.

Steve Allen, Robert Clark, and Ann McDermed (1986) used Ippolito methodology to simulate the losses in pension wealth associated with quitting a job, using pension data from the 1983 Employee Benefit Survey of Medium and Large Firms and samples of individuals from several micro data sets. They simulated representative pension plans and estimated the percentage of salary necessary to finance a quit pension and a stay pension each year.

Their findings, summarized in table 4.1, are similar to those of Kotlikoff and Wise (1989). After vesting, quit pension accrual as a share of salary rises each year until the onset of early retirement. In contrast, the stay pension provides a smoother accrual path. There is no spike in its accrual path at vesting since the stay pension assumes the worker will, in fact, stay until retirement age. The spike at early retirement is also less pronounced—15 rather than 27 percent of annual salary. The pattern of pension wealth loss they found, were the worker to leave under the implicit contract scenario, mirrors the accrual patterns. The pension loss associated with a quit builds until middle age, since the stay accrual taken from salary is greater than the legal accrual guaranteed to a quitter. Hence, the potential wealth loss generally peaks (at about one year's salary, according to Allen, Clark, and McDermed) in late middle age. After that, the pension loss associated with a quit rapidly falls and approaches zero as the worker approaches early retirement age.

Allen, Clark, and McDermed did not take into account the recent reduction (from 10 to 5) in the maximum years of tenure required before vesting occurs. But it is not likely that this would dramatically change their results. Reducing the maximum number of years until complete vesting will shift the spike in the quit pension value by five years and provide positive accrual to workers between their fifth and tenth years. It will have no effect on the stay pension value. It will reduce the penalty that worker who do leave the job with between 5 and 10 years of tenure pay, but it will not substantially alter the losses associated with quit-

Table 4.1
Simulation of Pension Contract Lifetime Compensation Patterns
for the Typical Manufacturing Firm with 1,000 or More Employees
for Its Professional and Administrative Staff

		Accrual as a percent of salary	
Age	Tenure	Quit pension	Stay pension
25	0	1.4	14.3
35	10	10.9	14.4
40	15	13.9	14.5
45	20	17.5	14.7
50	25	22.0	15.0
55	30	27.5	15.5
60	35	10.1	5.3
64	39	−1.7	−4.2
65	40	−3.3	−6.0
70	45	−15.3	−20.0

SOURCE: Compilation from Allen, Clark, and McDermed (1986).

ting, since both the quit and stay value of pensions at early ages are relatively small.

Pension Plans and Turnover

In a spot market framework, pensions are neutral with respect to job tenure with a firm. Since workers forego only the change in the quit value of a pension each year, they suffer no loss if they leave a firm. They collect all their past wage decrements on the way out. While it is true that they forego the ever-increasing accrual value of future years of tenure with the firm, it is assumed that their total compensation package in the future will be equal to their future productivity and, therefore, that they will receive similar benefits in alternative employment. In the less pristine real world, the operation of markets is not quite so smooth, but the presence or absence of pensions adds no complications to the spot market view of labor market turnover.

The implicit contract view, however, puts pension plans at the center of a theory of turnover. Workers who join a firm with a defined benefit pension plan agree to a wage package that defers some of the compensation until the end. The value of a worker's services to the firm equals the worker's total compensation only for those who stay until retirement age to collect a pension. Quits before the optimal retirement age result in a penalty, often a large one, to the worker.

While substantial evidence exists that workers in firms with pensions tend to stay longer and do have lower turnover rates, the studies do not adequately disentangle the incentives of the potential pension wealth loss from the fact that such firms may simply have higher overall compensation packages.[5] Empirical testing of the effects of pensions on turnover has been difficult for two reasons. First, few data sets provide both the detailed information on pension rules necessary to estimate accruals and quit penalties and the longitudinal data on the individuals necessary to test behavioral models. Second, to the extent workers recognize these penalties, those more likely to stay until retirement age will tend to choose firms with such plans. While this is exactly the matching that firms and workers desire, such matching at the start of career jobs may obscure the true importance of losses in pension wealth associated with an early quit on a sample of workers caught in mid-career.

Both Allen, Clark, and McDermed (1986, 1988a) and Alan Gustman and Thomas Steinmeier (1987, 1989a) have attempted to disentangle the ways in which pensions influence tenure with a firm. Allen, Clark, and McDermed (1986) used data from the Panel Study on Income Dynamics (PSID) and the National Longitudinal Surveys (NLS) to estimate a model of turnover that included pension coverage and the capital loss associated with a quit. Because workers who plan to stay with the firm are more likely to join firms that penalize moving, they first estimated a pension coverage equation to adjust for this sample selection bias.

Because neither the PSID nor the NLS contains detailed information on pension characteristics, Allen, Clark, and McDermed linked pension data from the 1983 Employee Benefit Survey for Medium and Large Firms (EBS) to these data sets. They assigned the modal pension formula for each industry-occupation cell in the EBS to workers in the PSID and NLS according to their industry and occupation. They estimated the likelihood that an employee with a given firm in 1975 would leave that firm by 1982 and found a strong negative relationship between pension coverage and a quit. This is consistent with the mobility literature. They found some evidence that the potential loss of pension wealth discouraged quitting, and concluded that the "loss in pension wealth associated with quitting substantially reduces the rate of mobility among workers covered by pension," and that "pension loss helps explain why older workers may be reluctant to leave a job even though market conditions may imply that future wage increases in his/her present job will be quite low."

In a later study with the same data sets, Allen, Clark, and McDermed (1988a) found that potential pension wealth losses had a larger effect on turnover than either vesting or overall compensation levels. The losses were mainly associated with lower layoff rates rather than quit rates, and they concluded that

> this evidence indicates either that deferred compensation schemes increase productivity (and thus reduce layoffs) or that employers are sufficiently concerned about layoff reputation and the ability to offer deferred compensation schemes in the future to prevent them from laying off workers and collecting a capital gain on their pensions.

Gustman and Steinmeier (1987) used data from the Survey of Consumer Finances (SCF) to test the importance of pensions on turnover. The SCF has excellent data on the pension characteristics of the individuals in the sample, so the authors did not have to assign modal formulas from another data source. In addition, they used a method of estimating pension losses very different from that proposed by Ippolito and by Allen, Clark, and McDermed. They estimated an age-earning profile for each person in their sample and then processed it through the rules of the individual's actual pension plan to calculate the path of "quit" pension accruals. With earnings data, this yielded age-compensation paths for all workers on their current jobs. They then estimated an alternative age-compensation path for each based on those who actually did change jobs over the period of the analysis. Finally, with these simulations from actual stayers and quitters, they estimated current and alternative job paths for all individuals in the sample.

Gustman and Steinmeier found that workers who switched jobs suffered for two reasons. First, their total pension wealth declined.[6] But, in addition, they tended to earn less on the alternative job. Hence, the appropriate comparison is the total compensation on the two jobs from the transition date until normal retirement age. They found that "lost" pension wealth (pension backloading) did matter. The higher the loss, the less likely the job switch. But they also argued that it was far less important than the lower wage workers could expect on a new job. They concluded that "compensation premia constitute a much more important fraction of the loss from job termination than does backloading of pension benefits [and] simulations . . . confirm that it is not backloading, but wage premia that accounts for the large difference in mobility between pension covered and noncovered jobs."

The papers by Ippolito and by Allen, Clark, and McDermed on the one hand, and those by Gustman and Steinmeier on the other, used different approaches to estimate the importance of pensions on turnover. They began with different views of how pension rules affect compensation across a worker's tenure with a firm, and they reached different conclusions about the importance of lost pension wealth on the decision of workers to quit a job. Both sets of authors did find some correlation between pension wealth loss and turnover, but Gustman and Steinmeier found that wealth loss was dominated by wage change effects. The difference in their conclusions reflects the currently unsettled debate on the precise nature of the effects of defined benefit pension plans on employee turnover.

Pension Liability

Since a firm can legally terminate a pension plan at any time, its pension liability is often estimated to reflect the current quit value of the obligations. Were the plan terminated, workers would only be eligible to receive pension benefits paid at the stipulated future retirement age, based on current nominal wages.

But if, in fact, workers have entered into an implicit contract to receive stay pensions based on nominal wages at the time of retirement, then this method dramatically underestimates the actual current pension liability of the firm. The amount of the underestimate depends on the age distribution of the firm's workforce, since the difference between quit and stay values rises and then falls as workers approach retirement age.

Once again, empirical evidence is scarce on the relative merits of these two alternative views of pension liability. Ippolito (1986) argued that stock traders are better judges of a firm's pension liability than are actuaries, and that one can examine stock prices for clues about which accounting method most accurately reflects true liability. Martin Feldstein and S. Seligman (1981) and Feldstein and Randall Morck (1983) found that when the traditional method of estimating liability (quit values) was incorporated into their stock market equations, the companies' stock appeared undervalued. When Ippolito used the larger stay value of pension liabilities, there was no evidence of either over- or undervaluation of stock. This suggests that the stock market views the higher liabilities implied by the implicit contract view of pensions as the relevant financial concept.

Social Security

Another Look at Accrual Rates

Much of the discussion concerning pensions in the previous section can be applied to the retirement component of Social Security. One can estimate the annual accruals of Social Security wealth. In fact, as we have seen in chapters 2 and 3, this is precisely what researchers have done to estimate the impact of Social Security on retirement. Social Security wealth and changes in that wealth are important theoretical and empirical components of modern economic models of retirement.

In the previous section, pension accruals were introduced as a means of differentiating between single-period and multiperiod models of labor contracts. The emphasis was on how pensions influence tenure with a single firm and on how alternative views of pension promises affect pension liabilities. There is little or no discussion on the impact of pensions on lifetime labor supply. In contrast, this is precisely the focus of the small amount of literature on Social Security and younger workers.

Social Security is similar to a defined-benefit pension plan, since the government promises workers a benefit at retirement based on a known formula. Normal benefits begin at age 65, with an early retirement option at 62. Cliff vesting exists since workers (aged 62 by 1991) must have worked in Social Security-covered employment for 10 years to be eligible for benefits. This requirement is not likely to be important for many workers since, unlike most employer pension plans, Social Security earnings are portable from one covered job to the next.

For workers aged 62 by 1990, retirement benefits are based on the highest 35 years of Social Security-covered earnings. A major change in the formula has occurred for those who were less than 63 years old in 1978. The highest years' earnings used in the benefit calculation formula are now indexed to economywide changes in nominal wage rates. In effect, they are blown up to current dollars before being averaged. If this change were applied to defined-benefit pension plans, it would dramatically reduce the current penalty to those who leave a job before retirement and remove the major penalty associated with quitting. It would allow those who left a job to receive the *real* value of their last year of work with the firm, adjusted not merely for inflation but also for growth in real wages, even if they left the job many years before retirement.

If one assumes that workers receive constantly increasing real wages and work the same number of hours per year, and if one ignores taxes and merely looks at the present discounted value of future benefits, then the accrual pattern for Social Security would look much like that for a private pension found by Kotlikoff and Wise (1989). From a quit-value perspective, accruals would be zero until vesting, and then show a large peak at 10 years. Accruals would then rise slowly for another 25 years, as additional years of work replace zeros in the calculation formula. After 35 years, current earnings would be replacing past (lower) earnings rather than zeros, and the accrual increases would taper off. As was seen in the last chapter, what happens at age 62 is a matter of considerable dispute. Some authors, such as Blinder, Gordon, and Wise (1980), argue that accruals remain positive (at least they did during the 1960s and 1970s) and therefore continue to subsidize work. Others have estimated small negative accruals and discussed work disincentives that would imply. All agree that Social Security accruals turn sharply negative after age 65.

What distinguishes a small, recent literature on this topic is a shift away from the assumption of constant hours over the work career and an emphasis on intertemporal labor supply shifts. Richard Burkhauser and John Turner (1981, 1982, 1985) have argued that, from a lifetime labor supply perspective in which workers can choose annual hours, it is irrelevant whether accrual rates are positive or negative after age 62. What is critical is whether these rates are higher or lower than they were in earlier years. Once annual hours are endogenous, it is in the worker's interest to shift away from hours that are less well rewarded and toward those that are better rewarded. If Social Security accrual rates peak at early retirement, as many private pensions do, this will encourage workers to work more when younger and less when old. In a recent paper, Stephan Gohmann and Robert Clark (1989) present a sophisticated retirement model that makes the same point.

As discussed in the last chapter, there is considerable evidence that the Social Security system reduces work effort at older ages. Empirical research on its importance earlier in the career is sparse. Burkhauser and Turner (1978) used time-series data to argue that Social Security is partly responsible for the leveling off of the decline in hours worked per week that took place after the first four decades of the twentieth century. They suggest that the market work of younger men would have fallen two to three hours more since 1936 without the presence of Social Security. Adrienne McElwain and James Swofford (1986) also used time-series data to show that younger men increase their hours worked in years when it is easier to earn an income above the Social Security taxable maximum. Both of these studies recognize the life-cycle effect of the tax and benefit components of Social Security in their labor supply estimates. This perspective is more fully developed in the next section.

An Alternative Measure of Social Security's Marginal Value

Those who recognize the relationship between Social Security contributions and future benefits know that the official Social Security tax does not represent their true tax rate. Future benefits offset current taxes to some degree. This reduces the true tax paid on work in the period.

If Social Security benefits and taxes were perfectly actuarially linked, the increase in the present discounted value of future benefits would exactly offset the taxes paid. Edgar Browning (1975) has shown that the Social Security tax should then have no effect on work behavior. Social Security would merely act as a neutral deferred compensation plan whose impact on current disposable income could be offset by lending and borrowing.

But no such exact actuarial relationship between taxes and benefits exists. Nevertheless, some relationship does exist, and it is only by understanding this that the effect of Social Security on workers throughout their work life can be understood. Burkhauser and Turner (1985) exploit this life-cycle view to analyze how the dramatic changes mandated for the twenty-first century by the 1983 amendments to the Social Security Act affect younger workers today.

Table 4.2 shows the legislated payroll tax (t) across the life of workers who retired and took Social Security benefits at age 65 in 1982. The legislated payroll tax increased from 4 percent in 1955 to 8.55 percent in 1978 (column 3). Column 4 shows the marginal benefits associated with an additional dollar of taxable income, and column 5 is the true payroll tax rate—the difference between columns 3 and 4.

Table 4.2
True Social Security Payroll Tax Rates for White Males Age 65 in 1982

Year[a]	Age	Legislated payroll tax[b] (%)	Worker		Worker with dependent spouse	
			Benefit increment[c] (%)	True payroll tax[d] (%)	Benefit increment (%)	True payroll tax[e] (%)
1955	--	4.00	0	4.00	0	4.00
1956	39	4.00	13.15	-9.15	25.77	-21.77
1962	45	5.75	13.18	-7.43	25.70	-19.95
1967	50	7.10	12.76	-5.66	24.68	-17.58
1972	55	8.10	13.20	-5.12	25.25	-17.15
1978	61	8.55	15.83	-7.28	29.45	-20.90

SOURCE: Burkhauser and Turner (1985).

a. We assume an increasing age-earning profile so all years prior to 1956 are not used in the AIME calculation. Hence, marginal benefits in those years are zero. Payroll tax rates varied between 2 percent and 4 percent over the period.

b. The tax rate is on an additional dollar of taxable income. It includes both employer and employee shares of OASI payroll tax.

c. Present discounted value of OASI benefits derived from an additional dollar of taxable income, expressed as the percentage per dollar.

d. Column 3 minus column 4. A negative value indicates a wage subsidy.

e. Column 3 minus column 6.

During the 23 years of earnings used in the calculation of Social Security benefits for a worker who reached age 62 in 1978, the expected marginal gain in Social Security benefits far exceeded the marginal taxes paid. For these years, the Social Security tax was actually a substantial wage subsidy. The subsidies were even larger for workers with dependent spouses, since, at no additional charge, Social Security pays an additional 50 percent benefit to the eligible spouse of a Social Security recipient. Note, however, that during the years not used in the calculations (in this case, those prior to 1956), the payroll tax was, in fact, a tax at the legislated rate. And after age 61, the 50 percent earnings test applied, reducing the marginal impact of a dollar earned below what it was a year before. Even if Social Security continued to provide a subsidy between ages 62 and 64, there would be an incentive to shift hours from years with low subsidy to years of high subsidy, as long as the actuarial adjustment was less than fair. This view assumes that workers know which years will and will not eventually be used in the calculation formula, an interesting assumption theoretically, but one whose accuracy is subject to question.

In the previous chapter, we argued that Social Security encourages older workers to retire after some age (certainly by 65) because of reductions in Social Security wealth. From a life-cycle view, the Social Security benefit formula is shown to twist net wage compensation toward middle years, encouraging workers to increase their work then and decrease it at both ends.

The divergence of legislated rates from benefit-adjusted rates for the new generation of workers entering the system in the 1980s is much less than that of the generation now retiring. The increase in the number of years used in the formula (which is 35 in 1990) is one explanation, as is the indexing of past wages in the averaging calculation. In addition, the increased labor force participation of women will mean fewer men will have dependent spouses.

This long-run trend toward convergence of legislated and actual tax rates was accelerated by recent amendments to the Social Security Act. Table 4.3 shows the legislated payroll tax rates for a male aged 22 in 1983 before and after the 1983 Social Security Amendments. The true tax rates are shown for men in the lowest and highest Social Security benefit calculation brackets. The numbers (0.32 and 0.15) refer to the increase in monthly benefits associated with a $1 increase in average monthly earnings. Even before the amendments, the true payroll taxes were larger, and the difference between legislated and true rates smaller than for the currently retiring generation of workers. For a worker without a dependent spouse, the tax was really a tax for most years. For those in the 0.15 bracket, the pre-1983 net tax was between 50 and 70 percent of the legislated rate (column 7).

The effect of the 1983 changes in benefits and legislated tax rates on true marginal tax rates is estimated in table 4.3. Column 4 shows the new legislated payroll tax rates over the work life of those workers. They represent an increase of about 1 percentage point (about 10 percent) over the pre-amendment rates. But by reconsidering the link between future benefits and current taxes, we see that the change in the true tax rates was substantially larger in both absolute and relative terms.

Concentration on changes in legislated payroll rates masks the changes in true tax rates implied by the alterations in the future benefit schedule. The 1983 act cut benefits by increasing the age of full benefits from age 65 to age 67 (for those reaching age 62 in 2022) and by taxing one-half of all Social Security benefits for high-income recipients.[7] Although this tax is now paid by only a small number of current Social Security recipients, it will be relevant for more workers in the future unless the tax thresholds are raised to offset inflation.

The exact changes in the true payroll tax are controversial. They depend critically on assumptions about discount rates and about the manner in which individuals perceive the future and act on those perceptions. Edgar Browning (1985), for instance, has argued that the 1 percent real discount rate used in Burkhauser and Turner (1985) and in a parallel study by Roger Gordon (1983) was unrealistically low, and that a much higher rate is appropriate. A more fundamental criticism by Browning is that workers do not know for certain which years will be included in the average earnings measure. Hence, it is not appropriate to divide work life into years that are used in the accounting period and years that are not. To do so results in low true marginal tax rates in the years

Table 4.3
Life-Cycle Marginal Social Security Payroll Tax Rates For White Males
Age 22 in 1983 Before and After 1983 Amendments

Year	Age	Legislated payroll tax rates		True tax rates			
				(0.32 bracket)		(0.15 bracket)	
		Preamendment (%)	Amendment (%)	Preamendment (%)	Postamendment (%)	Preamendment (%)	Postamendment (%)
				Worker			
1983	22	9.15	9.55	9.15	9.55	9.15	9.55
1991	30	10.20	11.20	3.94	6.27	7.27	9.15
2001	40	10.20	10.98	1.08	3.80	5.92	7.99
2011	50	10.20	10.98	1.81	4.37	6.27	8.23
2022	61	10.20	10.98	-0.20	2.78	5.32	7.56
				Worker with dependent spouse			
1983	22	9.15	9.55	9.15	9.55	9.15	9.55
1991	30	10 20	11.20	-2.14	1.48	4.42	7.15
2001	40	10 20	10.98	-7.60	-3.04	1.86	5.14
2011	50	10.20	10.98	-6.02	-1.79	2.60	5.66
2022	61	10.20	10.98	-9.16	-4.27	1.12	4.63

SOURCE: Burkhauser and Turner (1985).

used, since the earnings generate higher future benefits, and in true tax rates equal to the legislated rate in all other years. Browning suggested that if workers are not certain which years will be used in the averaging process, then the true rate should be some average of the two.

Taking these factors into account in his simulations, Browning argued that while "historically" the divergence between legislated and true payroll tax rates may have been great, the difference is much less for today's generation of workers. His simulation results suggest that true rates are in the range of 80 to 90 percent of actual rates. This is approximately the range of difference found for single workers in the 0.15 bracket of table 4.3. In any case, both papers provide a plausible reason for the reduced support for Social Security among younger workers. The well-known increases in taxes together with the less-publicized decreases in future benefits combine to reduce the value of Social Security to today's contributors. Only a life-cycle view of the process can combine the taxes and benefits and reveal the true redistributional impact of the program.

Summary

The life-cycle view of human behavior is intuitively and theoretically appealing. The basic idea is that labor supply, consumption, and savings decisions are based not only on one's current situation, but also on the past and on expectations of the future. In the very short run, this view is obviously accurate; people do not reduce consumption on the weekends because they are not earning income for two days. In the medium run, it also makes sense; consumption habits take time to alter, and people should be able to anticipate and incorporate likely changes in circumstances ahead. In the very long run, over a lifetime, the theory strains credulity, but still provides a useful construct with which to approach multiperiod issues.

Public and private retirement income programs are certainly multiperiod in nature. Work decisions today affect retirement benefits in the future. It is widely agreed that the incentives built into these schemes affect labor supply behavior late in life. It is reasonable to expect that there are implications earlier in the career as well, but the literature is much thinner and the empirical evidence less robust.

Richard Ippolito is a leading proponent of the view that employer pensions are part of an implicit contract that firms and employees expect to be long term in nature. The contract binds them together and is structured to penalize a job separation that is too early or too late. Reputational considerations discourage the firm from reneging on its part of the agreement, even though it might be profitable to do so in the short run. Pension promises and liabilities should be evaluated, then, on the assumption that the workers will be around to collect all the delayed compensation foregone during their work careers.

There is considerable evidence that financial penalties for early departure do exist and some evidence that workers respond to them when they are large enough to be important. Mobility is lower among workers with pensions, but it is not clear whether this is due to pension wealth losses, to wage decreases associated with moving, or to the fact that workers who intend to remain with one firm tend to choose firms with pensions. Research also suggests that the stock market views unfunded pension liabilities as larger than the quit value of current obligations, which is consistent with the implicit contract view. But this implicit contract literature is relatively new and the evidence to date is far from overwhelming.

Both Gustman and Steinmeier (1989b) and Ippolito (1987) have pointed out a number of puzzles and inconsistencies in the implicit contract story. A primary reason for pensions in this scenario is to reduce worker turnover and thereby reduce hiring and training costs. If so, then why are the implicit pension penalties so low during the early years of association with the firm, precisely when turnover is most likely? The penalties may deter mobility among mid-career workers, but they seem too inconsequential to do much at either end. Another hypothesized goal is to prevent shirking by the workers. If a substantial portion of deferred compensation will be forfeited if an individual is dismissed, then there are strong incentives not to give cause. But if this is important, why do these incentives generally disappear as soon as the worker reaches early retirement age, when pension wealth often declines with delayed receipt?[8]

Other objections are even more basic. The size of the penalty for early departure depends critically on the rate of inflation, a factor which is highly variable and totally out of the control of the contracting agents— the firm and the workers. Why would they rely so heavily on a penalty that they cannot control? In addition, the magnitude of these financial incentives varies dramatically from plan to plan. They are nonexistent in defined contribution plans and show great variety among defined benefit programs. For the implicit contract theory to make sense, these differences should reflect underlying differences in the firms, industries and occupations in which they are found. Very little research into these implications has been conducted. And finally, the entire story assumes that workers understand the details of their pension plans and the nature of these pension wealth incentives. Olivia Mitchell (1988) and others have cast some doubt on this.

When the pros and cons are weighed, some researchers, such as Ippolito, remain committed to the concepts behind the implicit contract theory and the new pension economics, even while acknowledging that many unanswered questions remain. Others, such as Gustman and Steinmeier, express considerably more skepticism and look to other motivations, like the redistribution of income among workers, to explain the structure of pension plans.

The Social Security system also creates an interesting set of incentives across the life cycle. The most dramatic and best understood occur near the end, and it is reasonable to argue that their effects—to induce older workers out of the labor force—are intentional. Whether there is any method to the variations in implicit tax rates over the rest of the work life is much less clear, as is the proposition that workers understand and respond to them during their younger and middle years.

That individuals respond rationally to incentives is appealing to economists. Most of our models assume it, and many of our empirical results confirm it. The research discussed in this chapter is new, innovative, and controversial, and the jury is still out on its accuracy and importance.

NOTES

1. The Omnibus Budget Reconciliation Act of 1986 requires continued pension credits and accruals for work after age 65, unless the worker has reached the maximum number of years of tenure that are counted in the benefit calculation formula (Herz and Rones 1989). The discussion here reflects the situation that existed when this research was done, and does not reflect the impact of this law on typical accrual patterns.

2. Current pension legislation requires firms to back up their explicit defined pension promises by holding reserves equal to the quit value of the pensions. This is consistent with this single-period view of labor contracts.

3. Becker and Stigler (1974) and Lazear (1979) were earlier proponents of the importance of pensions in implicit lifetime contracts.

4. Gustman and Steinmeier (1989b) have experimented with a model in which lifetime productivity and lifetime compensation have to be equal for all employees as a whole, but not for individual ones. They then simulate how pension features might be used to reallocate pay among different age cohorts of employees.

5. See, for example, Schiller and Weiss (1979), Viscusi (1979), Freeman (1980), Mitchell (1982), McCormick and Hughes (with British data [1984]), and Rebitzer (1986).

6. Clark and McDermed (1988) compared the total pension wealth of a worker with one 40-year job to that of a worker with an identical wage profile, but with four different employers, all with the same pension plan. In their baseline example, total real pension wealth at age 65 for the mobile workers was only 57 percent of that of the 40-year employee. The exact percentage depended on whether or not the worker could cash out his pension wealth upon termination, and if so, the interest rate at which these funds could be invested. But in all cases examined, final pension wealth was always lower for the worker who switched jobs, illustrating one cost of job mobility.

7. Single-tax filers with taxable income above $25,000 and joint filers above $32,000 pay taxes on half of their Social Security benefits as well.

8. There is a related story at the aggregate level. With delayed compensation to be repaid only at retirement, workers are actually creditors, like bondholders, to the firm. If the firm goes out of business, the employees stand to lose some of their accounts receivable. This should discourage the workers, as a whole, from making demands deleterious to the health of the firm.

– 5 –

Transitions from Career Jobs

As we discussed in chapters 2 and 3, there is voluminous literature on the economic determinants of the retirement decision, much of it very current. Over the past decade, economists have focused on the financial incentives embedded in the Social Security and private pension systems and on how these incentives affect individual behavior. The consensus is that strong incentives to retire do exist, that many individuals behave as though they understand and respond to these incentives and, therefore, that the incentives have some impact on aggregate retirement patterns.

Most economic models of retirement have focused either on retirement status or on hours of labor supply. The first concept is discrete; the latter, continuous. Analyses of retirement status have usually treated the concept as dichotomous—one is either retired or not—but have differed on how it should best be defined. For example, Boskin (1977) defined retirement as movement to quarter-time (or less) work. Burkhauser (1979, 1980) used the acceptance of pension or Social Security benefits. Quinn (1977), Gordon and Blinder (1980), and Burkhauser and Quinn (1983b) required complete labor force withdrawal. Fields and Mitchell (1984c) defined retirement as departure from a primary job, and Burtless and Moffitt (1985) looked for a sudden and discontinuous drop in hours worked. Quinn (1980, 1981) and Hausman and Wise (1985) used self-defined retirement status. But all of the above used their rules to define a dichotomous state. We show below that this oversimplification overlooks some very rich and interesting labor force withdrawal patterns and therefore misses much of the story.

Some researchers have also studied hours of work after retirement. These models generally posit a continuous budget constraint along which a worker chooses the optimal combination of income and leisure. As we have explained above, the actual budget constraint is kinked because of the vagaries of tax, Social Security, and pension rules, and true compensation can differ dramatically from the wage rate. Economists usually assume either that workers can choose to work any number of hours (e.g., Gordon and Blinder 1980), or that the number of hours is fixed (e.g., Fields and Mitchell 1984c, and Burtless and Moffitt 1984). Although there is some truth in each of these assumptions, neither captures the realities of actual behavior.

Relatively few economists have dealt seriously with the fact that retirement, in fact, includes a whole gamut of labor market activities. To label them all with a single term obscures the rich variety of behavior that actually exists.

In this chapter, we discuss the economics literature that explicitly models the diverse patterns of labor market withdrawal. Most of this treats the decision as trichotomous—one either retires completely, retires partly, or does not retire at all. We then describe the actual patterns of departure from full-time work on career jobs that we have observed in our Retirement History Study sample. Although traditional retirement (sudden and complete labor force withdrawal) remains the most common pattern, a substantial minority of Americans leave their career jobs via more complex routes. A few choose a period of partial retirement (reduced hours) on the career job. Others take a new part-time position. Some older workers move from one full-time job to another, and others retire completely, but then later return to the labor force in a full-time or part-time capacity.

We will establish several facts below. First, alternative routes to retirement, other than the traditional transition from full-time work to full-time leisure, are common among the American workforce. Second, most of the intermediate stages occur soon after departure from the career job. And finally, these transitional jobs last long enough to be interesting. In chapter 6, we will discuss some of the correlates and implications of the different exit patterns.

Partial Retirement

Self-Employed vs. Wage and Salary Workers

Using the initial 1969 cross section of the Retirement History Study, Joseph Quinn (1980, 1981) compared the retirement patterns of a sample of white married men aged 58 through 63. The focus of this research was twofold: to determine the extent of partial retirement among older Americans, and to compare the patterns of self-employed and wage and salary workers. The hypothesis was that partial employment would be more common among the self-employed, since they have more control over their work environment. They are less likely to be covered by compulsory retirement provisions or pension plans, and are generally unconstrained by institutional rules on the length of the workweek.

Retirement status was determined by the respondents, who described themselves as either completely retired, partly retired, or not retired at all. These subjective responses correlated well with more objective labor force status (in or out) and annual hours measures.[1]

Several interesting conclusions emerged. Among men approaching normal retirement age (58 to 63 in the 1969 cross section), partial retirement was a common phenomenon, particularly among the self-employed.[2] Five percent of the wage and salary workers and over 12 percent of the self-employed described themselves so (Quinn 1981). In fact, among the self-employed in this age range, partial retirement was more common than complete retirement.

Data on annual hours of work confirmed that the self-employed enjoy more hours flexibility. Among those not retired, the annual hours distribution of the wage and salary workers was completely dominated by the mode around 2,000 hours, reflecting full-year status at the standard workweek. Over 80 percent worked between 1,500 and 2,500 hours per year. In contrast, the self-employed "not retired" were more evenly distributed over the spectrum. Over half worked more than 2,500 hours per year, and another 8 percent worked less than 1,500 hours.

Retirement status was highly correlated with the age and health of the individual. The probability of partial retirement rose monotonically with age, and was always much more common among those with a health condition limiting the type or amount of work they could do. This suggests that the phenomenon may grow in importance as the nation ages. For every age and health combination, partial retirement was more likely among the self-employed than among wage and salary workers. Additional analyses suggested that retirement status was also influenced by pension and Social Security eligibility and by the amount of asset income.

Quinn (1980) also found that some of the self-employed (about one in eight) had become so only in the previous 10 years. This suggests that some people may utilize self-employment as a transitional step between a career job and retirement.

This early research was relatively unsophisticated. It did not utilize the longitudinal nature of the RHS, and the treatment of retirement income sources was very rudimentary. But it previewed some findings of later, more detailed research—that partial retirement is an important phenomenon among the American workforce, that its importance grows with the age of the individuals, that the behavioral patterns of wage and salary workers and the self-employed are different, and that some wage and salary workers turn to self-employment late in life. There was also some circumstantial evidence that one reason for the difference in retirement patterns is a lack of choice of hours in the wage and salary sector, a topic that Alan Gustman and Thomas Steinmeier later addressed in a much more sophisticated manner.

Victor Fuchs (1982) also analyzed the phenomenon of labor force withdrawal among the self-employed, using the first three waves of the RHS. He intentionally avoided the term "retirement," because the concept is so poorly defined. He began by observing, as seen in table 5.1, that the proportion of the workforce that is self-employed increases with age, and that this can be seen in both cross-sectional and longitudinal data. This relationship with age occurs partly because self-employment has declined in importance in the United States over the long run, so we tend to observe fewer self-employed among the young than among the old. But the trend is also found within cohorts as they age. This is either because the self-employed retire later than wage and salary workers, so their relative number among the employed grows as a cohort

Table 5.1
Self-Employed as Percent of Total Employment, By Age,
White Urban Males, 1969, 1970, 1971, 1973

| | Cross section | Birth cohort[b] | | | | | |
Age	1970[a]	1911	1910	1909	1908	1907	1906
55	14.9						
56	14.6						
57	15.2						
58	15.1	13.4	13.4				
59	14.6			13.5			
60	14.8	16.5	15.6	13.5	13.9		
61	13.8			15.6	13.9		
62	16.6	18.7		15.6	17.6	16.2	15.4
63	15.9		21.7	19.9	17.6	20.0	15.4
64	17.5			19.9		20.0	
65	21.5				25.4		24.2
66	23.6				25.4	21.3	24.2
67	25.6					21.3	34.2
68	26.2						
69	26.5						

SOURCE: Fuchs (1982).

a. 1/100 sample, 1970 Census of Population.

b. Retirement History Study, 1969, 1971, 1973.

ages, or because some wage and salary workers become self-employed late in life.

Using a sample of white urban men in the RHS, Fuchs found that both reasons were important. At every age between 58 and 65, those already self-employed were less likely to stop working and this difference generally grew with age. In addition, 4 to 5 percent of the wage and salary workers switched over to self-employment in each of the two-year transition periods studied.

In order to understand why some workers switched to self-employment late in life, Fuchs estimated transition equations for those who were initially wage and salary workers. He found that workers were more likely to switch if they had had some periods of self-employment earlier in their careers, or if their career jobs had characteristics similar to self-employment. In particular, managers, professionals, and sales workers, many of whom have considerable discretion on the job, and those already working particularly short (less than 35 hours) or long (more than 50 hours) weeks were significantly more likely to become self-employed. The probabilities were considerably lower for those eligible for pensions or subject to mandatory retirement provisions, both of which are uncommon among the self-employed. In other words, those wage and salary workers whose work habits already resembled those of the self-employed were more likely to become so around retirement age.

Fuchs then combined all of those initially working (wage and salary and self-employed) and asked why some continued to work while others did not. Not surprisingly, he found that the probability declined with age, with evidence of poor health, and with pension or mandatory retirement coverage. But he also found that the probability of continuing work was significantly higher if the respondent was self-employed. In fact, holding all the other economic and demographic variables constant, the probability of continuing work over a two-year period was nearly 8 percentage points higher for the self-employed. Interaction terms between class of worker and age suggested that this difference was important only at ages 61 and above.

In a final set of regressions, Fuchs showed that among men initially working more than 35 hours per week, the self-employed were more likely to reduce their weekly labor supply below 35 hours two years later than were wage and salary workers. This suggests that the additional hours of flexibility enjoyed by the self-employed may be part of the reason why they are more likely to continue working late in life.

In summary, Fuchs has emphasized an important transition route for workers leaving career jobs, namely, a switch to self-employment. This change often involves a reduction in hours worked. He suggested that many of those who do switch have been self-employed in the past or are leaving wage and salary jobs that resemble self-employment in important ways, although he does not explicitly compare the old and new jobs. We will pursue this line of inquiry below.

Minimum-Hours Constraints

In a long series of articles beginning in 1983, Alan Gustman and Thomas Steinmeier have added considerable insight to our understanding of the labor supply choices facing older workers, and have developed sophisticated theoretical models and econometric techniques to deal with the complexity they found. Their major contribution has been to emphasize the importance of partial retirement—a transitional period of reduced hours between full-time employment and complete labor force withdrawal. They show that this transitional stage often occurs on a job other than the career job and usually at a significantly lower wage rate. They maintain that this occurs because most jobs have a minimum-hours constraint, so that many people have to leave their career jobs in order to work part time. They argue that models that ignore this phenomenon of gradual retirement can be very misleading.

With a sample of wage and salary white men, Gustman and Steinmeier (1984b) demonstrated again the importance of partial retirement in the labor force withdrawal process, utilizing the same subjective definition used by Quinn (1980, 1981).[3] Although they found that being "not retired" dominated up through age 63 and full retirement dominated thereafter, the intermediate status was an important phenomenon nonetheless. Fewer than 10 percent of those below age 62 described themselves as partially retired, but the proportion rose to between 15 and 20 percent among those aged 65 to 69. In fact, for those over 65, partial retirement was much more frequent than nonretirement. When the authors combined the first four waves of the RHS data, they found that about a third of the respondents were partially retired at some time during that six-year period.

Gustman and Steinmeier (1984a) also studied job change among older workers and found that the vast majority of the partially retired were no longer on their main jobs (defined as the full-time job held at age 55). Partial retirement usually involves a job change. In contrast, most of those not retired were still on the same job they held at 55. This difference would not be surprising if those partially retired had all faced mandatory retirement on their previous jobs, but this was not the case. Even those partly retired who had not and would not have faced mandatory retirement were much more likely to be on a new job. This was true even for the subset with no health problems and with neither a pension nor mandatory retirement on their main jobs.

A final piece of the puzzle was that those who did switch to a new job usually did so at a wage rate lower than what they had previously earned.[4] Why then do older workers change jobs? Why do they not simply reduce hours on their career jobs? Gustman and Steinmeier conclude that they do not because they cannot. Most jobs, they claim, have a minimum-hours constraint. Although the RHS did not inquire about this, some other data sets have. For example, over half (56 percent) of those who answered the appropriate question on the Michigan Panel Study of Income Dynamics claimed that they could not have worked less if they had wanted to.[5] In a survey of employers, only 15 percent (and only 10 percent in manufacturing) had a program in which workers could reduce hours as they approached retirement (Gustman and Steinmeier 1983). The authors concluded from these various sources that between 60 and 90 percent of workers face minimum-hours constraints on their jobs and, therefore, are unable to reduce hours as they age.

Gustman and Steinmeier also showed that ignoring these constraints can lead to erroneous conclusions. For example, the discontinuous labor supply shifts (in hours and employers) observed for most workers who choose partial retirement may be attributed to dramatic changes in preferences in a model that does not include the minimum-hours constraint. Similarly, the "choice" to move to a job with a lower wage rate will be puzzling unless one realizes that a reduction in hours on the original high-wage job was not possible. The authors demonstrated that ignoring the partial retirement option can significantly change the coefficients in a retirement model, because those partially retired have to be combined either with those retired or those not retired in a dichotomous world. Those who define retirement as complete labor force status would call them "not retired" and not differentiate between partial retirement and continued full-time work on the original job. Those with a definition based on hours or work or pension receipt would label many of them as retired, and equate partial retirement and complete labor force withdrawal. Since there is a sizable number of people in this intermediate category, particularly among those 65 and over, the empirical results are affected by how they are defined.[6]

A Structural Retirement Model

Gustman and Steinmeier (1986a) have developed a structural model of retirement that incorporates changes in individual preferences and budget constraints over time. In contrast to most of the retirement literature, their model permits individuals to reduce their hours to less than full time, but only at a reduced wage rate. This corresponds to the actual options described above.

Graphically, the worker faces the budget constraint shown in figure 5.1, which is drawn for a particular moment in time. *Point* A corresponds to full-time work at the full-time wage rate. No other hours options are permitted at this wage rate. To work less, the worker must take a lower wage rate, either on the main job or, more likely, on a different job. If this choice is made, the worker faces the budget constraint BCDE, kinked because of the mechanics of the Social Security system. Point E represents full retirement. Y(t) is current earnings, and, therefore, is zero at E.

Figure 5.1
Choice of Income and Leisure at Time *t*,
With Different Part-Time and Full-Time Wages

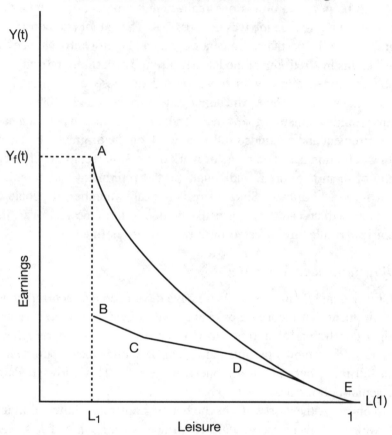

SOURCE: Gustman and Steinmeier (1986a), p. 561.

The complete budget constraint includes point A and line segments BCDE. The labor supply choice depends on this budget constraint and on the shape of the individual's indifference curves. A person with a very flat set of indifference curves (for whom a small increase in income would compensate for a large loss in leisure) will remain at point A and continue full time on the career job. People with steep indifference curves (a strong preference for leisure) will prefer point E and withdraw from the labor force. Workers with very curved indifference sets may be found working part time, along BCDE.

The individual faces a life-cycle labor supply problem, with each year treated as a separate period. Both the budget constraints and individual preferences change over time. Gustman and Steinmeier hypothesize that the indifference curves steepen as the worker ages, and therefore that most people eventually end up at point E, that is, out of the labor force.

In their empirical work, they estimated the parameters of a utility function, which the individual maximizes subject to a changing budget constraint. The parameters were chosen to maximize the likelihood of observing the retirement patterns actually observed in a sample drawn from the first four waves of the RHS.[7] Because of the complexity of the estimation procedure, only one of every 10 eligible households was chosen, and only a very sparse set of explanatory variables was used.

The variables determining the shape of the indifference curves included age, year of birth, and a dummy variable denoting a serious health problem lasting a year or more. Compensation (separately for full- and part-time work) had three components: wages, and pension and Social Security benefits. Full-time and part-time wage profiles were imputed from wage equations.[8] The pension and Social Security components of compensation were defined as the changes in the present discounted values of the streams of benefits that would occur with an additional year's work.[9]

The coefficient estimates were all significant in the expected direction. As anticipated, they indicated that indifference curves steepen significantly with age and with the onset of a health problem. The wage terms were modest in size. The authors estimated that a 10 percent change in the wage rate in the year of retirement would change the date of retirement by about five months.

The Gustman and Steinmeier model (1986a) had two innovative components: two different wage rates (for full-time and part-time work), and variable hours on the part-time job. To isolate which of these features was more important, they reestimated their equations in models in which there is (1) one wage and fixed hours (*a la* Fields and Mitchell); (2) one wage and variable hours (*a la* Gordon and Blinder); and (3) two wages, but partial retirement hours are fixed. It turned out that the important feature empirically was the introduction of the part-time wage rate, an innovation that they consider essential to understanding actual retirement patterns.

The authors (1986a) tested the overall quality of their model by simulating retirement patterns based on their parameter estimates, and comparing them with the patterns actually observed. Their results did a remarkable job of duplicating the retirement peaks observed at ages 62 and 65 without the use of dummy variables denoting these two ages. The simulated peaks were due entirely to smooth changes in the slope of the indifference curves and to the sudden changes in financial incentives embedded in the Social Security and pension rules. When the effects of Social Security, pension, and mandatory retirement were eliminated from the compensation function, both simulated peaks disappeared. When the single-wage model simulations were compared, they did an inferior job of tracing actual retirement behavior.

Gustman and Steinmeier (1985b) used their model to simulate the effects of three components of the 1983 Social Security reforms:

(1) the increase in the normal retirement age from 65 to 67,

(2) the increase in the annual delayed retirement credit after age 65 from 3 to 8 percent, and

(3) the decrease in the benefit reduction rate (the earnings-test tax) from 50 to 33 percent, which has already gone into effect for those aged 65 to 69.

Their simulated impacts are long-run in that they assumed that workers faced these rules all along. They are less than long-run, however, because the model does not permit other institutions (like pensions) to adjust to the new Social Security environment.

Their simulations suggested a decline in retirement behavior around 65. The authors predicted that the percentage of Americans over age 65 working full time would increase and the percentages working part time and fully retired would decrease. Disaggregation indicated that most of the impact was due to the increase in the actuarial adjustment for delayed retirement after age 65, which would reduce or eliminate the surreptitious pay cut that Social Security imposes then. There was very little effect prior to age 65 and a slight increase in retirement activity at age 67. In proportional terms, some of these predicted changes were substantial, because the changes occurred on such a small base of workers over 65. But because of the small base, the overall impact of these changes on the labor force would be minimal.[10]

The delay in the age of normal retirement is equivalent to a decrease in Social Security benefits. With no other changes, it would decrease the income levels of older Americans. But the increased incentives to work beyond age 65, because of a delayed retirement adjustment that is closer to actuarially fair, will induce some additional labor supply and partly offset this income loss.

In a subsequent paper, Gustman and Steinmeier (1986b) simulated the impact of the 1983 Social Security legislation on retirement behavior and lifetime income. Without any labor supply response, all groups would lose lifetime income equal to about 11 to 14 percent of Social Security wealth because of the 1983 amendments. All of the groups offset this loss, to some extent, with additional work. But the degree of offset varied. Those in good health made up nearly half of the loss, while those in poor health made up only a fifth.

In summary, Gustman and Steinmeier have added two important and realistic dimensions to their behavioral models: minimum-hours constraints and partial retirement at reduced wages. They have confirmed that partial retirement is an important phenomenon among older Americans (about one-third of their RHS sample reported themselves as partially retired at some time between 1969 and 1975) and that most people have to switch jobs in order to reduce hours. The price paid for this additional flexibility is a decrease in hourly pay.

Most of the previous research had ignored the partial retirement option and labeled those in this intermediate category as either retired or not retired. Gustman and Steinmeier have shown that this dichotomy is unrealistic and that empirical results change when it is relaxed.

Partial Retirement as an Earnings Reduction

In a series of recent papers, Giora Hanoch, Marjorie Honig, and Cordelia Reimers have emphasized the importance of partial retirement between full-time employment and complete labor force withdrawal. They also have found that partial retirement is common and that its duration is significant, and concluded that traditional models of dichotomous retirement miss important aspects of the story.

Honig and Hanoch (1985) adopted an objective definition of partial retirement, in contrast to the subjective concept used by Quinn and by Gustman and Steinmeier. According to Honig and Hanoch, retirement means a reduction in earnings. They use as a measure of earnings reduction "the ratio of current to potential earnings (in real terms), the latter defined as the individual's maximum earnings during the greater part of his adult life." They defined those with no earnings as fully retired, those earning less than half of their highest annual real earnings as partially retired, and all others as not retired. For the ends of the spectrum—those fully retired and those not retired—this definition correlates very well with subjective self-definitions by the respondents themselves. But fewer than half of those whom the authors defined as partially retired described themselves in the same way. Nearly 40 percent called themselves fully retired, despite their (usually small) positive earnings.

Decreases in earnings can result from lower wages, lower hours, or both. Honig and Hanoch found that both occurred among older workers and that the latter appeared both as decreases in hours per week and in weeks per year. But they found the strongest association between partial retirement and diminished hours per week. Those partially retired averaged 34 hours compared to 43 for the nonretired.

With their definition, Honig and Hanoch found a significant amount of partial retirement among older American men. During the four years between 1969 and 1973, between 14 and 27 percent (depending on age in 1969) of the white married wage and salary men in the Retirement History Study sample moved from nonretirement into partial retirement. And this ignores those initially self-employed, who are more likely to utilize a period of partial retirement.

Not only was partial retirement fairly likely, but it was also of significant duration. The average partially retired person had been so for over two years, and nearly a fifth had been so for four or more years. And since these respondents were still partially retired in 1973, the eventual duration would be even longer.

The authors also found that partial retirement was very likely to continue or to develop into full retirement. There were, however, a small number of irregular patterns; for example, a transition from full retirement back to partial or to nonretirement, or a move from partial to nonretirement. These odd patterns were most likely to occur among the younger respondents.

Honig and Hanoch discovered some interesting differences between the partially retired and others. Not surprisingly, the former were much less likely to be on the same job they had had two years previously, since some became partially retired by switching jobs. But they also were more likely than the others to have experienced earlier interruptions in Social Security-covered earnings, were less likely to have pension coverage, and were much more likely (than the nonretired) to report health limitations.

The authors tested several models of the decisionmaking process. They concluded that the most likely involved recursive decisions: first, people decide whether or not to continue working, and then, if they do continue, they decide whether to work full or part time. Labor force participation was correlated with good health, low family income, a lack of pension coverage, and high Social Security entitlement. The last finding may seem surprising, since high Social Security wealth can finance leisure. Here it seems to encourage continued work. The answer may lie in the intertemporal incentives embedded in the Social Security system. The annual Social Security benefit cannot capture the complicated impacts of current work decisions on future benefits and, hence, on Social Security wealth.

For those who did decide to continue working, the likelihood of partial retirement (as opposed to nonretirement) increased with age, the onset of health limitations, education, and high family income, and decreased with pension coverage and the size of the potential annual Social Security benefit.[11]

In more recent work, Reimers and Honig (1989) changed the time unit of analysis and the definition of partial retirement and found even more of the phenomenon. They utilized information in the RHS regarding the exact timing of job transitions to interpolate a month-by-month job history, and then examined transitions from one month to the next. They defined partial retirement to occur whenever real *monthly* earnings fell below *80 percent* of peak lifetime monthly earnings, compared to the 50 percent annual threshold used above. This may be an overly liberal definition of partial retirement, since monthly earnings can change for many reasons other than an intentional change in labor supply status.

With this new definition, the authors concluded that men aged 58 to 61 leaving nonretirement were more likely to end up in partial retirement than in full retirement. This contrasts the Honig and Hanoch conclusions mentioned above, in which transitions to full retirement were always more frequent, and shows the sensitivity of the results to the choice of time interval and the definition of partial retirement used. Reimers and Honig found that most of the transitions from nonretirement to partial retirement occurred while the respondent stayed working for the same employer. This implies a far greater degree of intrafirm hours flexibility than found by Gustman and Steinmeier, who claim that most people have to switch jobs in order to reduce labor supply, or by us (below), with a more severe "hours-only" definition of partial retirement.

Different definitions obviously lead to different estimates about the magnitude of partial retirement. Reimers and Honig adopted a lenient definition (less than 80 percent of one's highest real monthly pay) and therefore found a lot of it. But nearly all of the evidence suggests that partial retirement is important, and that by ignoring it, as much of the retirement research does, one overlooks some very interesting behavioral responses. Reimers and Honig (1989) conclude that

> retirement has often been viewed as an "either-or" proposition: either one is working full-time or not at all, with the transition occurring in the early sixties for Americans. It has become increasingly clear, however, that retirement in the U.S. is a more complex phenomenon. In particular, significant numbers of older workers are spending time in the intermediate stage of partial retirement.

Job Reentry after Retirement

In some recent work, George Sweeney, J.S. Butler, Richard Burkhauser, and Kathryn Anderson (1989) have shown that a life-cycle model modified to allow uncertainty about the date of one's death yields good predictions about who returns to work after leaving the labor force. They suggest that reentry after retirement may be part of a rational plan of consumption over the life cycle. Behavior changes when new information becomes available. While aging, people must reevaluate their own life expectancies and levels of assets, and may find that returning to work after having been retired makes sense.

To test the model, the authors analyzed a sample of men and women drawn from the RHS who were working in 1968, but later stopped and reported themselves fully retired. They found that 23 percent of the sample returned to work—most within two years after retirement. The longer one was out of the workforce, the less likely was reentry. Increases in Social Security and pension wealth significantly reduced the probability of reentry, with Social Security having the larger effect. The authors argued that this may reflect the fact that Social Security benefits are reduced when earnings exceed the exempt amount, which creates a work disincentive not found in most pension plans.

Butler, Anderson, and Burkhauser (1989) have brought the literature on health and retirement to bear on the decision to return to work in older years. The main innovation in this paper is the use of a competing-risks model that allows unobservables that influence both health and the probability of returning to work to be correlated. They found that these unobservables are correlated, and that including this correlation changes the impact of Social Security and pension income.

Both of these papers shed some light on the decision to reenter the labor market at older ages. However, neither distinguishes between exits from career jobs and exits from what may be one of several post-career jobs. In addition, little information is provided on the type or duration of the new jobs.

In our research discussed below, we also consider the extent of labor market reentry, or "unretirement." We have a stricter definition of the phenomenon, since we will define as retired only those who have been out of the labor market for at least two years. Since Butler, Anderson, and Burkhauser report that most of their reentries occurred during the first two years, we will find fewer unretirements than they did. It is really a matter of definition whether someone who moved from one job to another with a six-month hiatus really retired and then reentered, or merely switched jobs with a little time off in the interim. For younger workers, we would certainly not label the interim as "retirement" and we prefer not to here either. But the important point on which we all agree is that very interesting patterns of labor market withdrawal are being observed. People are leaving the labor market in many different ways, and once out, some decide to return. This is in stark contrast to most of the recent retirement literature in which the retirement decision is modeled as dichotomous and permanent.

Although the research on partial retirement is limited, it has made some important points. The authors all agree that the traditional dichotomous treatment of the retirement decision that dominates the literature is inadequate, that it overlooks some common and interesting withdrawal patterns, and that it can result in misleading conclusions. In fact, many people do utilize periods of partial retirement between full-time work and full-time leisure. Most do so on new jobs, and often at significantly lower wage rates. A primary reason appears to be the hours flexibility that is unavailable in their career jobs.

In the section below, we describe in detail the exit patterns of a large sample of older American workers, using all 10 years of the Retirement History Study. The evidence confirms that nontraditional retirement patterns are common and suggests that the scope of future research should be broadened to include them.

Exit Patterns from Career Jobs

In chapter 1, we argued that career jobs are important in America. Despite all the discussion about the mobility of American workers, most spend a considerable amount of time on a single job. Among the men in the 1969 wave of the Retirement History Study, for example, 55 percent remained on their longest job for at least 20 years, and nearly 80 percent stayed at least 10 years (table 1.6). For the women in the sample, the analogous figures are smaller—28 and 55 percent—but still substantial.

In this study, we are concentrating on the patterns of disengagement from career jobs. Since we are utilizing the Retirement History Study, which follows for 10 years a sample of people initially aged 58–63, we observe exits only between ages 58 and 73. Before turning to the topic at hand, we will discuss our definition of a career job and the derivation of the samples used in the tables below.

Definition of a Career Job

Our definition of current employment on a *career job* is simple: the respondent must be working full time (at least 35 hours per week) on a job held for at least 10 years. We experimented with several alternative definitions. We found that requiring 40 hours per week decreased the sample size appreciably, but that relaxing the definition to 30 or 25 hours made very little difference. Since many full time jobs now involve fewer than 40 hours of work per week, the 35-hour definition seemed most appropriate. Increasing the tenure requirement to 15 or 20 years on the job diminished the sample size significantly. Since we consider a full-time job of 10 years' duration to represent a significant commitment to an employer—even if the job is not the longest job held— we chose the 10-year definition. [12] From this perspective, an individual could hold more than one career job; we are studying the transition from the last one.

Sample

Of the more than 11,000 respondents in the 1969 RHS sample, nearly 4,500 met our definition of current employment on a career job (table 5.2). Almost all of those individuals who did not fit our definition were either out of the labor market altogether or working on jobs of less than 10 years' duration. Since the retirement patterns of wage and salary and self-employed workers are very different, we disaggregated along this dimension. About 21 percent of the men and 7 percent of the (non-married) women were self-employed.[13] Since the absolute number of self-employed women is so small (50), they are excluded from further analysis.

Table 5.2
Selection of Sample of Workers on Career Job in 1969

Number	Men	Women	Total
RHS sample in 1969	8,131	3,021	11,152
–not employed in 1969	1,550	1,315	2,865
–bad data on tenure or hours	365	73	438
–tenure less than 10 years	2,239	807	3,046
–hours less than 35 per week	216	115	331
RHS sample employed on a career job in 1969	3,761	711	4,472
–wage and salary	2,956	661	3,617
–self-employed	805	50	855

SOURCE: Retirement History Study.

As seen in table 5.3, the vast majority (about 80 percent) of the wage and salary men and women changed their labor force status between 1969 and 1979, the end of the RHS surveys. Of those who did not, nearly all either died or disappeared from the survey while still on their career jobs. Fewer than 3 percent remained employed full time until 1979.

Table 5.3
Disposition of Sample of Workers on Career Job in 1969

	Wage and salary men	Self-employed men	Wage and salary women	Total
Total	2,956	805	661	4,422
–bad data on disposition	–75	–23	–12	–110
–good data on disposition	2,881	782	649	4,312
Remained full time on career job				
–until 1979	57 (2%)	113 (14%)	17 (3%)	187 (4%)
–until death	256 (9%)	95 (12%)	22 (3%)	373 (9%)
–until disappeared	306 (11%)	92 (12%)	75 (12%)	473 (11%)
Left full-time status on career job	2,262 (79%)	482 (62%)	535 (82%)	3,279 (76%)
–without 4 years of additional data after exit	816	241	167	1,224
–with 4 years of additional data after exit	1,446	241	368	2,055

SOURCE: Retirement History Study.

The disposition of those who were self-employed in 1969 is very different. Only about 60 percent left full-time status on that job and of the other 40 percent, over a third were still working full time in 1979. The others died or disappeared.

We are primarily interested in those individuals who stopped doing full-time work on their career jobs. As we will see below, those who stopped did so in many different ways—some moved to part-time work on the same job, others took new jobs, and still others left the labor market and were never observed working again.

There is a potential problem here, however, since some of those whom we never observed working again may have left the sample after leaving their jobs. Some died, some refused to be reinterviewed, and others could not be located. For another group, those first observed out of their full-time career jobs in 1979, the last year of the RHS, there was simply not another opportunity to contact them again. Some of these respondents may well have taken another job, but we do not know. To diminish this problem, we have chosen a subsample of those for whom we have four years (two RHS interviews) of data after their departure from the career job.[14] There are 1,446 wage and salary men, 241 self-employed men, and 368 wage and salary women in this category (table 5.3). With this sample, which we use below, we are more confident that the transitions listed are accurate. "Out of the labor force" now means out for at least four years.

Exit Patterns

In table 5.4, we show the exit patterns of the RHS respondents who were still in career jobs in 1969, who subsequently left these full-time positions and whom we could follow for four additional years. Of the wage and salary men, over a quarter did something other than withdraw from the labor force. More than 20 percent left and took a new job, and those were about evenly split between new full-time and new part-time positions. A small proportion (5 percent) moved to part-time status on the same career job—i.e., reduced their labor supply below 20 hours per week.[15] The remaining 73 percent of the sample were never observed working again.

The least likely transition was to part-time work on the career job, even though, as we will see, the earnings from this move usually exceeded the earnings on a new part-time job. The low probability of becoming a part-time worker on one's career job may be because this choice was generally not available to wage and salary workers, as Gustman and Steinmeier (1983) suggest, or because the workers chose to leave in order to collect pension benefits and prevent a loss in pension wealth. Pension accruals usually fall after early retirement age, and the loss in pension wealth might be even larger for those who worked part time on the career job. Not only would they be likely to face actuarial adjustments that inadequately reward continued work, but the part-time work might decrease the earnings base on which the pension benefits are calculated, if they are based on the last (as opposed to the highest) few years. Hence, for some workers, a lower wage on a new job may exceed the true net wage for part-time work on the career job.

Table 5.4
Exit Patterns from Career Jobs, for Those
with Four Years of Subsequent Data
(vertical percentage)

Type of transition	Wage and salary men	Self-employed men	Wage and salary women
Part time on career job	5%	25%	10%
Part time on new job	10%	13%	10%
Full time on new job	12%	13%	7%
Out of labor force	73%	49%	74%
(Sample size)	(1,446)	(241)	(368)

SOURCE: Retirement History Study.

For self-employed men, the withdrawal patterns were very different. Only half of the sample left the labor force when they stopped full-time work on a career job, and of those who did not, a transition to part-time work on the same job was by far the most likely choice. A quarter of the sample reduced their hours in this way, which undoubtedly reflects the greater control over hours enjoyed by the self-employed. Another quarter moved to a new job, equally split between full time and part time.

The fact that the self-employed were five times more likely than wage and salary workers to continue to work part time on their career jobs suggests that more of the latter might do the same if there were fewer direct restrictions on part-time work, and if defined benefit pension plans did not penalize that choice. This might substantially decrease the percentage who move directly from full-time work to full retirement.

The (nonmarried) wage and salary women in the sample resembled the wage and salary men. About three-quarters of them chose the traditional labor force withdrawal. The quarter that did not was more evenly divided among the three choices: part-time work on the career job, or part-time or full-time work on a new job.

Age of Respondent

The exit patterns varied with the age of the respondent at the time of departure (table 5.5). Most of these men and women left their career jobs between the ages of 62 and 64, which is now normal retirement age. Those who left earlier, between 58 and 61, were by far the most likely to take another full-time job—about one in four of the wage and salary men, one in three of the self-employed men, and one in five of the women did so. Only one-half to two-thirds of these younger workers left the labor market for at least four years.

In the older categories, new full-time employment was much rarer and transitions to part-time work were more popular. Only a small minority of the wage and salary workers stayed on career jobs past age 65 (6 percent of the men and 11 percent of the women). This group was the least likely to leave the labor force for good. About 40 percent made a nontraditional exit and over half of them moved to part time

Table 5.5
Exit Patterns from Career Jobs by Age of Worker at Time of Exit
(horizontal percentage)

| Group | | Type of Transition | | | | |
Age	Part time on career job (%)	Part time on new job (%)	Full time on new job (%)	Out of labor force (%)	Total	
Wage and salary men						
58–61	2	8	23	66	327 (23%)	
62–64	2	10	10	77	825 (57%)	
65	8	12	5	74	200 (14%)	
66–70	21	14	4	61	94 (5%)	
					1,446 (100%)	
Self-employed men						
58–61	11	7	35	48	46 (19%)	
62–64	19	18	11	52	118 (49%)	
65	44	16	0	41	32 (13%)	
66–70	40	4	4	51	45 (19%)	
					241 (100%)	
Wage and salary women						
58–61	1	12	17	70	69 (19%)	
62–64	10	8	4	77	215 (58%)	
65	7	19	0	74	42 (11%)	
66–70	21	5	12	62	42 (11%)	
					368 (100%)	

SOURCE: Retirement History Study.

on their career jobs. This may seem odd, but the very fact that these men and women stayed on their career jobs past 65 (a rare phenomenon these days) indicates either that their preferences were different from those of most older workers or that they held career jobs that were more flexible with respect to retirement options. The popularity of the part-time option suggests that the latter may be the case.

The patterns of the self-employed also differed by age. Overall, about half took nontraditional exits. Younger workers (58 to 61) who kept working were most likely to move to another full-time job, and over a third did; those 62 to 64 were most likely to drop to part-time employment, either on the same or on a new job; and the older workers (65 and older) very rarely switched jobs. They either reduced hours on career jobs or dropped out of the labor force completely.

Timing of Transitions

The transitions in table 5.4 could have occurred at any time within four years of departure from full-time work on the career job. The RHS data permit one to calculate exactly when each transition occurred, unless the transition was to part-time on the same job.[16] In this case we assumed it took place immediately. The distributions for the wage and salary men are shown in table 5.6, along with the probability of each type of exit occurring during each six-month period.

Most of the transitions happened immediately or soon after the departure from the career job. Nearly half of the wage and salary men who moved to a new part-time job and over 60 percent of those who took a new full-time job did so during the first year. The same story is told by the transition rates in table 5.6. The probability that someone leaving a full-time job took a new full-time job in the first six months was nearly 7 percent. Of those who were still not working after six months, only 2 percent took a full-time job during the next six months. The likelihood of a new full-time job for those not working past one year continued to fall. The probability of a move to new part-time work also declined with time out of work, but not as dramatically.

The timing patterns for self-employed men were slightly different. They took even less time off between jobs. Over 60 percent of those who

Table 5.6
Marginal Probabilities of Various Transitions Within Four Years of Leaving Career Job Wage and Salary Men
(horizontal percentage)

Months after exit from career job	Number entering period	Part time on career job	Part time on new job	Full time on new job	Still out of labor force
			Type of transaction		
0–6	1,446	4.7%	3.4%	6.9%	84.9%
7–12	1,236		1.9%	2.0%	96.2%
13–18	1,191		1.5%	1.4%	97.0%
19–24	1,156		1.5%	1.2%	97.3%
25–30	1,125		1.3%	0.8%	97.9%
31–36	1,101		1.0%	0.7%	98.3%
37–42	1,082		1.3%	0.4%	98.3%
43–48	1,064		0.6%	0.4%	99.0%
Total	(1,446)	(65)	(151)	(176)	(1,054)

SOURCE: Retirement History Study.

took a new part-time job and nearly 90 percent with new full-time employment began the new job within a year. The patterns for women were mixed. Those who claimed new full-time jobs generally did so very quickly, like the men. But the women who moved on to new part-time jobs took their time. Fewer than 40 percent made this transition during the first year.

Duration of the Transition Job

The tables above suggest that nontraditional exits from full-time work on a career job are fairly common. About a quarter of the wage and salary respondents and about half of the self-employed men did something other than simply leave the labor force. One interesting question is whether these intermediate stages last long enough to be important and worthy of analysis. If workers use them to delay complete retirement by only a couple of months, then there is little here to study. On the other hand, if the transitional steps last for several years, then this is a phenomenon worth investigating.

The next three tables show the status of the transitional jobs one and two years after the transition, for those who dropped to part-time status on their career jobs (table 5.7) or took new part-time (table 5.8) or new full-time (table 5.9) jobs.[17] In table 5.10, the data are aggregated across demographic groups and transition types.

Several important points emerge. The main one is that these transitional jobs do last sufficiently long to be of interest. Nearly three-quarters of those respondents who left their full-time career jobs for something else were still on that transitional job a year later, and nearly 60 percent remained after two years (table 5.10). Some had quickly moved on to a second transition job—11 percent after one year and 17 percent after two years. The remainder had left the labor market altogether. For the 18 percent of the sample who stopped working within a year after starting the transitional job, this job may have been a mistake—something that looked better than it turned out to be. Another 7 percent left during the second year. But the other three-quarters of those career-job-leavers who continued to work had at least another two years of labor market activity ahead of them.

Table 5.7
Tenure of Part-Time Status on Career Job
(horizontal percentage)

Group	Status 1 and 2 years after transition				
Tenure	Part time on new job	Full time on new job	Out of labor force	Full time on career job	Still part time on career job
Wage and salary men (N=82)[a]					
after 1 year	2	0	17	b	80
after 2 years	7	1	26	9	57
Self-employed men (N=100)[a]					
after 1 year	0	0	8	b	92
after 2 years	1	2	17	24	56
Wage and salary women (N=46)[a]					
after 1 year	0	0	7	b	93
after 2 years	0	0	15	13	72
Total (N=228)					
after 1 year	1	0	11	b	88
after 2 years	3	1	20	16	60

SOURCE: Retirement History Study.

a. See chapter 5, footnote 17.

b. The RHS questionnaires did not ask when during the two-year period the respondent resumed full-time status on the career job.

Table 5.8
Tenure of Part-Time Status on a New Job
(horizontal percentage)

Group Tenure	Status 1 and 2 years after transition				
	Part time on another new job	Full time on another new job	Out of labor force	Full time on the new job	Still part time on the new job
Wage and salary men (N=168)[a]					
after 1 year	11	2	18	0	70
after 2 years	20	5	26	0	49
Self-employed men (N=36)[a]					
after 1 year	6	6	19	0	69
after 2 years	14	6	28	6	47
Wage and salary women (N=44)[a]					
after 1 year	14	7	18	0	61
after 2 years	14	9	23	0	55
Total (N=248)					
after 1 year	10	3	18	0	68
after 2 years	18	6	25	1	50

SOURCE: Retirement History Study.
a. See chapter 5, footnote 17.

Table 5.9
Tenure of Full-Time Status on New Job
(horizontal percentage)

Group Tenure	Status 1 and 2 years after transition				
	Part time on another new job	Full time on another new job	Out of labor force	Part time on the new job	Still full time on the new job
Wage and salary men (N=203)[a]					
after 1 year	5	11	26	0	57
after 2 years	7	16	33	0	44
Self-employed men (N=34)[a]					
after 1 year	9	9	6	0	76
after 2 years	12	9	15	0	65
Wage and salary women (N=30)[a]					
after 1 year	7	3	20	0	70
after 2 years	10	7	30	0	53
Total (N=267)					
after 1 year	6	10	23	0	61
after 2 years	8	14	30	0	48

SOURCE: Retirement History Study.
a. See chapter 5, footnote 17.

Table 5.10
Tenure of First Transitional Job,
Status 1 and 2 Years After Transition

Tenure (N=743)	On another job (%)	Out of labor force (%)	Still on transitional job (%)
After 1 year	11	18	72
After 2 years	17	25	57

SOURCE: Retirement History Study.

The disaggregated tables reveal some interesting detail. For those who became part time on their career jobs, that was usually the end of the line (table 5.7). Some (16 percent) returned to full-time status on that same job (primarily the self-employed) and others (20 percent) left the labor market, but very few (4 percent) went on to a new job within the next two years.

In contrast, many of those who moved from a career job to a new part-time or full-time job (tables 5.8 and 5.9) continued to experiment. Within two years, nearly a quarter of those respondents had moved on to another postcareer job. The part-timers tended to stay part time, and the full-timers, full time. The latter were slightly more likely to leave the labor force within two years of starting the transitional job.

Unretirements

Most of the people who made labor market transitions late in life did so soon after leaving their career jobs. But there is a small minority who spent a significant amount of time out of the labor force, and then reconsidered and reentered. Table 5.11 suggests that about 10 percent of those out for at least two years "unretired." These estimates provide a lower boundary for the phenomenon, because some additional people may have reentered, but after they had ceased contact with the RHS.[18]

Table 5.11
Unretirements—Labor Market Reentries
After At Least Two Years Out

Group Time period	Part time on new job	Full time on new job	Stayed out of labor force
Wage and salary men (N=1,125)			
after 2–3 years	26	17	
after 3–4 years	20	8	
after 4 or more years	20	14	
Total	66 (6%)	39 (3%)	1,020 (91%)
Self-employed men (N=126)			
after 2–3 years	5	0	
after 3–4 years	2	1	
after 4 or more years	2	1	
Total	9 (7%)	2 (1%)	115 (91%)
Wage and salary women (N=286)			
after 2–3 years	6	1	
after 3–4 years	6	2	
after 4 or more years	8	1	
Total	20 (7%)	4 (1%)	262 (92%)

SOURCE: Retirement History Study.

The likelihood of a late reentry was about the same for wage and salary men, self-employed men, and wage and salary women. For all the groups, unretirees were much more likely to return to part-time rather than to full-time employment.

Summary

Most of the research by economists on retirement patterns in the United States has viewed the individual's decision as either a dichotomous choice between work and leisure or as a choice of hours of labor supply along a continuous budget constraint. Recent work suggests that both of these modes of modeling assumptions can be misleading. In fact, older workers take a variety of routes between full-time work and full-time retirement. The paths are so varied that the phrase "retirement"—defined by dozens of authors in dozens of different ways—may well conceal more than it reveals. What we are observing and describing are labor market transitions, and they are not easily categorized by a single term.

Using data from the Social Security Administration's Retirement History Study, we have analyzed the exit patterns of a large sample of men and women who were aged 58 through 63 and still employed on a career job in 1969. Career employment was defined as full-time work on a job of at least 10 years' duration. We found that the vast majority of these older workers (about 80 percent of the wage and salary workers and 60 percent of the self-employed) were observed leaving full-time career employment over the next decade. Of the remainder, most either died (9 percent) or disappeared prematurely from the sample (11 percent) while still fully employed. Only a very few (4 percent, and predominantly the self-employed) stayed fully employed on a career job through 1979.

The focus of this chapter is on the patterns of disengagement from career jobs. In most of the tables, we required at least four years of good data (two more waves of questionnaire information) after the initial transition. This left us with a sample of about 2,000 individuals for study.

The primary finding is that a sizable minority of these older Americans utilized a nontraditional route to leave the labor force. Although the abrupt change from full-time work to complete withdrawal was still the most frequent transition, over a quarter of the wage and salary workers in the sample did something different.[19] Approximately 10 percent of the men moved to part-time work on another job, and a similar proportion took a new full-time position. Relatively few (only 5 percent) were able to reduce hours to part-time status on their career jobs.[20]

The self-employed behaved very differently. Only half withdrew completely from the labor force and of those who did not, a transition to part-time work on the same career job was by far the most likely occurrence.

There were interesting differences by age at departure from full-time work on the career job. Through age 65, part-time positions (new and on the career job) became more likely the older the worker, while new full-time positions became less so. Nontraditional exit routes (particularly part-time on the career job) were the most likely for the few individuals who stayed on their career jobs until after age 65.

Most of the transitions occurred very soon after departure from the career job—usually within a year. Nonetheless, a significant minority (about 10 percent) waited at least two years before returning to work, and some even longer. These "unretirements" may have been planned all along, or may have been responses to unforeseen changes in circumstances.

These transitional jobs were of sufficient duration to represent an important part of the retirement process. Nearly three-quarters of the jobs lasted more than one year, and almost 60 percent lasted at least two years. Part-time positions on the career job lasted the longest, followed by part-time work on another job, and then by new full-time work. But even half of the new full-time jobs lasted two years or more. These intermediate jobs were most likely to end with complete labor force withdrawal, although some individuals experimented with more than one transitional position.

In summary, something is happening. Part-time and full-time work on a new job is a serious alternative to continued work on the career job and to complete labor force withdrawal. These findings suggest that a substantial number of older Americans are willing and able to continue working despite the financial disincentives that often penalize the decision to do so.

NOTES

1. Over 99 percent of those who described themselves as not retired were in the labor force (Quinn 1981). Almost 90 percent of the completely retired were out of the labor force. Among the self-defined partly retired, seven-eights of the self-employed and three-quarters of the wage and salary workers were in the labor force. Some of those not in the labor force may have been part-year workers who happened not to be working at the time of the survey.

2. As we will see below, self-employment status is not exogenous, since many workers switch to self-employment status late in life. Quinn (1980) found that about 12 percent of the self-employed had become so within the previous 10 years. In the research we report below, we are only analyzing workers still employed full time on career jobs—jobs held for at least 10 years.

3. The primary advantage of this definition (fully retired, partly retired, or not retired) is its simplicity. It eliminates the need for arbitrary distinctions based on labor supply or earnings. Its disadvantage is that in a small number of cases it does not correspond well to more objective measures. For example, Gustman and Steinmeier (1986a) redefine as fully retired a few individuals who called themselves partially retired, despite having held no job for two years or more.

4. Gustman and Steinmeier (1985a) reported a significant wage drop for individuals who reported themselves as not retired in one RHS wave, and partially retired two years later. The wage decrease was observed for those partially retired on the same job and those partially retired on a new job. More people were in the latter category, and the wage drops were larger for those who had changed jobs.

5. This may underestimate the extent of minimum-hours constraints. Some of those who said they could have worked less may have been working overtime and referring to a reduction to full time. They may have faced a minimum-hours constraint below that. When the sample was limited to only those working 42 hours or fewer per week, 61 percent said they could not work less (Gustman and Steinmeier 1983).

6. In some early empirical work, Gustman and Steinmeier (1984a) estimated reduced-form equations to explain individuals' choices to be retired, not retired, partially retired on their main jobs, or partially retired on a new job. They then showed the importance of the definition by which partially retired people would be assigned to a *dichotomous* retirement status. The magnitude—and often the direction—of the effect on the probability of retirement of the main job wage rate, the presence of mandatory retirement, marital status, and health condition changed depending on whether those in the partially retired categories were counted as retired or not retired.

7. In each of the four waves of the RHS, each respondent was categorized as working full time (f), working part time (p), fully retired (r) or status indeterminate (x). With four years and four states, there are 256 potential patterns. In the full RHS sample, 49 percent of the observations moved directly from full-time work to full retirement, and remained there. Another 9 percent were fully retired in all four waves. Of the remaining, many had patterns involving partial retirement, the most common of which were *fffp, ffpp, ffpr, fprr* and *fppp* (Gustman and Steinmeier 1986a).

8. Two full-time wage equations were computed, one for jobs started before age 55 and another for jobs started after 55. The former was based on a sample drawn from the Panel Study on Income Dynamics, the latter on an RHS sample. People were assumed to stay on their full-time jobs until mandatory retirement age. After that age, where applicable, the full-time wage was based on the full-time wage equation, with the variable "tenure on the job" set to zero. All of the wage equations are shown in Gustman and Steinmeier (1986a).

9. Annual pension benefit amounts were obtained from the RHS, and actuarial adjustments for delayed retirement were based on industrywide averages. Benefits were assumed to be frozen in nominal terms after retirement. The Social Security adjustments were based on Social Security rules and the earnings records appended to the RHS. See Gustman and Steinmeier (1986a) for additional details.

10. As noted above, the authors assumed that the incentives in pension plans would not change in response to the 1983 Social Security reforms. If the age of normal retirement in pensions were increased to age 67 as well, the changes at ages 65 and 66 would be augmented. On the other hand, if pension incentives were altered to *offset* the Social Security changes, then the simulations presented here would be overestimates.

11. In a related article, Honig (1985) reported very similar results for the nonmarried women in the RHS sample.

12. In a series of very interesting papers on the transition from work to retirement, Chris Ruhm (1988, 1989 and 1990) defined the career job as the longest job held, regardless of when the respondent left it. With this definition, he finds even more transitional behavior (bridge jobs, in his terminology) than we do.

13. The initial RHS sample included as respondents men and nonmarried women. Married women were excluded because it was thought that their retirement would be defined largely in terms of their husbands' behavior, and therefore that there was less to be learned from them than from a larger sample of the included categories. For this reason, there are no married women in our sample.

14. In this analysis, we are implicitly treating the RHS as a four-year longitudinal survey, but one that starts for each respondent not at a particular calendar date, but rather at the moment of departure from the career job. We include only those respondents on whom we have data over this subsequent four-year period.

15. Our definition of a career job requires full-time employment, meaning over 35 hours per week. Many of the respondents were very near 35 hours. We did not want to overstate the number of job transitions by including those with small decreases, to just under 35 hours per week. Therefore, for the purposes of this transition, movement to part time required a decrease to below 20 hours per week. This probably understates the number of transitions, by excluding from the count some workers who would have described themselves as moving from full to part time.

16. In this case, detailed questions on the timing of the move were not asked. We assumed that all these transitions occurred within the first six months.

17. For these samples, we required only two years of data after the respondent left the career job. If we knew that a respondent made a transition at any time within four years of leaving the career job, then that respondent was included in this sample. Therefore, the sample sizes are slightly larger here than in earlier tables.

18. For the individuals in table 5.10, we have a minimum of four years of good data after their departure from the career job. For many, we have more than four years. But some may have reentered after four years, but after the RHS had ceased (1979) or lost track of them.

19. With the career job defined as the longest job held, Ruhm (1988) concludes that the majority of individuals leave their career jobs well before retirement, and utilize a transitional job-stopping process before leaving the labor force. The qualitative nature of his results is consistent with ours. The quantitative differences stem from the fact that we consider any full-time job lasting at least 10 years to be a career job, whereas Ruhm would define it a bridge job if the individual had held a longer job earlier. We think that job transitions by middle-aged people (for example, those in their 40s and younger, when nearly a quarter of Ruhm's sample leave their "career" jobs) are not really part of the retirement transition.

20. Ruhm's (1988) results are perfectly consistent with ours on this point. He found that only 6 percent of his RHS sample partially retired on their career jobs.

– 6 –

Correlates of
Career Job Transitions

Nontraditional routes to retirement are important in America. As the nation ages and the relative supply of younger workers diminishes, the labor supply decisions of the elderly will become more and more important. Over the past decade, Congress has moved in several important ways to encourage work at older ages. The 1983 amendments to the Social Security Act will slowly reduce work disincentives after age 65. Legislation concerning labor-management contracts has also been modified. Congress first raised the minimum age at which firms could force mandatory retirement from 65 to 70, and then, for most workers, outlawed mandatory retirement at any age. In addition, 1986 amendments to the Age Discrimination in Employment Act require that employees who work beyond a pension plan's normal retirement age receive credit in the plan's benefit formula. This was intended to reduce negative pension accruals and therefore reduce the disincentives to work in later years.

Employers can also choose on their own to alter private pension incentives and other personnel policies in order to entice older workers to remain on the job. One attractive mechanism may be the introduction of more flexible hours alternatives, to make the options faced by wage and salary workers more like those already enjoyed by the self-employed. Another would be to reduce even further the loss in pension wealth that generally accompanies work at older ages.

Before proposing further changes, however, it is important to understand the rich diversity of withdrawals from career jobs that are possible and the circumstances under which current choices are being made.

As we have seen, many older Americans are already choosing to leave the labor force in stages, by moving from full-time career employment to part-time work or to a transitional new job. Others leave the labor force entirely and then return later.

In this chapter, we first describe some of the correlates of these different patterns. How did the choices vary with the health or education of the individual? Did they differ by industry and occupation or by the financial circumstances facing the worker? Did the decisions depend on why the person left the career job? We then turn to a comparison of the old and new jobs of those who actually changed employment. Did these workers continue to do what they had done before, or were they embarking on new and different careers?

Correlates of Transitions

Health

A major determinant of the well-being of the elderly is health. Health status, defined in many ways, both subjectively and objectively, has always played a central role in the retirement literature (see chapter 3). Its dominance has diminished somewhat during the past several decades, as researchers have begun to concentrate on the financial incentives surrounding the retirement decision, but no one would deny that it is still a major factor. In a very recent study using all 10 years of the Retirement History Study, for example, Gary Burtless (1987) found that a self-defined health variable is a very significant and important determinant of employment status. He estimates that "at age 62 the average probability of working full-time for a man in good health is 82 percent. For a man with a health limitation the probability is only 63 percent, or nearly a quarter less."[1]

The sample we are studying includes only individuals who were employed full time on career jobs in 1969. Therefore, much of the population with serious health impairments is excluded from our group because most of them had already left the labor market before the start of the survey. Within our sample, however, there is still a range of health conditions and, given the longitudinal nature of the data set, we are able to observe subsequent changes in the health of those who started out in good shape.

The health variable used here is subjective—the respondents' self description of their health relative to that of their peers.[2] We measure health in the survey *prior* to the individual's departure from the career job—in different years and at different ages, therefore, for different members of the sample.

As seen in table 6.1, only about 10 percent of these individuals claimed health worse than that of their peers. We are studying a relatively healthy cross section of the older population. Although the behavioral differences were modest, men with poorer health were the most likely to withdraw completely from the labor force. Those in better health were more likely to remain on the career job part time or move to a new job. This was particularly true of the self-employed, for whom the differences were more dramatic. The patterns were less clear among the women, perhaps due to the very small number (32) of these women in "worse" health.

Education

The patterns by level of education were not clear (table 6.2). Among the largest group, the wage and salary men, the likelihood of a non-traditional route seemed to increase with educational attainment above "some high school," and it was substantially higher for those with a college degree. But this generalization did not hold for the other groups. For the self-employed men (over half of whom had no formal high school education, and many of whom were farmers), there was no pattern, and among the women (with the highest average education), nontraditional paths decreased with years in school.

Pension and Mandatory Retirement Status

Current pension status appears to have played an important role in the retirement decision.[3] According to table 6.3, those eligible to receive a pension at the time they left their career jobs were much more likely

Table 6.1
Exit Patterns from Career Jobs by Health Prior to Exit
(horizontal percentage)

Group Health status[a]		Type of transition			
	Part time on career job (%)	Part time on new job (%)	Full time on new job (%)	Out of labor force (%)	Total[b]
Wage and salary men					
Better	4	10	13	73	526 (38%)
Same	5	11	12	72	724 (52%)
Worse	3	8	9	79	149 (11%)
Self-employed men					
Better	29	18	15	37	65 (28%)
Same	23	11	13	54	133 (58%)
Worse	24	9	9	58	33 (14%)
Wage and salary women					
Better	8	10	10	72	159 (44%)
Same	11	8	5	76	173 (48%)
Worse	9	19	3	69	32 (9%)

SOURCE: Retirement History Study.

a. Self-defined health status, relative to peers, in the interview prior to exit from the career job.

b. Sample with good health data.

Table 6.2
Exit Patterns from Career Jobs by Level of Education
(horizontal percentage)

Group	Type of transition				
Educational attainment	Part time on career job (%)	Part time on new job (%)	Full time on new job (%)	Out of labor force (%)	Total[a]
Wage and salary men					
0–8 years	5	11	10	74	576 (40%)
9–11 years	2	8	11	79	298 (21%)
12–15 years	4	11	14	71	432 (30%)
16+ years	7	11	18	64	123 (9%)
Self-employed men					
0–8 years	26	13	12	49	120 (50%)
9–11 years	19	14	19	48	42 (18%)
12–15 years	27	10	14	49	59 (25%)
16+ years	29	18	6	45	17 (7%)
Wage and salary women					
0–8 years	12	10	4	75	113 (31%)
9–11 years	12	8	10	71	52 (14%)
12–15 years	9	11	8	72	151 (41%)
16+ years	6	8	8	78	49 (13%)

SOURCE: Retirement History Study.
a. Sample with good education data.

Table 6.3
Exit Patterns from Career Jobs by Age and Pension Status
(horizontal percentage)

| Group | Type of transition | | | | |
Age at exit Pension status[a]	Part time on career job (%)	Part time on new job (%)	Full time on new job (%)	Out of labor force (%)	Total[b]
Wage and salary men					
58–61					
Not eligible	6	7	38	50	120
Eligible	0	9	15	76	201
62+					
Not eligible	12	14	15	58	369
Eligible	2	9	6	83	726
Total					
Not eligible	11	12	20	56	489
Eligible	1	9	8	82	927
Wage and salary women					
58–61					
Not eligible	0	13	23	63	30
Eligible	3	5	14	78	37
62+					
Not eligible	25	11	8	55	130
Eligible	1	8	2	90	166
Total					
Not eligible	21	11	11	57	160
Eligible	1	7	4	88	203

SOURCE: Retirement History Study.
a. Pension eligibility refers to eligibility for a pension on the career job when the individual left the career job.
b. Sample with good pension eligibility data.

to withdraw completely from the labor force. Over 80 percent of the eligible men did, compared to only 56 percent of those not eligible.[4] The difference was even higher for women (88 versus 57 percent). Much of the difference stems from the fact that those eligible were much less likely to stay part time on the career job. The reason for this is clear— unlike Social Security, most pensions require one to leave the job in order to draw benefits. In addition, if benefits are based on the last several years' earnings, a move to part time could lead to a substantial reduction in pension wealth. But the probability of taking a new job (especially full time) was also diminished by pension eligibility on the career job, suggesting that a key motivation for the transitional jobs may be the earnings they provide.

When the sample is further disaggregated by age (with age 62, the earliest age of Social Security eligibility, as the cutoff), the same patterns are observed, although the younger workers were always more likely to continue working. This was particularly true for new full-time employment. Nearly 40 percent of the younger (aged 58 to 61) men and nearly a quarter of the younger women who were ineligible for a pension started a new full-time job. This was true for only 15 percent of the men and less than 10 percent of the women aged 62 and older.

Pension eligibility and mandatory retirement frequently came hand-in-hand prior to the 1983 legislation that virtually outlawed mandatory retirement before age 70. As seen in table 6.4, both current pension eligibility and mandatory retirement increased the likelihood of a traditional retirement—directly from full-time career work to complete labor force withdrawal—among men. Pensions appear to have had the larger effect, and when they were combined, they were complimentary but far less than additive. The influence of the two together is dramatic— the proportion continuing to work after leaving the career job dropped from nearly one in two to only one in eight when both factors were in effect. But mandatory retirement only increased the probability of movement out of the labor force by 6 percentage points once pension eligibility was already established. This suggests that these two institutions may be viewed as alternative means to the same ends, and that changes in the mandatory retirement laws should have only marginal effects while the pension incentives remain in effect.[5]

Table 6.4

Exit Patterns from Career Jobs by Current Mandatory Retirement and Pension Status
(horizontal percentage)

Group	Type of transition				
MR and pension status[a]	Part time on career job (%)	Part time on new job (%)	Full time on new job (%)	Out of labor force (%)	Total[b]
Wage and salary men					
No MR, no pension	14	14	19	54	373
MR only	3	10	11	76	62
Pension only	2	9	8	81	658
MR and pension	0	9	5	87	237
Wage and salary women					
No MR, no pension	24	11	10	54	136
MR only	0	18	0	82	11
Pension only	2	6	3	90	142
MR and pension	0	14	2	84	51

SOURCE: Retirement History Study.

a. Status at time of exit from the full-time career job. Pension eligibility refers to eligibility for a pension on the career job when the individual left the career job.

b. Sample with good pension and mandatory retirement data.

Industry and Occupation

Transition patterns differed dramatically by industry and occupation, as shown in tables 6.5 and 6.6. Among wage and salary workers, over half of those in the agricultural and private household industries and over 40 percent of those in construction and retail trade chose a non-traditional route to retirement. This contrasts the experience of those in manufacturing, transportation, and public utilities and mining, where only about one in five did so. When the industries are ranked in ascending order of traditional retirement, as they are in table 6.5, the industries go loosely from service to manufacturing, and from low to high union presence. This is interesting in view of recent trends in America toward a more service-oriented economy—and one in which the proportion of the work force that is unionized has shrunk—and suggests that nontraditional retirement routes may increase in importance in the future.

Certain figures stand out in table 6.5. Part-time work on the career job was very rare, except in agriculture and private household work (both of which are small industries) and in finance, insurance, and real estate. In the latter, employees are often paid on commission, so firms are less interested in imposing hours constraints. Among women, part-time work on career jobs was more common, especially in private household work and retail trade.

In several industries, movement to a new job was very common. About a third of the men in construction, retail trade, and public administration did so. For some reason, it was much less common among the women in these same industries.

The distribution by occupation tells a similar tale. Nontraditional retirement patterns were more likely among white-collar than among blue-collar workers. About a third of managers, sales, and service workers did not leave the labor force in one move. Laborers, craftsmen, and foremen were much more likely to do so.

Gary Burtless (1987) has pointed out that the relationship between industry and occupation and labor force status may have an intermediate factor—health. It may be that certain jobs cause bad health, and that this,

Table 6.5
Exit Patterns from Career Jobs by Industry
(horizontal percentage)

Group		Type of transition			
Industry[a]	Part time on career job (%)	Part time on new job (%)	Full time on new job (%)	Out of labor force (%)	Total[b]
Wage and salary men					
Private household	19	24	14	43	21
Agriculture	14	14	29	43	14
Construction	5	7	30	58	97
Retail trade	8	15	17	60	84
Public administration	3	12	17	69	108
Finance, insurance & real estate	13	8	10	69	83
Other service	7	10	12	71	120
Wholesale trade	5	14	8	73	37
Manufacturing–nondurable	3	11	13	74	238
Manufacturing–durable	1	11	8	80	403
Transportation & public utilities	3	7	10	80	213
Mining	7	7	4	82	28
Total	5	10	12	73	1,446

Wage and salary women

Private household	37	4	11	48	27
Retail trade	16	9	2	73	45
Public administration	0	0	5	95	20
Finance, insurance & real estate	6	10	13	71	31
Other service	5	13	8	73	119
Manufacturing–nondurable	10	8	5	77	60
Manufacturing–durable	0	5	8	87	39
Transportation & public utilities	0	15	0	85	13
Other	c	c	c	c	14
Total	10	10	7	74	368

SOURCE: Retirement History Study.

a. In ascending order of "out of the labor force" for wage and salary men.

b. Sample with good industry da.a.

c. Cells with sample sizes smaller than 10.

Table 6.6
Exit Patterns from Career Jobs by Occupation
(horizontal percentage)

Group Occupation[a]	Type of transition				
	Part time on career job (%)	Part time on new job (%)	Full time on new job (%)	Out of labor force (%)	Total[b]
Wage and salary men					
Farm labor & managers	23	15	23	38	13
Sales workers	9	12	23	56	43
Managers	6	14	14	66	200
Service workers	6	13	15	66	93
Professional & technical	4	12	12	72	139
Clerical workers	3	12	12	72	97
Transportation equipment operators	6	13	8	73	62
Craftsmen & foremen	4	8	13	75	439
Nonfarm laborers	7	6	9	78	102
Operatives	1	10	9	81	252
Private household workers	c	c	c	c	3
Total	4	10	12	73	1,443

Wage and salary women					
Sales workers	24	6	0	71	17
Managers	14	0	19	67	21
Service workers	10	17	5	68	41
Professional & technical	4	8	8	79	73
Clerical workers	7	13	6	74	116
Operatives	7	7	4	82	72
Private household workers	47	7	7	40	15
Other	c	c	c	c	11
Total	10	10	7	74	366

SOURCE: Retirement History Study.

a. In ascending order of "out of the labor force" for wage and salary men.

b. Sample with good occupation data.

c. Cells with sample sizes smaller than 10.

not the job *per se,* is responsible for the difference in retirement patterns. He tested this hypothesis and found that there are, in fact, significant correlations between industry and occupation and current health, and that the differences can be extreme.[6] Nonetheless, even though health is an important determinant, he found that the impact of industry and occupation remained strong in a multivariate framework. There was an independent influence over and above the indirect effect through health.

Olivia Mitchell, Phillip Levine, and Silvana Pozzebon (1988) have also found important occupational and industrial differences in retirement patterns. They suggest that part of this may be due to differences in job risk (those on the riskier jobs retire earlier) or age/productivity profiles.

Wage Rate, Earnings, and Wealth

In table 6.7, we disaggregate our three samples by the wage rates that the respondents were earning prior to the job transition. An interesting, nonlinear pattern emerges among the male wage and salary workers. Those at the ends of the wage spectrum were the most likely to continue working when they ended full-time employment on a career job. For example, nearly 40 percent of the men earning less than $7.50 per hour (the bottom quintile) and 30 percent of those earning more than $20 per hour (the top 7 percent) stayed in the labor force after this transition. In contrast, only about 20 percent of those earning between $7.50 and $20 per hour did so. The same pattern appears at the bottom end of the women's distribution—low-wage women were the most likely to continue working. Since only 5 percent of the women earned more than $15 per hour, it is difficult to draw conclusions here. For the smaller number of self-employed men, no pattern appears.

Data on annual earnings on the career job prior to the transition tell a similar story (table 6.8). Among the wage and salary men, the probability of complete labor force withdrawal increases through the $20,000 to $30,000 category and then falls, although the decrease at the top is smaller than in the wage rate data. The data for women are similar, although the smaller sample sizes, especially at the top, reduce our confidence in the results.

In table 6.9, we disaggregate by the level of traditionally defined wealth in the survey year prior to departure from a career job. This wealth includes financial assets and real estate, including the home. It excludes human capital, durables, and the asset value of retirement income rights. The figures are adjusted for inflation and are all expressed in 1971 dollars.

A similar pattern emerges, although it is not as distinct as it was in the wage data. Those most likely to move directly out of the labor force were those in the middle wealth categories. The very poor (including those in debt) and the very wealthy were the most likely to utilize intermediate stages.

These findings suggest that nontraditional exit routes may be popular among two very distinct groups—those at the bottom and those at the top of the socioeconomic scale. The motivations may be very different. The poor may have no choice but to continue working because they have so few assets to spend during retirement. The rich, on the other hand, may choose postcareer work even when there is no financial need, either because their commitment to work is greater or because the jobs they can choose are more enjoyable or amenable to part-time work.

In addition, there may be a cause in common among members of these diverse groups. It may be that the relative scarcity of defined-pension benefit plans among very low- and very high-wage workers means that there is relatively little change in their true wage rates if they work part-time on their career jobs. Note that those earning less than $5 per hour are the only wage and salary group more likely to work part time on a career job than part time on a new job (table 6.7). The same is true for those in the highest wealth category (table 6.9). While low-wage workers are unlikely to have employer pensions of any kind, the wealthy may have pensions related to profits or stock prices rather than traditionally determined pension benefits. Although this evidence is far from conclusive, it is consistent with the hypothesis that subtle changes in compensation late in life affect labor supply decisions.

Table 6.7

Exit Patterns from Career Jobs by Wage Rate before Exit
(horizontal percentage)

Group	Type of transition				
Wage rate[a]	Part time on career job (%)	Part time on new jobs (%)	Full time on new job (%)	Out of labor force (%)	Total[b]
Wage and salary men					
Less than $5/hour	18	13	14	55	77
$5–7.50/hour	7	11	15	67	187
$7.50–10/hour	2	9	8	81	351
$10–15/hour	3	11	9	77	537
$15–20/hour	2	6	15	77	125
More than $20/hour	5	9	15	70	91
Total	4	10	11	75	1,368
Self-employed men					
Less than $5/hour	15	10	15	60	92
$5–7.50/hour	33	16	12	40	43
$7.50–10/hour	25	30	0	45	20
$10–15/hour	25	4	4	67	24
More than $15/hour	21	5	11	63	19
Total	22	12	11	55	198

Wage and salary women					
Less than $5/hour	21	12	10	57	58
$5–7.50/hour	9	6	6	78	125
$7.50–10/hour	6	12	6	76	84
$10–15/hour	3	9	6	82	66
More than $15/hour	13	6	0	81	16
Total	9	9	7	75	349

SOURCE: Retirement History Study.

a. Wage rate in 1984 dollars.

b. Sample with good wage rate data.

Table 6.8

Exit Patterns from Career Jobs by Annual Earnings before Exit
(horizontal percentage)

Group	Type of transition				
Annual earnings[a]	Part time on career job (%)	Part time on new job (%)	Full time on new job (%)	Out of labor force (%)	Total[b]
Wage and salary men					
Less than $10K	22	20	14	44	64
$10–20K	4	8	11	77	501
$20–30K	2	10	10	78	548
$30–40K	4	11	10	75	157
$40–50K	4	6	19	72	54
More than $50K	4	11	16	70	57
Total	4	10	11	75	1,381
Self-employed men					
Less than $10K	16	15	12	57	75
$10–20K	24	13	16	47	62
$20–30K	28	9	6	56	32
$30–50K	14	0	0	86	14
More than $50K	18	18	9	55	11
Total	21	12	11	56	194

Wage and salary women					
Less than $10K	18	10	7	65	71
$10–20K	7	10	8	76	196
$20–30K	2	7	2	90	59
$30–40K	13	7	0	80	45
More than $40K	13	0	13	75	8
Total	9	9	7	75	349

SOURCE: Retirement History Study.

a. Earnings in 1984 dollars.

b. Sample with good annual earnings data.

Table 6.9

Exit Patterns from Career Jobs by Wealth before Exit

(horizontal percentage)

Group		Type of transition			
Wealth[a]	Part time on career job (%)	Part time on new job (%)	Full time on new job (%)	Out of labor force (%)	Total[b]
Wage and salary men					
In debt	9	10	13	68	114
$0 to 10K	4	14	12	70	93
$10 to 30K	4	9	13	75	216
$30 to 50K	5	12	11	72	231
$50 to 100K	3	12	12	73	417
$100 to 250K	3	10	10	77	234
More than $250K	9	4	19	67	67
Total	4	11	12	73	1,372
Self-employed men					
In debt	c	c	c	c	6
$0 to10K	c	c	c	c	5
$10 to 30K	22	19	26	33	27
$30 to 50K	20	13	7	60	15
$50 to 100K	20	17	15	48	54

$100 to 250K	24	11	9	56	82
More than $250K	39	11	11	39	28
Total	24	14	14	48	217
Wage and salary women					
In debt	15	15	8	62	52
$0 to 10K	9	7	7	76	68
$10 to 30K	14	11	6	69	64
$30 to 50K	2	8	4	85	48
$50 to 100K	9	9	5	77	57
$100 to 250K	9	11	15	65	46
More than $250K	c	c	c	c	5
Total	10	10	7	73	340

SOURCE: Retirement History Study.

a. Wealth includes financial, business, and real estate assets, and is in 1971 dollars.

b. Sample with good wealth data.

c. Cells with sample sizes less than 10.

Reasons for Exit from the Career Job

The Retirement History Study asked those who left a job why they did so. (The question was not asked of those who became part-timers on the same job.) The answers appear in table 6.10, listed in order of frequency of response by the largest subsample, wage and salary men. The most popular answer was retirement benefits—precisely the answer that was almost never mentioned in the old days of retirement research, as we saw in chapter 2. Thirteen percent of those mentioning benefits took a new part-time job, and only 7 percent a new full-time job. This is consistent with workers being sensitive to Social Security benefit reductions after an exempt amount is earned.

Among the wage and salary men who claimed that they left the job because of age or health or simply because they wanted to, only 16 percent remained in the labor market. But among those who were laid off (only 4 percent of the sample) or left for "other" reasons (another 11 percent), more than half continued to work, primarily by embarking on new full-time jobs. Here is where many of the interesting transitions occur. It is unfortunate that the reasons are unknown for most of these workers.

A Comparison of New and Old Jobs

About one-quarter of the men and women in our sample who left career jobs took other jobs within four years of the exit. Most did so very soon after the departure. In this section, we compare the old and the new jobs to see whether people were primarily continuing old careers with new employers, or beginning new lines of work.

Class of Worker

Table 6.11 documents some transitions that have been discussed by Fuchs (1982). About 10 percent of the wage and salary men who switched jobs became self-employed. The percentage was about the same among those coming from the private sector and those from government. The percentages were smaller for women. What is surprising is

Table 6.10
Exit Patterns from Career Jobs by Reason for Exit
(horizontal percentage)

Group	Type of transition			
Reason	Part-time on new job (%)	Full-time on new job (%)	Out of labor force (%)	Total[a]
Wage and salary men				
Retirement benefits	13	7	80	429 (31%)
Age	11	6	83	325 (24%)
Health	8	8	84	252 (18%)
Wanted to stop	8	8	84	150 (11%)
Laid off	9	40	52	58 (4%)
New job	13	87	0	16 (1%)
Other	12	40	48	151 (11%)
Total	11	13	76	1,381 (100%)
Self-employed men				
Retirement benefits	19	0	81	16 (9%)
Age	9	9	83	23 (13%)
Health	11	12	87	65 (36%)
Wanted to stop	22	0	78	18 (10%)
Other	25	36	39	59 (33%)
Total	17	17	66	181 (100%)
Wage and salary women				
Retirement benefits	13	2	85	95 (29%)
Age	10	3	86	86 (26%)
Health	8	4	89	53 (16%)
Wanted to stop	5	5	90	41 (12%)
Laid off	13	27	60	15 (5%)
Other	16	30	53	43 (13%)
Total	11	8	81	333 (100%)

SOURCE: Retirement History Study.

a. Sample who left their career jobs.

Table 6.11

Class of Career and New Jobs by Sex for Those Who Changed Jobs (vertical percentage)

Sex	Class of career job			
Class of new job	Private sector	Government sector	Self-employed	Total
Men				
Private sector	87%	71%	69%	318 (82%)
Government sector	3%	18%	16%	31 (8%)
Self-employed	9%	11%	15%	40 (10%)
Total	261	66	62	389
	(67%)	(17%)	(16%)	(100%)
Women				
Private sector	82%	a	a	50 (82%)
Government sector	14%	a	a	8 (13%)
Self-employed	4%	a	a	3 (5%)
Total	51	10	0	61
	84%	16%	0%	(100%)

SOURCE: Retirement History Study.

a. Cells with sample sizes less than 10.

that 85 percent of the former self-employed who switched jobs became salaried workers, most in the private sector. The net result, in this sample at least, was a net decrease in the number of self-employed, contrary to what those who studied just wage and salary workers have found. Of course, these figures exclude those who became part-timers on the career job. This is only a small proportion of the wage and salary men and women (5 and 10 percent, respectively), but a significant fraction of the self-employed (25 percent).

Occupation and Industry

Table 6.12 suggests that there are a lot of changes underway. About 60 percent of the men who switched jobs changed occupations and an equal number changed industries, defined by one-digit categories.[7] Wage and salary workers were more likely to change industry and occupation if they were undertaking a new part-time (as opposed to full-time) job. The self-employed, on the other hand, were more likely to change with a new full-time job. Women were slightly more stable, and only half of them moved to a new occupation or industry.

Table 6.12
Occupation and Industry[a] Change for Those Who Changed Jobs (vertical percentage)

Group	Type of transition		
Status	Part time on new job	Full time on new job	Total[b]
Wage and salary men			
Same occupation	36%	48%	42%
Different occupation	64%	52%	58%
Same industry	30%	48%	40%
Different industry	70%	52%	60%
Sample size	151	176	327
Self-employed men			
Same occupation	29%	16%	23%
Different occupation	71%	84%	77%
Same industry	42%	29%	35%
Different industry	58%	71%	65%
Sample size	31	31	62
Wage and salary women			
Same occupation	47%	58%	52%
Different occupation	53%	42%	48%
Same industry	47%	65%	55%
Different industry	53%	35%	45%
Sample size	36	26	62

SOURCE: Retirement History Study.

a. One-digit Census industry and occupation codes.

b. Sample with good industry and occupation data on career and new jobs.

When we ranked jobs by white-collar and blue-collar status and by skill level (table 6.13), we observed job-changers moving toward blue-collar and toward less-skilled categories.[8] Fewer than half of the men in skilled white-collar career positions remained there.[9] About a quarter moved into sales and clerical jobs, and another quarter became blue-collar workers. Nearly all (92 percent) of those originally in less-skilled white-collar positions either remained there or moved to blue-collar employment. And almost none of the blue-collar workers moved up into white-collar jobs. A third of those in blue-collar skilled work dropped to less-skilled categories, and 70 percent of those in the bottom category remained there. Fewer than 10 percent of them became white-collar workers in the new job.

When we analyzed specific occupational categories, we found that the largest net outflow occurred in manufacturing. Of the men originally in durable and nondurable manufacturing, only about a third stayed there on their next job. Seventeen percent moved into trade, 16 percent into finance, insurance, and real estate, and nearly 20 percent went into other services. Other large percentage net outflows were found in transportation and public utilities and in public administration. The largest net gainers were finance, insurance and real estate, and other services.

Wage Rates

In table 6.14, we compare the wage rates before and after the job transition. Using four categories of hourly pay, we observed declines for both male and female wage and salary workers. For men, the proportion of earnings less than $5 per hour rose from 10 to nearly 40 percent; for women, from less than 30 to more than 50 percent. Although most workers did stay in the same category, those who moved were much more likely to slide down than to climb up.[10]

We then disaggregated further by the type of the transition, for male wage and salary workers only (table 6.15). The wage changes were the smallest for the small minority who moved to part-time status on their career jobs. This is as expected, since the specific human capital acquired on the job remains applicable. For those who began a new job, especially a part-time one, the wage losses were often severe.[11]

Table 6.13
Occupational Change
Wage and Salary Men Who Changed Jobs
(vertical percentage)

New job	Career job				
	White-collar skilled[a]	White-collar other	Blue-collar skilled	Blue-collar other	Total[b]
White-collar skilled	47%	8%	7%	0%	55 (17%)
White-collar other	28%	44%	9%	9%	60 (18%)
Blue-collar skilled	13%	13%	50%	20%	103 (32%)
Blue-collar other	11%	36%	33%	70%	107 (33%)
Total	89	39	152	45	
	(27%)	(12%)	(47%)	(14%)	

SOURCE: Retirement History Study.

a. See chapter 6, footnote 7 for definitions.

b. Sample with good occupation data on career and new jobs.

Only about one in 10 of those who moved to new part-time employment was earning less than $5 per hour before the move; over half of them were afterwards. The decreases were significant but less severe for new full-time work.

In table 6.16, we show the actual wage rate losses, in dollars per hour, by type of transition. We have aggregated small wage rate changes (less than $2.50 per hour) into a central category and looked at gains and losses larger than that. Over 40 percent of the wage and salary men who remained on the same job, but reduced their hours to part-time status, continued to earn approximately the same wage. Of those who did not, more enjoyed an increase than suffered a loss.

This was very different from the experience of those who found new employment. Of the new part-timers, two-thirds lost more than $2.50 per hour and 45 percent lost at least $5 per hour in the transition. Only one in 10 found work at a higher hourly wage. For new full-time workers, nearly half approximated their old wage, but among the others there were many more losers than gainers. These results are entirely consistent with those of Gustman and Steinmeier (1985a), who reported wage decreases among RHS respondents who described themselves as partially retired. The decreases were especially large for those who had changed jobs.

Earnings and Social Security Thresholds

Some of this loss in earnings may have been intentional. Most workers aged 62 and over are eligible to receive Social Security benefits. If they earn less than a threshold amount, they can work and receive the entire benefit to which they are entitled. After that exempt amount of earnings, benefits are reduced by 33 percent (for those aged 65–69) or 50 percent (for those aged 62-64) of additional earnings, until the benefits are reduced to zero. At this point, the individual ceases to be a Social Security recipient.

In tables 6.17 and 6.18, we compare each individual's earnings with the threshold for the appropriate year. Before the transition, nearly all of these respondents were earning well above the threshold. This is not

Table 6.14
Change in Wage Rate
Wage and Salary Men and Women Who Changed Jobs[a]

Sex	Career job wage rate[b]				
New job wage rate[b]	$0–5 per hour	$5–10 per hour	$10–15 per hour	$15+ per hour	Total[c]
Wage and salary men					
Less than $5/hour	71%	37%	35%	29%	132 (39%)
$5–10/hour	23%	49%	39%	21%	130 (38%)
$10–15/hour	3%	11%	15%	3%	36 (11%)
More than $15/hour	3%	3%	11%	45%	44 (13%)
Total[b]	35	129	122	56	342
	(10%)	(38%)	(36%)	(16%)	
Wage and salary women					
Less than $5/hour	72%	45%	42%	d	43 (52%)
$5–10/hour	16%	45%	42%	d	31 (36%)
$10–15/hour	4%	2%	17%	d	4 (5%)
More than $15/hour	8%	9%	0%	d	7 (8%)
Total[b]	25	47	12	3	84
	(29%)	(54%)	(14%)	(3%)	

SOURCE: Retirement History Study.
a. Including part time on the same job.
b. Wage rate in 1984 dollars.
c. Sample with good data on career and new job wage rates.
d. Cells with sample sizes smaller than 10.

Table 6.15
Change in Wage Rate
Wage and Salary Men Who Changed Jobs[a] by Type of Transition
(vertical percentage)

| Transition | Career job wage rate[b] | | | | |
New job wage rate[b]	$0-5 per hour	$5-10 per hour	$10-15 per hour	$15+ per hour	Total[c]
Part time on same job					
Less than $5/hour	71%	24%	14%	12%	18 (32%)
$5-10/hour	21%	33%	43%	12%	17 (30%)
$10-15/hour	7%	33%	14%	0%	10 (18%)
More than $15/hour	0%	10%	29%	75%	12 (21%)
Total[b]	14 (25%)	21 (37%)	14 (25%)	8 (14%)	57
Part time on new job					
Less than $5/hour	70%	57%	48%	47%	71 (53%)
$5-10/hour	20%	35%	41%	20%	47 (36%)
$10-15/hour	0%	4%	5%	7%	6 (4%)
More than $15/hour	10%	4%	5%	27%	10 (7%)
Total[b]	10 (7%)	51 (38%)	58 (43%)	15 (11%)	134

Full time on new job					
Less than $5/hour	73%	25%	26%	24%	43 (28%)
$5–10/hour	27%	67%	34%	24%	66 (44%)
$10–15/hour	0%	9%	26%	9%	21 (14%)
More than $15/hour	0%	0%	14%	42%	21 (14%)
Total[b]	11	57	50	33	151
	(7%)	(38%)	(33%)	(22%)	

SOURCE: Retirement History Study.

a. Including part time on the same job.

b. Wage rate in 1984 dollars.

c. Sample with good data on career and new job wage rates.

Table 6.16
Absolute Change in Wage Rate
Those Who Changed Jobs[a]
(vertical percentage)

Group	Type of transition		
Change in wage rate[b]	Part time on career job	Part time on new job	Full time on new job
Wage and salary men			
−$10/hr. or more	2 ⎫	11 ⎫	11 ⎫
−$5 to −$10/hr.	18 ⎬ 24	34 ⎬ 68	18 ⎬ 42
−$2.5 to −$5/hr.	4 ⎭	23 ⎭	13 ⎭
−$2.5 to +$2.5/hr.	42	21	46
+$2.5 to +$5/hr.	11 ⎫	2 ⎫	10 ⎫
+$5 to +$10/hr.	9 ⎬ 36	4 ⎬ 11	1 ⎬ 12
+$10/hr. or more	16 ⎭	5 ⎭	1 ⎭
Sample size[c]	57	134	151
Self-employed men			
−$10/hr. or more	7 ⎫	4 ⎫	5 ⎫
−$5 to −$10/hr.	5 ⎬ 24	17 ⎬ 29	9 ⎬ 19
−$2.5 to −$5/hr.	12 ⎭	8 ⎭	5 ⎭
−$2.5 to +$2.5/hr.	37	46	50
+$2.5 to +$5/hr.	12 ⎫	13 ⎫	14 ⎫
+$5 to +$10/hr.	7 ⎬ 40	4 ⎬ 25	18 ⎬ 32
+$10/hr. or more	21 ⎭	8 ⎭	0 ⎭
Sample size[c]	43	24	22
Wage and salary women			
−$10/hr. or more	6 ⎫	0 ⎫	0 ⎫
−$5 to −$10/hr.	6 ⎬ 18	28 ⎬ 41	4 ⎬ 17
−$2.5 to −$5/hr.	6 ⎭	13 ⎭	13 ⎭
−$2.5 to +$2.5/hr.	69	44	83
+$2.5 to +$5/hr.	3 ⎫	0 ⎫	0 ⎫
+$5 to +$10/hr.	0 ⎬ 12	3 ⎬ 16	0 ⎬ 0
+$10/hr. or more	9 ⎭	13 ⎭	0 ⎭
Sample size[c]	32	32	23

SOURCE: Retirement History Study.
a. Including part time on career job.
b. Wage rate in 1984 dollars.
c. Sample with good data on career and new job wage rates.

Table 6.17
Ratio of Earnings to Social Security Threshold on New Jobs[a] by Type of Exit
(vertical percentage)

Group	Type of transition			
Earnings/SS threshold	Part time on career job	Part time on new job	Full time on new job	Total
Wage and salary men				
0–0.5	7	17	3	9
0.5–1.0	41	49	3	27
1.0–1.5	24	15	2	11
1.5–2.0	5	9	13	10
More than 2.0	24	10	79	43
Sample size[b]	59	136	154	349
Self-employed men				
0–0.5	23	29	9	21
0.5–1.0	26	42	5	25
1.0–1.5	9	13	14	11
1.5–2.0	19	4	18	15
More than 2.0	23	13	55	28
Sample size[b]	43	24	22	89
Wage and salary women				
0–0.5	16	16	0	11
0.5–1.0	63	47	17	45
1.0–1.5	16	25	0	15
1.5–2.0	0	6	13	6
More than 2.0	6	6	70	23
Sample size[b]	32	32	23	87

SOURCE: Retirement History Study.
a. Including part time on career job.
b. Sample with good data or the earnings/threshold ratio.

surprising, since our sample included only full-time workers on career jobs. After the transition from full-time career work, however, many of the people who moved to part-time employment were earning just below the amount where the earnings test went into effect.[12] Among the male, (formerly) wage and salary workers, nearly half of those working part time earned between 50 and 100 percent of the threshold. For the small number of women, the proportion in this range was even higher (55 percent), and it was somewhat lower for the self-employed men. Among those who moved to new full-time work, not surprisingly, nearly all were above—and most considerably above—the threshold.

If this is due to a Social Security effect, we expect the behavior to be correlated with age. Those below age 62 suffer no Social Security loss with continued work; in fact, their Social Security wealth rises because of the effect of the additional earnings on future benefits. Those over 65 suffer the most when earning over the threshold, because the actuarial adjustment for delayed receipt of benefits after age 65 is far from actuarially fair. The sign and size of the penalty in the 62-to-64 age range are matters of debate, as we discussed earlier. It depends on whether the adjustment to future benefits is sufficient to compensate for the loss of current benefits. The effect on Social Security wealth of earning more than the earnings-test threshold goes from positive to ambiguous to negative as we consider those less than age 62, those 62 through 64, and those 65 and over.

Table 6.18 is certainly consistent with the Social Security hypothesis. The proportion of wage and salary men who earned just under the threshold (between 0.5 and 1.0) after leaving full-time career employment rises from 9 to 27 to 36 percent as we consider the three age groups. If we include those earning less than half of the appropriate threshold (between 0.0 and 0.5), the numbers climb from 16 to 34 and 49 percent. Similar patterns exist for the smaller numbers of women and self-employed men. Of course, this could be just an age effect—older workers prefer fewer hours and therefore earn less than younger workers. There is undoubtedly an age effect in these figures, but the dramatic differences between those under and over 62 and the smaller differences at the age 65 break suggest that there is more than age at work. Many people eligi-

Table 6.18
Earnings/Social Security Threshold on New Jobs[a]
by Age at Return
(vertical percentage)

Group	Age at exit		
Earnings/SS threshold	58–61	62–64	65+
Wage and salary men			
0–0.5	7	7	13
0.5–1.0	9	27	36
1.0–1.5	4	11	15
1.5–2.0	4	8	15
More than 2.0	76	47	22
Sample size[b]	76	130	143
Self-employed men			
0–0.5	0	18	32
0.5–1.0	8	25	30
1.0–1.5	17	8	14
1.5–2.0	8	15	16
More than 2.0	67	35	8
Sample size[b]	12	40	37
Wage and salary women			
0–0.5	8	8	17
0.5–1.0	23	58	39
1.0–1.5	8	8	25
1.5–2.0	8	0	11
More than 2.0	54	26	8
Sample size[b]	13	38	36

SOURCE: Retirement History Study.
a. Including part time on career job.
b. Sample with good data on the earnings/threshold ratio.

ble for Social Security benefits seem to be designing their work careers late in life to avoid the high tax rate in the official Social Security earnings test.

Job Characteristics

The 1969 wave of the Retirement History Study included the three-digit industry and occupation codes for all the employed recipients. A cross-classification matrix made it possible to calculate the probability that an individual fell into each of the approximately 14,000 jobs listed in the Department of Labor's *Dictionary of Occupational Titles*. Each of these jobs, in turn, was linked to a set of specific job characteristics. Therefore, we could calculate the expected values of these characteristics for each of the three-digit Census categories.

Unfortunately, subsequent waves of the RHS included only the very broad one-digit categorizations. One can take another set of expected values and calculate the expected job characteristics for each one-digit occupation. We have done this and asked how the characteristics on the career and new jobs compared.[13] But the level of aggregation required to do this makes the conclusions suggestive at best.[14]

Table 6.19 is consistent with our other evidence about the career and the new jobs. The new jobs, for those working both full and part time, generally required lower levels of specific vocational preparation (SVP) and general educational development (GED).[15] For example, among those who moved to new part-time jobs, nearly one-quarter were in positions requiring fewer than six months training. Only 13 percent had left jobs like this. At the other end of the spectrum, 27 percent had left jobs requiring at least four years of vocational preparation, and only 14 percent ended up on such jobs. It is interesting to note that the quality of the new jobs, measured by SVP or GED, was generally higher among those with new full-time positions.

This table also suggests the workers had less personal discretion in carrying out their duties on the new jobs. They were less likely to exercise "direction, planning, and control" or perform a "variety of duties characterized by frequent change." Conversely, the new employment was more likely to involve "repetitive or short-cycle operations" or

Table 6.19
Comparisons of Job Characteristics on Career and New Jobs
Wage and Salary Men

Job characteristic	Part time on new job		Full time on new job	
	Career job (%)	New job (%)	Career job (%)	New job (%)
Direction, planning, and control	32	17	30	25
Variety of duties	70	64	78	74
Repetitiveness	41	59	37	44
Specific instructions	37	48	33	37
Specific vocational preparation required				
0–6 months	13	24	9	18
7–12 months	30	38	31	29
13–48 months	30	24	37	35
48 months +	27	14	23	18
General education development required				
Levels 1,2	16	23	11	19
Level 3	28	42	32	29
Level 4	45	25	47	43
Levels 5,6,7	12	10	11	9

SOURCE: Retirement History Study.

''doing things only under specific instructions.'' Because of the extreme level of aggregation involved in these statistics, it would be unwise to draw conclusions from these numbers alone. But they are useful as confirmation of a picture already drawn.

Summary

Nontraditional retirement transitions are common in the United States, even though abrupt changes from full-time work to complete labor force withdrawal are still more likely. The patterns of exit we observed were correlated with individuals' circumstances at the time of the change. Those in relatively poor health were more likely to drop out completely, as were those eligible for employer pensions or subject to mandatory retirement. There were interesting differences by industry and occupation, with intermediate stages most likely among workers in the nonunion service sectors. There was weak evidence suggesting that nontraditional transitions were more common among those at the ends of the socioeconomic scale (the poor and the rich) than among those in the middle, suggesting that the motivations for partial retirement stages may differ.

When we compared the old and new jobs of those who changed employment, we found a great deal of industrial and occupational movement. When the sample was analyzed by white-collar/blue-collar status and by skill level (skilled/other), the most common transition involved remaining in the same general category. But most of the movement that did exist was down—toward blue-collar and less-skilled positions. Rough estimates of job characteristics suggested that the new jobs had lower specific vocational and general educational requirements. They also appeared to be jobs on which workers exercised less personal discretion in performing their duties, and were more likely (than on the career jobs) to be doing repetitive tasks or working under specific instructions.

Wages showed similar decline; most workers earned less, and often considerably less, after the transition, especially those who took new part-time positions. Large flows were noted out of manufacturing and into finance, insurance and real estate, and other services. These occupations, we suspect, allowed more hours flexibility than did the jobs the individuals had left. And they did so while permitting the individuals to collect pension benefits, and thus avoid the wealth losses (and implicit pay cuts) that would have accompanied continued work on their career jobs.

NOTES

1. Burtless (1987) acknowledged that the measure of health that he used (the answer to a question on whether health limited the respondent's capacity for work) is suspect, since some people may use health as a socially acceptable reason for retirement even when other factors were key. To diminish the importance of this phenomenon, Burtless also estimated his employment equation using a predetermined index of health—the answer to the same health question from the previous questionnaire. The estimated health effect remained strong and statistically significant.

2. See Stern (1989) for some evidence on the usefulness of these subjective health variables.

3. Filer and Petri (1988) have proposed another interpretation of the correlation between pension eligibility and retirement age. They contend that the causation may not be from pensions to retirement, but rather from basic job characteristics to both pensions and retirement. Those in jobs with intense physical demands, stress, or repetitive working conditions, they hypothesize, plan to retire early and therefore have employment contracts (i.e., pensions) that anticipate this.

4. The self-employed are excluded from the pension tables, since so few of them had formal pension plans.

5. This is consistent with a much more detailed analysis of the impact of mandatory retirement and the effect of the 1983 legislation found in Burkhauser and Quinn (1983b).

6. Burtless (1987) found that "a miner aged 62 is 50 percent more likely to suffer a work limitation than is the average worker . . . and he is twice as likely . . . than is a worker in a professional industry. Similarly, a worker in a professional occupation is one-third less likely to face a work limitation than is an average worker . . . and he is 57 percent less likely to be limited than a laborer."

7. This is very similar to the results reported by Parnes and Less (1985b), who used data from the National Longitudinal Surveys. They reported that almost two-thirds of their postretirement job-changers crossed broadly defined industry lines.

8. Using the 1970 Census occupational codes, we defined our categories as follows:
　　White-collar skilled:
　　　Professional, technical, and kindred workers
　　　Teachers
　　　Managers and officials (excluding farm)
　　White-collar, other:
　　　Sales workers
　　　Clerical and kindred workers
　　Blue-collar skilled:
　　　Craftsmen, foremen, and kindred workers
　　　Operatives and kindred workers
　　　Transportation equipment operatives
　　　Farm managers

Blue-collar, other:
  Nonfarm laborers
  Private household workers
  Service workers
  Farm laborers
Omitted:
  Members of the armed forces

9. These results are also consistent with those of Parnes and Less (1985b), who found the majority of NLS job-changers moved down the socioeconomic hierarchy.

10. Parnes and Less (1985b) found that most of the NLS men they studied had lower real wages on the new job. Ruhm (1990), with a sample from the RHS, reported the same for those who switched industry or occupation or both.

11. Herz and Rones (1989) reported that hourly wages tend to decline by 30 to 40 percent when full-time workers become part-time employees.

12. Burtless and Moffitt (1985) and Iams (1987) have also reported this clustering around (and primarily below) the exempt amounts. Iams also showed that the earnings of benefit recipients aged 65 to 71 were consistently higher than the earnings of those aged 62 to 64. The median earnings for the younger group was $4,391, only $9 less than their (1982) exempt amount of $4,400. For the older recipients, with $6,000 in exempt earnings, the median earnings were about $5,500.

13. Holden (1988) has shown that those in physically demanding jobs in the year before they started receiving Social Security benefits were less likely to continue working in retirement. Since the analysis here includes only those who did change jobs and continue working, the distribution of job attributes for this sample will differ from that of the older population as a whole.

14. For the job held in 1969, we had both the one-digit and three-digit job descriptions, and therefore could calculate expected job characteristics for each person at the detailed or at the highly aggregated level. Since the new jobs were at only the one-digit level, we used only the one-digit information for the career jobs in table 6.19. The conclusions drawn from an analogous table with the more accurate three-digit descriptions of the 1969 characteristics, however, were very similar to those drawn above.

15. The specific vocational preparation descriptions refer to the actual number of months of training time required for the worker to acquire the knowledge and abilities necessary for average performance on the job. The general education development descriptions, on the other hand, are not in units of time. Rather, each gradation (1 through 7) is characterized by higher levels of mathematical and language development. The numbers, however, are merely ordinal.

– 7 –

Summary and Conclusions

A major goal of this book is to summarize and discuss recent research by economists on individual retirement decisions and aggregate retirement trends. This is a fascinating time to study these phenomena. As we saw in chapter 1, dramatic demographic shifts are underway in the United States. The population is aging and the ratio of those of traditional working age to those of traditional retirement age is falling significantly. In addition, the work and retirement patterns of older Americans, especially men, have undergone major changes. During the past two decades, the labor force participation rates of men aged 62 to 70 have dropped by well over a third. Percentage declines are also substantial for those as young as 55. For older women, participation rates have remained fairly stable, but have declined relative to the labor supply increases of younger women.

Among the declining numbers still in the labor force, other changes are underway. The proportion of older employees working part time (and nearly all voluntarily so) has increased steadily. Older workers are disproportionately self-employed, and those who are have retirement patterns very different from those of wage and salary workers.

What is responsible for these dramatic changes in the work behavior of older Americans? On what do individual retirement decisions and aggregate trends depend? Circumstantial evidence points to our public and private retirement income systems as likely influences. At the same time that participation rates were declining, both Social Security and employer pensions were growing substantially. Real Social Security expenditures (excluding Medicare) have increased about fivefold since 1960 and have more than doubled since 1970. Retirement patterns reveal definite spikes at ages 62 and 65—the ages of early and normal Social Security eligibility. In addition, since 1950, employer pension coverage has increased from one-quarter to nearly one-half of private sector workers, and the number of pension recipients has increased significantly. It seems very likely that these large and growing institutions, aimed specifically at the labor supply decisions of older workers, would have had some impact on individual and aggregate retirement behavior.

On the other hand, years of surveys by the Social Security Administration and others found very little mention of these retirement programs. When asked why they had stopped work, most retirees named health or an employer-initiated separation as the primary reason and very few mentioned Social Security or pension benefits. Were they important or not?

The stage was set. Several interesting and important demographic phenomena were underway. Past research yielded some insights, but circumstantial evidence led in other intriguing directions. Two outstanding new microeconomic data sets appeared with which to test alternative hypotheses. The result was the dramatic increase in economic research on retirement issues that we have discussed. What have we learned?

Work, Retirement, and Pensions: A Life-Cycle View

A major advance, we believe, is a growing consensus that the financial incentives embedded in our Social Security and employer pension plans influence work decisions throughout an individual's life. Social Security and pension plans certainly affect labor supply late in life, and they probably do so earlier as well.

The key to understanding these relationships is the recognition that retirement income eligibility—the right to a future stream of income—is a component of compensation. For employees covered by Social Security or a defined benefit pension plan, the value of these rights varies in nonlinear ways with continued employment with the firm. Workers can control both the timing and the magnitude of these benefits, subject to the rules of the plan. Benefits claimed later are fewer in number, but generally larger in size. Their total value can rise or fall with continued work (delayed receipt), depending on whether the future increments are sufficient to compensate for the earlier benefits foregone.

Since retirement benefits are paid out over time, the entire income stream is best viewed in present discounted value terms—as the *asset* or *stock of wealth* that could generate this stream. The value of this asset depends on when it is first claimed. In each year of continued employment with a firm, an individual's pension and Social Security wealth changes. These *changes* in retirement income wealth are part of annual compensation. If the asset values are increasing, pension (or Social Security) accrual is positive, and true compensation exceeds the paycheck by the amount of the increase. On the other hand, if the wealth values are declining, true compensation is less than it appears.

An important advance in the theory of pensions is the realization that pensions can influence the decision to leave the firm throughout one's career. If one follows Richard Ippolito (1987) and makes the distinction between the "quit" and the "stay" value of a pension, then the penalty in foregone pension wealth for quitting "too soon" rises through middle age and then falls. During early years with the firm, the "quit" accrual—that is, the change in the present discounted value of the pension required by law—is less than the wages foregone by the worker to finance the eventual ("stay") value of the pension (the value received by a worker who remains until retirement age). The firm owes the worker. Around middle age, the accruals equal and then surpass the implicit wage reductions, as the firm begins to make up the previous shortfalls in compensation. After the age of eligibility for early retirement, defined benefit pension accruals usually fall and often turn negative. The decrease in accrual is like a pay cut. It discourages continued employment with the firm.

Robert Clark and Ann McDermed (1988) and others have shown how much pension wealth workers can lose from job changes. The losses occur because pensions are backloaded—accruals rise until the age of early retirement eligibility. Therefore, overall compensation on a job already held for 20 years will exceed that on a new job with the identical wage and pension plan. Workers who switch jobs lose because they move from the gravy of one plan to the gruel of another and miss out on the pension accrual repayment they had coming.

Alan Gustman and Thomas Steinmeier (1989a) have an additional perspective on the cost of job mobility. They agree that losses in pension wealth can occur, but disagree with the conclusion that these losses are significant. Rather, they argue, mobility is discouraged much more by the fact that wages on the new job are likely to be lower than on the previous job.

These various models all agree that pensions can change the pattern of lifetime compensation. They predict that pension incentives should reduce turnover at younger ages and encourage it later. The authors differ, however, on the magnitude of the effect and the strength of the evidence. Thus far, a consensus view has not emerged.

There has been a great deal of empirical research on the financial incentives of the Social Security system. Although the rules are complicated, there is only one set of rules and researchers know them. There is general agreement that the Social Security system subsidizes work prior to age 62, since future benefits are rising and there are no benefits foregone, and penalizes it after age 65, often severely. Between ages 62 and 65, the delayed retirement credit is close to actuarially fair, and whether Social Security provides a small subsidy or a small tax on earnings depends on assumptions about life expectancies and discount rates.

The pension side is much more complicated. There are hundreds of thousands of employer pension plans, each with its own rules and regulations, and these details are frequently unknown to the researcher. Economists who have chosen to use the large microeconomic data sets (such as the Retirement History Study and the National Longitudinal Surveys) must rely on assumptions rather than facts on many pension plan details. Industrywide averages about key parameters (for example, the rewards for delayed receipt) are frequently used, but the rich variety that exists in the individual plans is lost. Fortunately, other researchers have taken another tack and analyzed the complex details of a smaller number of actual plans. They know more about the actual financial incentives but are less able to discern the impact of the plans, because they do not have as much other information about the individuals in their samples.

The consensus on pensions is that defined benefit plans are rarely actuarially fair. Their asset values generally rise or fall with continued work—they *are* affected by the timing of initial benefit receipt. But there is tremendous variety among the individual plans. We now know that the accrual values of defined benefit pensions usually peak around the earliest year of benefit eligibility. Income from working exceeds income from retiring, but the difference between the two declines over time. In other words, true compensation remains positive but diminishes after some age, even if simple wage growth is constant. Most workers can continue to work after that age, but only for smaller and smaller pay, and many decide to leave.

That these work incentives and disincentives exist does not necessarily mean that they are understood or, even if they are, that they influence individual behavior. This is the empirical question that has been the focus of much of the recent work by economists. The consensus is that these financial incentives *do* influence individual retirement decisions. When the changes in Social Security and pension wealth that would accompany another year of work are entered as explanatory variables in behavioral equations, they are generally statistically significant. Older Americans behave as though they understand and respond to these incentives. They are sensitive to their true compensation, and when this falls, as it inevitably does because of retirement income wealth losses, they are less likely to stay on the job.

Although these financial incentives are statistically significant, they are only part of the story. Individual decisions obviously depend on a vast number of factors, only some of which we can observe and measure. Physical and mental health, social networks, attitudes toward work and leisure, living arrangements, job characteristics, dependents, local labor market conditions, climate, and expectations about the future are all undoubtedly important. They interact with the financial incentives on which we have focused to bring about the final result.

Several economists have used their empirical models to estimate the aggregate impact of various Social Security reforms that have been proposed and, in some cases, enacted. They use simulation methods to predict individual decisions on the basis of the behavioral equations they have estimated and the new policy parameters that have been proposed. In these experiments, the Social Security amendments do affect aggregate behavior, but only modestly. The delays in the average retirement age are on the order of months, not years.

Why then do we concentrate so much attention on an issue of limited influence? There are several good reasons. First, unlike many of the factors listed above, these financial incentives are the direct product of specific public policy initiatives. Congress created the Social Security system and all of its details, and Congress can change it. This is in stark contrast to many of the other important factors in the retirement decision, such as attitudes, job characteristics, social networks, and expectations. Even with those that are subject to public policy, such as labor market conditions and health, the linkages between government action and the eventual outcome are much more tenuous. It is much easier to change ages of eligibility, benefit reduction rates, or delayed retirement credits than it is to improve the general level of health or expectations of older Americans.

In addition, the simulations on Social Security reform estimate first-round effects only. The researchers have altered Social Security rules but have left the employer pension environment unchanged. We are convinced that pension incentives, which exhibit considerably more variety than does Social Security, are extremely important in determining individual and aggregate behavior. A key variable about which little is known is how the employer pensions will respond to amendments in Social Security rules. Will pension changes augment or offset Social Security initiatives? Will pension changes be nullified by other components in the compensation package? In short, how will the long-run, general equilibrium impacts compare to the short-run effects that have been studied?

This is an area of extreme uncertainty. It involves predicting both personal and corporate behavior. What we now know is that such decisions by firms, unions, and workers will make a difference. Most people do not retire because they can no longer find or perform work, as we once thought. Some do, but many others now retire voluntarily, when they are still able to work and there is demand for their services. They do so partly because of the tradeoffs they see in the market. There are always people at the margin, and these people will alter their behavior in response to changes in the choices they face.

Exit Patterns from Career Jobs

A second goal of this book is to discuss the ways in which older Americans leave their career jobs. We pointed out in chapter 1 that most workers spend a considerable portion of their employed life with a single firm. The departure from this position is therefore an important event. We decided to concentrate on this transition, rather than on retirement *per se,* and thereby sidestep the debate on the appropriate definition of retirement. We defined a career job as a full-time job held for at least 10 years. Our primary focus was on the subset of the Retirement History Study sample who were still employed on career jobs in 1969, when they were all between 58 and 63 years of age.

Complete retirement from a career job is only one form of job exit. What makes transitions at older ages different from those earlier is that many workers do go from a full-time career job to full-time retirement— they leave the job and the labor force simultaneously. But this is not the only way to leave. The other transitions—to part-time work on the same job or part-time or full-time work on a new job—are very important, but poorly understood. Policy research that has concentrated on labor force participation has missed the importance of Social Security and pensions on the paths that workers take between career work and complete retirement.

It is ironic that while our understanding of the determinants of retirement, particularly the importance of financial incentives, has grown so dramatically, relatively little work was being done on describing the actual behavior under study. Most of the effort has concentrated on the right-hand side of the equation and relatively little on the left. Most researchers (including ourselves) described retirement as an either-or phenomenon. They disagreed on how retirement should be defined, but agreed that an individual either is or is not retired, whatever the definition. Our current analysis of the actual exit patterns chosen by career workers shows that this dichotomy can be misleading and will lead one to overlook some very interesting retirement transitions.

The traditional retirement pattern involves a one-time movement from full-time labor market activity to complete labor market withdrawal. We found that this was still the modal pattern during the 1970s—about 70 percent of those who left their career jobs did so in this fashion. During the subsequent four years they did not report working again.

The other 30 percent, however, exited in nontraditional ways. Over 20 percent of the wage and salary men found new work when they left, and they were evenly distributed between full-time and part-time status. Only a few (5 percent of the total) were able to reduce their hours to part-time (less than 20 hours per week) on their same career jobs. The experience of the (nonmarried) women in the sample was similar. About one-quarter did not leave the labor market completely. They were more able than the men to stay part time on their career jobs. The self-employed men were the most likely to keep working after leaving full-time career work. Only half of this group left the labor force during the decade they were observed. One-quarter found new employment, and the other one-quarter reduced their hours of work to part time on their career jobs.

We found that these intermediate jobs were not just brief way stations on the road to retirement. Although most of these workers eventually did leave the labor force, only one-quarter of them did so within the first two years after the transition. The majority of the remainder were still employed on their first transitional job after two years, and about one-fifth had moved on to yet another job.

Whether or not those who leave full-time career status but continue to work should be labeled as retired or not is a matter of debate. In some ways they do not seem retired. They are still employed, often for a considerable number of hours per year, and some are working full time, but on a new job. In other ways they do seem retired. Many claim pension benefits, some collect Social Security, and most earn significantly less than they had prior to the transition. Some describe themselves as retired, but many do not.

Exit patterns varied by the age at transition. The youngest and the oldest groups were the most likely to do something nontraditional. Nearly a quarter of those aged 58 to 61 found new full-time jobs, compared to fewer than 10 percent of those 62 to 64, and fewer than 5 percent of those 65 and over. The oldest category (aged 66–70) contained the workers least likely to leave the labor force completely. This may be surprising until one realizes that these people had already chosen to work beyond age 65, which makes them a very nonrepresentative sample of the population—probably individuals with a particular propensity to work or with insufficient resources to stop.

We saw this pattern when we looked at the wage rates, earnings, or wealth of our sample. For all three variables, those in the tails of the distributions were the least likely to leave the labor force completely. We suspect that those at the bottom continued to work because they had to; they did not have the financial means to do otherwise. They were also unlikely to face dramatic age-specific wage cuts, since they were usually not covered by employer pension plans. Those at the upper end could afford to retire, but had either jobs or hours flexibility that made continued work the more attractive alternative. It is interesting to note that men in the highest wealth category (more than $250,000) were the most likely to stay on in part-time employment on their career jobs.

Health and pension status were both important. Those with poor health were the most likely to leave the labor force. Those in good health (the same or better than their peers) were the most likely to move on to a new job. The health differences in this sample were modest and greatly understate the overall impact of health on the retirement decision. The reason is that our sample included only those still employed full time on their career jobs at ages 58 to 63. Most of those with severe health problems would have already left their career jobs by then, and therefore be excluded from the study.

Pension status was highly correlated with transition patterns. Those eligible for pension benefits when they left were much more likely to leave the labor force completely. Very few remained part time on the career job, since employer pensions rarely permit one to do so and draw benefits. Earnings from other jobs, however, usually do not affect eligibility. The fact that relatively few pension recipients took new part-time or full-time positions suggests that the pension benefits had the usual income effect, increasing the demand for leisure.

There were interesting differences by industry and occupation. Traditional retirement was most common in the unionized manufacturing sectors, and least likely in construction, trade, and services. By occupation, nontraditional transitions were more frequent among white-collar workers. This is an interesting finding since the labor market is moving toward more white-collar service employment. This may mean that traditional retirement will be even less common in the future.

Retirement History Study respondents were asked why they had left their last jobs. Since much of the earliest research was based on questions of this nature, it is interesting to note that the most frequent response, among wage and salary men and women, was retirement benefits. Age and health were the next most common reasons given. This is in stark contrast to the early research findings, in which health always dominated and retirement income sources were rarely mentioned.

We looked carefully at the subset of our sample who switched employers. With the exception of the self-employed, most had to do this in order to keep working after leaving full-time status on their career jobs. (Many of the self-employed just reduced the hours on their same jobs.) Most did so with very little time between jobs, although a few returned after as many as four years out of the labor force. A comparison of the career and new jobs reveals that most of these job-switchers moved to different lines of work. About three of every five wage and salary men moved to a new (one-digit) industry and occupation. The percentage was even higher for self-employed men—three-quarters began new occupations, as did about half of the women.

When we ranked jobs by skill level and by white-collar/blue-collar status, we noticed a drift down the occupational scale. Although about half of the job-changers stayed in the same category, many more slid down than climbed up. Wages told the same story. They were generally lower on the new jobs, especially for those moving to part-time work with a new employer. Over half of the part-timers earned less than $5 per hour, even though only 7 percent had on their previous jobs. Comparisons of the new earnings levels with the thresholds for the Social Security earnings test hinted that some of the earnings loss may have been intentional. Many earned just under the threshold, and this behavior was correlated with age. Only 9 percent of those less than age 62 (and therefore ineligible for Social Security retirement benefits) did so, compared to over a quarter of those 62 through 64 and over a third of those 65 and over.

The data on specific job characteristics are not very precise, because they are one-digit industrywide averages. These averages, however, indicated that job-switchers were moving from jobs in which they had a variety of different duties and control over the tasks performed to ones more likely to involve repetitive tasks under specific instructions. The levels of specific and general training required were noticeably lower in the new positions.

In summary, we find that nontraditional retirement patterns are common among older Americans. Many workers stay in the labor force after they leave their career jobs. Of those who remain employed, most take on a new position quickly and stay in it for several years. The new positions often represent a new line of work, lower on the socioeconomic scale and often at considerably lower pay. Many workers augment these earnings with Social Security and/or pension benefits.

This research suggests that work after retirement—after departure from full-time status on a career job—is a common occurrence. But such transitional jobs are still in the minority, and substantial changes in both Social Security and pension structures are required before the majority of workers are likely to stay at work beyond their early 60s.

What Will Future Retirement Behavior Look Like?

It is little wonder that the labor force participation rates of older workers have fallen dramatically over the last two decades, given the weak labor markets of the 1970s and the incentives embedded in our retirement income programs. But we have seen that despite the overall trend, many older workers who left their career jobs went on to work at new jobs, which they then held for a considerable length of time.

Very little empirical evidence exists on the influence of Social Security or pension policy on these nontraditional job transitions, because they have not been the major focus of study. What is known is that current attempts to increase the labor force participation of older workers by changing Social Security rules alone are likely to have only modest effects. Changes in the earnings-test exempt amount, the benefit reduction rate, the age of normal retirement, and the delayed retirement credit after age 65 will not by themselves create dramatic changes in the length of stay on the career job. And it is this labor market decision that primarily determines work effort at older ages.

Most defined benefit pension plans continue to encourage workers to leave the career job at the earliest possible retirement age. It is likely that changes in pensions, rather than Social Security, will have the greater effect on full-time career work. If employers are concerned about a shortage of labor early next century, as they well might be, then we may see substantial changes in pension policy. If they are not concerned, then employers may tilt lifetime benefits even more toward those who leave at early retirement age in order to offset the scheduled reductions in Social Security work disincentives.

Current pension rules sometimes offset Social Security changes automatically. This happens when employer pension plans are "integrated"; that is, when pension benefits depend on the size of an individual's Social Security payment. If Social Security benefits decline, the pension increases and makes up a portion (usually half) of the loss. The majority of full-time participants in defined benefit plans are in such integrated plans (Herz and Rones 1989). A smaller percentage receives pension supplements if they retire early, to compensate for the loss in Social Security benefits (Bell and Marclay 1987). If employers want to buck the Social Security trend even more than these integration features already do, it will not be easy to prevent them from doing so. For instance, the 1986 Omnibus Budget Act requires firms with pension plans to continue providing service credit to those who continue with the firm past normal retirement age.[1] But this does not prevent the firm from making early retirement benefits even more generous in order to offset this rule.

The ability to offset government policy, however, does not necessarily mean that employers will do so. In fact, one might well argue that private pensions will conform to the new Social Security incentives, even if they have not yet. They often have in the past. For example, age 65 has most frequently been chosen (in domestic pension plans) as the normal retirement age because the Social Security system adopted that age initially. One of the original goals of Social Security policy was to encourage older workers out of the labor force. Until 1972, earnings above a small amount were taxed at 100 percent, and benefits postponed beyond age 65 earned no actuarial credit at all. Given these strong disincentives to full-time work, it is not surprising that private firms developed institutions that conformed. To do otherwise would have required them to pay workers higher wages after age 65 to offset the losses in Social Security wealth.

The establishment of early Social Security benefits at age 62 may have encouraged private firms to do likewise, to the degree that workers perceived Social Security pension accrual to fall past that age. The changes in Social Security benefit rules scheduled for the next decade will reduce work disincentives and alter the institutional structure on which private pensions are built. How employer pensions respond will determine how work at older ages will change in the next century.

A final issue concerns the influence of retirement income benefit changes on the type of work we can expect at older ages. If pension rules do not adjust, we foresee increased part-time and full-time work on new postcareer jobs. This is because the easing of Social Security disincentives will make work more attractive, while pension rules continue to penalize those who stay on their career jobs. Workers will leave the firm, collect the career job pension while its asset value is high, and move to another employer. If private firms, rather than doing nothing, actually counter Social Security changes with even stronger retirement incentives of their own, then we will see even more of this postcareer employment. But if firms foresee labor shortages ahead and match the Social Security initiatives by flattening their own pension accrual patterns across the life cycle, then the age at which workers leave career jobs will begin to rise.

An important variation on this theme is the possibility of part-time work *on the career job,* a pattern that is already common among the self-employed. We suspect that many workers would find this an attractive alternative.[2] A gradual rather than instantaneous reduction of hours from full time to zero makes sense, and the option of doing so on the same job reduces the loss in specific human capital and the wage reduction that usually accompanies a job change. Current pension rules make this a poor choice for workers in defined benefit plans. Part-time employment with the firm usually prevents the receipt of any pension benefits, and future benefits are often a function of the last few years' earnings. But current pension rules are not written in stone.

Other nations have introduced programs to promote partial or gradual retirement. Barry Mirkin (1987) points out that many of them were initially designed to encourage earlier retirement in nations with high and persistent levels of unemployment. But they can be used to encourage later retirement as well. In Norway, for example, with a normal retirement age of 67, traditionally low levels of unemployment, and an age structure considerably older than that in the United States, workers aged 67 to 70 could claim various fractions of their old-age pensions, as long as the sum of pensions plus earnings did not exceed 80 percent of previous pay (Ginsburg 1985). Denmark (Petersen 1989) and Finland (Sundberg 1989) have similar plans.

In 1976, Sweden introduced a much more popular partial pension option designed to smooth the transition from full-time work to full-time retirement (Laczko 1988; Kruse and Söderström 1989). Under this plan, eligible workers aged 60 to 64 who reduce their hours to part-time have 65 percent of the loss in earnings made up by a partial pension.[3] Because of the high tax rates, the change in net pay is often small. Since 1977, between 12 and 27 percent of those eligible have opted for the plan each year. It is popular among both blue- and white-collar workers, and especially among women. Because it enjoys the support of both the unions' and the employers' confederations, the hours' reductions have proceeded smoothly. Employees usually work fewer days per week or alternate weeks, although shorter days are popular among women. Nearly all of these workers stay with the same employer and on the same job. Helen Ginsburg (1985) reported that both recipients and firms were pleased with this alternative. Workers' health and productivity improved while absenteeism and disability declined.

Partial retirement is possible under Social Security rules in the United States, although the earnings test is more restrictive for those aged 62 to 64 than for those 65 and over. It will be even more attractive now that the benefit reduction rate has dropped from one-half to one-third for those 65 and older. But employer pensions rarely offer these options. This implies that partial retirement usually means a job change and, as we have seen, a significant decrease in pay.

In the United States, there is a trend away from work disincentives for older workers. This is good, as long as our policies do not neglect those who cannot continue to work. Mandatory retirement has virtually been eliminated. Social Security changes scheduled to go into effect over the next several decades will make the system much more age neutral so that the value of Social Security rights will depend much less on when the benefits are first claimed. In the pension world, there is a trend toward defined contribution plans, which do not have the kind of work disincentives we have emphasized. But defined benefit plans, which generally do, still remain the dominant form of primary coverage.

The research on the retirement decision over the past decade shows the power of applied microeconomics. Our society has built programs with strong retirement incentives, and people have responded to them as economic theory and common sense would predict. As pension and Social Security accruals, and therefore total compensation, decline with age, some workers decide to stop working. We now know a great deal about this decision, but relatively little about the many other possibilities that exist—options involving job changes and second careers that some people already use as intermediate stops on the road to complete retirement. Other nations have been more imaginative than the United States in designing flexible programs that support workers' efforts to withdraw more gradually from the labor force. We are convinced that older Americans would respond to changed incentives in the future as they have in the past. What remains to be seen is whether the market—firms responding to labor shortages on the horizon—will introduce the appropriate changes themselves, or whether a more active government role is required.

NOTES

1. The law still permits caps on the total number of years of tenure that are counted in the benefit calculation formula and limits on the maximum benefit, so it is still possible for workers who stay on to get no increment to future pensions (Herz and Rones 1989). The difference is that this situation can no longer be a direct function of age.

2. According to Morrison (1983), Jondrow, Brechling, and Marcus (1987), and the U.S. Special Committee on Aging (1988, p. 90), national surveys suggest that many older workers indicate a strong preference for part-time work after their career jobs, and that many are interested in jobs the same as or similar to their preretirement employment. They conclude that many workers would take advantage of more flexible work policies if they were more widespread.

3. An important detail of the scheme is that these part-time earnings usually have little effect on the eventual state earnings-related pension, since the benefit is based on the 15 years of *highest* earnings, not the 15 final years of employment. A partial retirement plan in Great Britain failed partially because most employees in occupational pension schemes have their benefits based on their *final* salary, whether it be full time or part time (Laczko 1988).

REFERENCES

Aaron, Henry J. *Economic Effects of Social Security*. Washington, D.C.: The Brookings Institution, 1982.

Aaron, Henry J., Barry P. Bosworth, and Gary Burtless. *Can America Afford to Grow Old?* Washington, D.C.: The Brookings Institution, 1989.

Addison, John T. and Alberto C. Castro. "The Importance of Lifetime Jobs: Differences Between Union and Nonunion Workers." *Industrial and Labor Relations Review* 40 (April 1987): 393-405.

Akerlof, George A. and Brian G. M. Main. "An Experience-Weighted Measure of Employment and Unemployment Durations." *American Economic Review* 71 (December 1981): 1003-1011.

Allen, Steven G. and Robert L. Clark. "Unions, Pension Wealth, and Age-Compensation Profiles." *Industrial and Labor Relations Review* 39 (July 1986): 502-517.

Allen, Steven G., Robert L. Clark, and Ann A. McDermed. "Job Mobility, Older Workers and the Role of Pensions." Mimeographed. North Carolina State University, October 1986.

_____ . "Why Do Pensions Reduce Mobility?" Industrial Relations Research Association, Proceedings of the Fortieth Annual Meeting, Madison, Wisconsin, 1988a.

_____ . "Pensions and Lifetime Jobs: The New Industrial Feudalism Revisited." Mimeographed. North Carolina State University, 1988b.

Allen, Steven G., Robert L. Clark, and Daniel A. Sumner. "Postretirement Adjustments of Pension Benefits." *Journal of Human Resources* 21 (Winter 1986): 118-137.

Anderson, Kathryn H. and Richard V. Burkhauser. "The Retirement-Health Nexus: A New Measure of an Old Puzzle." *Journal of Human Resources* 20 (Summer 1985): 315-330.

Anderson, Kathryn H., Richard V. Burkhauser, and Joseph F. Quinn. "Do Retirement Dreams Come True? The Effect of Unanticipated Events on Retirement Plans." *Industrial and Labor Relations Review* 39 (July 1986): 518-526.

Ball, Robert M. "The Original Understanding on Social Security: Implications for Later Developments." In *Social Security: Beyond the Rhetoric of Crisis,* edited by Theodore R. Marmor and Jerry L. Mashaw, 17–39. Princeton: Princeton University Press, 1988.

Bane, Mary Jo and David T. Ellwood. "Slipping Into and Out of Poverty: The Dynamics of Spells." *Journal of Human Resources* 21 (Winter 1986): 1-23.

Barfield, Richard E. and James N. Morgan. *Early Retirement: The Decision and the Experience*. Ann Arbor: University of Michigan Press, 1969.

Bazzoli, Gloria J. "The Early Retirement Decision: New Empirical Evidence on the Influence of Health." *Journal of Human Resources* 20 (Spring 1985): 214-234.

Becker, Eugene H. "Self-employed workers: an update to 1983." *Monthly Labor Review* 107 (July 1984): 14-18.

Becker, Gary S. and George J. Stigler. "Law Enforcement, Malfeasance, and Compensation of Enforcers." *Journal of Legal Studies* 3 (January 1974): 1-18.

Bell, Donald and William Marclay. "Trends in retirement eligibility and pension benefits." *Monthly Labor Review* 110 (April 1987): 18-25.

Berkovec, James and Steven Stern. "Job Exit Behavior of Older Men." *Econometrica,* forthcoming.

Berkowitz, Monroe. "Functioning Ability and Job Performance as Workers Age." In *The Older Worker,* edited by Michael E. Borus et al., 87–114. Madison, WI: Industrial Relations Research Association, 1988.

Bernheim, B. Douglas. "Social Security Benefits: An Empirical Study of Expectations and Realization." In *Issues in Contemporary Retirement,* edited by Rita Ricardo Campbell and Edward Lazear, 312–345. Stanford, CA: Hoover Institution Press, 1988.

Blau, David M. "A Time Series Analysis of Self-Employment in the United States." *Journal of Political Economy* 95 (June 1987): 445-466.

Blinder, Alan S., Roger H. Gordon, and Donald E. Wise. "Reconsidering the Work Disincentive Effects of Social Security." *National Tax Journal* 33 (December 1980): 431-442.

_____ . "Rhetoric and Reality in Social Security Analysis—A Rejoinder." *National Tax Journal* 34 (December 1981): 473-478.

Boskin, Michael J. "Social Security and Retirement Decisions." *Economic Inquiry* 15 (January 1977): 1-25.

Boskin, Michael J. and Michael D. Hurd. "The Effect of Social Security on Early Retirement," *Journal of Public Economics* 10 (December 1978): 361-377.

Brennan, Michael J., Philip Taft, and Mark B. Schupack. *The Economics of Age.* New York: W. W. Norton, 1967.

Browning, Edgar. "Labor Supply Distortions of Social Security." *Southern Economic Journal* 42 (August 1975): 243-252.

_____ . "The Marginal Social Security Tax on Labor." *Public Finance Quarterly* 13 (July 1985): 227-252.

Bulow, Jeremy. "What Are Corporate Pension Liabilities?" *Quarterly Journal of Economics* 97 (August 1982): 435-452.

Burkhauser, Richard V. "The Pension Acceptance Decision of Older Workers." *Journal of Human Resources* 14 (Winter 1979): 63-75.

_____ . "The Early Acceptance of Social Security: An Asset Maximization Approach." *Industrial and Labor Relations Review* 33 (July 1980): 484-492.

Burkhauser, Richard V. and Joseph F. Quinn. "The Effect of Pension Plans on the Pattern of Life Cycle Compensation." In *The Measurement of Labor Cost,* edited by Jack E. Triplett, 395-415. Chicago: The University of Chicago Press, 1983a.

_____ . "Is Mandatory Retirement Overrated? Evidence from the 1970s." *Journal of Human Resources* 18 (Summer 1983b): 337-358.

Burkhauser, Richard V. and John A. Turner. "A Time Series Analysis of Social Security and Its Effect on the Market Work of Prime Age Men." *Journal of Political Economy* 86 (1978): 701-715.

_____ . "Can Twenty-Five Million Americans Be Wrong? A Response to Blinder, Gordon, and Wise." *National Tax Journal* 34 (December 1981): 467-72.

_____ . "Labor Market Experience of the Almost Old and the Implications for Income Support." *American Economic Review* 72 (May 1982): 304-308.

_____ . "Is the Social Security Payroll Tax a Tax?" *Public Finance Quarterly* 13 (July 1985): 253-267.

Burkhauser, Richard V. and Jennifer L. Warlick. "Disentangling the Annuity from The Redistributive Aspects of Social Security in the United States." *Review of Income and Wealth* 27 (December 1981): 401-421.

Burtless, Gary. "Social Security, Unanticipated Benefit Increases, and the Timing of Retirement." *Review of Economic Studies* 53 (1986): 781-805.

_____ . "Occupational Effects of the Health and Work Capacity of Older Men." In *Work, Health and Income Among the Elderly,* edited by Gary Burtless, 103-142. Washington, D.C.: The Brookings Institution, 1987.

Burtless, Gary and Robert A. Moffitt. "The Effect of Social Security Benefits on the Labor Supply of the Aged." In *Retirement and Economic Behavior,* edited by Henry J. Aaron and Gary Burtless, 135-171. Washington, D.C.: The Brookings Institution, 1984.

_____ . "The Joint Choice of Retirement Age and Postretirement Hours of Work." *Journal of Labor Economics* 3 (April 1985): 209-236.

_____ . "Social Security, Earnings Tests, and Age at Retirement." *Public Finance Quarterly* 14 (January 1986): 3-27.

Butler, J. S., Kathryn H. Anderson, and Richard V. Burkhauser. "Work and Health After Retirement: A Competing Risks Model with Semiparametric Unobserved Heterogeneity." *Review of Economics and Statistics* 71 (February 1989): 46-53.

Butler, J. S., Richard V. Burkhauser, Jean M. Mitchell, and Theodore P. Pincus. "Measurement Error in Self-Reported Health Variables." *Review of Economics and Statistics* 69 (November 1987): 644-650.

Campbell, Colin D. and Rosemary G. Campbell. "Conflicting Views on the Effect of Old-Age and Survivors Insurance on Retirement." *Economic Inquiry* 14 (September 1976): 369-388.

Carey, Max L. "Occupational tenure in 1987: many workers remain in their fields." *Monthly Labor Review* 111 (October 1988): 3-12.

Chapman, Steven H., Mitchell P. LaPlante, and Gail Wilensky. "Life Expectancy and Health Status of the Aged." *Social Security Bulletin* 49 (October 1986): 24-48.

Chirikos, Thomas N. and Gilbert Nestel. "Impairment and Labor Market Outcomes." In *Work and Retirement: A Longitudinal Study of Men,* edited by Herbert S. Parnes, 93-131. Cambridge, MA: MIT Press, 1981.

Clark, Robert L. and Ann A. McDermed. "Pension Wealth and Job Changes: The Effects of Vesting, Portability and Lump Sum Distributions." *The Gerontologist* 28 (August 1988): 524-532.

Clark, Robert L. and Stephan F. Gohmann. "Retirement and the Acceptance of Social Security Benefits." *National Tax Journal* 36, 4 (December 1983): 529-534.

Epstein, Lenore A. and Janet H. Murray. *The Aged Population of the United States: The 1963 Social Security Survey of the Aged.* Research Report No. 19 of the Social Security Administration, Office of Research and Statistics. Washington, D.C.: U.S. Government Printing Office, 1967.

Feldstein, Martin and Randall Morck. "Pension Funds and the Value of Equities." *Financial Analysts Journal* 39 (September/October 1983): 29-39.

Feldstein, Martin and S. Seligman. "Pension Funding, Share Prices and National Savings." *Journal of Finance* 36 (September 1981): 801-824.

Fields, Gary S. and Olivia S. Mitchell. "Economic Determinants of the Optimal Retirement Age: An Empirical Investigation." *Journal of Human Resources* 19 (Spring 1984a): 245-262.

————— . "The Effects of Social Security Reforms on Retirement Ages and Retirement Incomes." *Journal of Public Economics* 25 (November 1984b): 143-159.

————— . *Retirement, Pensions, and Social Security.* Cambridge, MA: The MIT Press, 1984c.

Filer, Randall K. and Peter A. Petri. "A Job Characteristics Theory of Retirement." *The Review of Economics and Statistics* 70 (February 1988): 123-129.

Freeman, Richard B. "The Exit-Voice Tradeoff in the Labor Market: Unionism, Job Tenure, Quits, and Separations." *Quarterly Journal of Economics* 94 (June 1980): 643-673.

Fuchs, Victor. "Self-Employment and Labor Force Participation of Older Males." *Journal of Human Resources* 17 (Summer 1982): 339-357.

Ginsburg, Helen. "Flexible and partial retirement for Norwegian and Swedish workers." *Monthly Labor Review* 108 (October 1985): 33-43.

Gohmann, Stephan F. and Robert L. Clark. "Retirement Responses to Social Security Changes." *Journal of Gerontology* 44 (November 1989): 218-225.

Golden, Claudia. "Life Cycle Labor Force Participation of Married Women: Historical Evidence and Implications." *Journal of Labor Economics* 7 (January 1989): 20-47.

Gordon, Margaret S. "Income Security Programs and the Propensity to Retire." In *Processes of Aging, Volume II,* edited by Richard William, Clark Tibbitts, and Wilma Donahue, 436-458. New York: Atherton Press, 1963.

Gordon, Roger H. "Social Security and Labor Supply Incentives." *Contemporary Policy Issues* 3 (April 1983): 16-22.

Gordon, Roger H. and Alan S. Blinder. "Market Wages, Reservation Wages and Retirement Decision." *Journal of Public Economics* 14 (October 1980): 277-308.

Grad, Susan. "Income and Assets of Social Security Beneficiaries by Type of Benefit." *Social Security Bulletin* 52 (January 1989): 2-10.

Guralnick, Jack M., Machiko Yanagishita, and Edward L. Schneider. "Projecting the Older Population of the U.S.: Lessons from the Past & Prospects for the Future." *The Generational Journal* 2 (April 1989): 115-120.

Gustman, Alan A. and Thomas L. Steinmeier. "Minimum Hours Constraints and Retirement Behavior." *Contemporary Policy Issues* 3 (April 1983): 77-91.

_____ . "Partial Retirement and the Analysis of Retirement Behavior." *Industrial and Labor Relations Review* 37 (April 1984a): 403-415.

_____ . "Modeling the Retirement Process for Policy Evaluation and Research." *Monthly Labor Review* 107 (July 1984b): 26-33.

_____ . "The Effects of Partial Retirement on the Wage Profiles of Older Workers." *Industrial Relations* 24 (Spring 1985a): 257-265.

_____ . "The 1983 Social Security Reforms and Labor Supply Adjustments of Older Individuals in the Long Run." *Journal of Labor Economics* 3 (April 1985b): 237-253.

_____ . "A Structural Retirement Model." *Econometrica* 54 (May 1986a): 555-584.

_____ "A Disaggregated Structural Analysis of Retirement by Race, Difficulty of Work, and Health." *Review of Economics and Statistics* 68 (August 1986b): 509-513.

_____ . "Pensions, Efficiency Wages and Job Mobility." National Bureau of Economic Research Working Paper No. 2426, November 1987.

_____ . " An Analysis of Pension Benefit Formulas, Pension Wealth, and Incentives from Pensions." In *Research in Labor Economics,* Vol. 10, edited by Ronald G. Ehrenberg, 53-106. Greenwich, CT: Jai Press, 1989a.

————. "Evaluating Pension Policies in a Model with Endogenous Contributions." National Bureau of Economic Research, Working paper No. 3085, August 1989b.

————. "The Stampede Toward Defined Contribution Pension Plans: Fact or Fiction?" National Bureau of Economic Research, Working Paper No. 3086, August 1989c.

————. "Changing the Social Security Rules for Workers Over 65: Proposed Policies and Their Effects." National Bureau of Economic Research, Working Paper No. 3087, August 1989d.

Haber, Sheldon E., Enrique J. Lamas, and Jules H. Lichtenstein. "On their own: the self-employed and others in private business." *Monthly Labor Review* 110 (May 1987): 17-23.

Hall, Arden and Terry Johnson. "The Determinants of Planned Retirement Age." *Industrial and Labor Relations Review* 33 (January 1980): 241-255.

Hall, Robert E. "The Importance of Lifetime Jobs in the U.S. Economy." *American Economic Review* 72 (September 1982): 716-724.

Halpern, Janice. "Raising the Mandatory Retirement Age: Its Effect on the Employment of Older Workers." *New England Economic Review* (May/June 1978): 23-35.

Hatch, Sara. "Financial Retirement Incentives in Private Pension Plans." Washington, D.C.: Urban Institute report to the Department of Labor, #J-9-P-0-0163, 1981.

Hausman, Jerry A. and David A. Wise. "Social Security, Health Status, and Retirement." In *Pensions, Labor, and Individual Choice,* edited by David A. Wise, 159-191. Chicago: The University of Chicago Press, 1985.

Haveman, Robert, Barbara Wolfe, and Jennifer Warlick. "Labor Market Behavior of Older Men: Estimates from a Trichotomous Choice Model." *Journal of Public Economics* 36 (July 1988): 153-175.

Herz, Diane E. "Employment characteristics of older women, 1987." *Monthly Labor Review* 111 (September 1988): 3-12.

Herz, Diane E. and Philip Rones. "Institutional barriers to employment of older workers." *Monthly Labor Review* 112 (April 1989): 14-21.

Holden, Karen C. "Physically Demanding Occupations, Health, and Work After Retirement: Findings From the New Beneficiary Survey." *Social Security Bulletin* 51 (November 1988): 3-15.

Holden, Karen C. and W. Lee Hansen. "Retirement Behavior and Mandatory Retirement in Higher Education." In *The End of Mandatory Retirement: Effects on Higher Education,* edited by Karen C. Holden and W. Lee Hansen, 33-49. San Francisco: Jossey-Bass Series, New Directions in Higher Education, 1989.

Honig, Marjorie. "Partial Retirement Among Women." *Journal of Human Resources* 20 (Fall 1985): 613-621.

Honig, Marjorie and Giora Hanoch. "Partial Retirement as a Separate Mode of Retirement Behavior." *Journal of Human Resources* 20 (Winter 1985): 21-46.

Hutchens, Robert M. "Delayed Payment Contracts and a Firm's Propensity to Hire Older Workers." *Journal of Labor Economics* 4 (October 1986): 439-457.

_____ . "Do Job Opportunities Decline With Age?" *Industrial and Labor Relations Review* 42 (October 1988): 89-99.

Iams, Howard M. "Jobs of Persons Working After Receiving Retired-Worker Benefits." *Social Security Bulletin* 50 (November 1987): 4-19.

Ippolito, Richard A. "The Labor Contract and True Economic Pension Liabilities." *American Economic Review* 75 (December 1985): 1031-1043.

_____ . *Pensions, Economics and Public Policy.* Homewood, IL: Dow Jones-Irwin, 1986.

_____ . "The Implicit Pension Contract: Developments and New Directions." *Journal of Human Resources* 22 (Summer 1987): 441-467.

_____ . *The Economics of Pension Insurance.* Homewood, IL: Irwin, 1989.

_____ . "Towards Explaining Earlier Retirement After 1970." *Industrial and Labor Relations Review* (1990) forthcoming.

Irelan, Lola M. *Almost 65: Baseline Data from the Retirement History Study.* U.S. Social Security Administration, Office of Research and Statistics, Research Report No. 49. Washington, D.C.: U.S.Government Printing Office, 1976.

Jondrow, Jim, Frank Brechling, and Alan Marcus. "Older Workers in the Market for Part-Time Employment." In *The Problem Isn't Age: Work and Older Americans,* edited by Steven H. Sandell, 84-99. New York, NY: Praeger, 1987.

Kahn, James A. "Social Security, Liquidity, and Early Retirement." *Journal of Public Economics* 35 (February 1988): 97-117.

Kingson, Eric R. "The Health of Very Early Retirees." *Social Security Bulletin* 45 (September 1982): 3-9.

Kotlikoff, Laurence J. and Daniel E. Smith. *Pensions in the American Economy.* Chicago. The University of Chicago Press, 1983.

Kotlikoff, Laurence J. and David A. Wise, *The Wage Carrot and the Pension Stick.* Kalamazoo, MI: W.E. Upjohn Institute, 1989.

Krueger, Alan B. and Jorn-Steffen Pischke. "The Effect of Social Security on Labor Supply: A Cohort Analysis of the Notch Generation." Princeton University, Industrial Relations Section, Working Paper No. 255, June 1989.

Kruse, Agneta and Lars Soderstrom. "Early Retirement in Sweden." In *Redefining the Process of Retirement: An International Perspective,* edited by Winfried Schmahl, 39–61. Berlin: Springer Verlag, 1989.

Laczko, Frank. "Partial retirement: An alternative to early retirement? A comparison of phased retirement schemes in the United Kingdom, France and Scandinavia." *International Social Security Review* 41/2 (1988): 149-169.

Lazear, Edward P. "Why Is There Mandatory Retirement?" *Journal of Political Economy* 87 (December 1979): 1261-1284.

Levine, Martin Lyon. *Age Discrimination and the Mandatory Retirement Controversy.* Baltimore: The Johns Hopkins University Press, 1988.

Long, Clarence D. *The Labor Force Under Changing Income and Employment.* Princeton: Princeton University Press, 1958.

Luzadis, Rebecca A. and Olivia S. Mitchell. "Explaining Pension Dynamics." National Bureau of Economic Research, Working Paper No. 3084, August 1989.

McCormick, Barry and Gordon Hughes. "The influence of pensions on job mobility." *Journal of Public Economics* 23 (February/March 1984): 183-206.

McElwain, Adrienne M. and James L. Swofford. "The Social Security Payroll Tax and the Life-Cycle Work Pattern." *Journal of Human Resources* 21 (Spring 1986): 279-287.

Meyer, Charles W. *Social Security: A Critique of Radical Reform Proposals.* Lexington, MA: Lexington Books, 1987.

Mirkin, Barry Alan. "Early retirement as a labor force policy: an international overview." *Monthly Labor Review* 110 (March 1987): 19-33.

Mitchell, Olivia S. "Fringe Benefits and Labor Mobility." *Journal of Human Resources* 17 (Spring 1982): 286-298.

_____ . "Fringe Benefits and the Cost of Changing Jobs." *Industrial and Labor Relations Review* 37 (October 1983): 70-78.

_____ . "Worker Knowledge of Pension Provision." *Journal of Labor Economics* 6 (January 1988): 21-39.

Mitchell, Olivia S. and Gary S. Fields. "The Effects of Pensions and Earnings on Retirement: A Review Essay." In *Research in Labor Economics.* Vol. 5, edited by Ronald E. Ehrenberg, 115-155. Greenwich, CT: JAI Press, 1982.

_____ . "The Economics of Retirement Behavior." *Journal of Labor Economics* 2 (January 1984): 84-105.

_____ . "Rewards for Continued Work: The Economic Incentives for Postponing Retirement." In *Horizontal Equity, Uncertainty, and Measures of*

Well-Being, edited by Martin David and Timothy Smeeding, 269-286. Chicago: The University of Chicago Press, 1985.

Mitchell, Olivia S., Phillip B. Levine, and Silvana Pozzebon. "Retirement Differences by Industry and Occupation." *The Gerontologist* 28 (August 1988): 545-551.

Mitchell, Olivia S. and Rebecca Luzadis. "Changes in Pension Incentives Through Time." *Industrial and Labor Relations Review* 42 (October 1988): 100-108.

Moen, Jon. "The Labor of Older Men: A Comment." *The Journal of Economic History* 47 (September 1987): 761-767.

Moffitt, Robert A. "Trends in Social Security Wealth by Cohort." In *Economic Transfers in the United States,* edited by Marilyn Moon, 327-347. Chicago: The University of Chicago Press, 1984.

_____ . "Life-Cycle Labor Supply and Social Security: A Time-Series Analysis." In *Work, Health and Income Among the Elderly,* edited by (Gary Burtless, 183-220. Washington, D.C.: The Brookings Institution, 1987.

Montgomery, Sarah. "Findings from the CEFHE Studies." In *The End of Mandatory Retirement: Effects on Higher Education,* edited by Karen C. Holden and W. Lee Hansen, 51-62. San Francisco: Jossey-Bass Series, New Directions in Higher Education, 1989.

Morrison, Malcolm. "The aging of the U.S. population: human resource impl-cations." *Monthly Labor Review* 106 (May 1983): 13-19.

_____ . "Changes in the Legal Mandatory Retirement Age: Labor Force Participation Implications." In *Issues in Contemporary Retirement,* edited by Rita Ricardo Campbell and Edward Lazear, 378-405. Stanford, CA: Hoover Institution Press, 1988.

Nestel, Gilbert. "Retirement Expectation and the Timing of Retirement." In *Retirement Among American Men,* by Herbert S. Parnes et al. Lexington, MA: Lexington Books, 1985, 79-89.

Organisation for Economic Co-operation and Development (OECD). *Aging Populations: The Social Policy Implications.* Paris: Organisation for Economic Co-operation and Development, 1988.

Packard, Michael D. and Virginia P. Reno. "A Look at Very Early Retirees." *Social Security Bulletin* 52 (March 1989): 16-29.

Palmore, Erdman. "Retirement Patterns Among Aged Men: Findings of the 1963 Survey of the Aged." *Social Security Bulletin* 27 (August 1964): 3-10.

Parnes, Herbert S. et al. *Retirement Among American Men.* Lexington, MA: Lexington Books, 1985.

Parnes, Herbert S. and Lawrence J. Less. "The Volume and Pattern of Retire-ments, 1966-1981." In *Retirement Among American Men,* by Herbert Parnes et al., 57-77. Lexington, MA: Lexington Books, 1985a.

_____ . "Economic Well-Being in Retirement." In *Retirement Among American Men,* by Herbert Parnes et al., 91-118. Lexington, MA: Lexington Books, 1985b.

Parsons, Donald O. "The Male Labour Force Participation Decision: Health, Reported Health and Economic Incentives." *Economica* 49 (February 1982): 81-91.

Pechman, Joseph A., Henry J. Aaron, and Michael K. Taussig. *Social Security: Perspectives for Reform.* Washington, D.C.: The Brookings Institution, 1968.

Perkins, Frances. *The Roosevelt I Knew.* New York: The Viking Press, 1946.

Petersen, Jorn H. "The Process of Retirement in Denmark: Trends, Public Discussion and Institutional Framework." In *Redefining the Process of Retirement: An International Perspective,* edited by Winfried Schmahl, 63–81. Berlin: Springer Verlag, 1989.

Pozzebon, Silvana and Olivia S. Mitchell, "Married Women's Retirement Behavior." *Journal of Population Economics* 2 (March 1989): 39-53.

Quinn, Joseph F. "Microeconomic Determinants of Early Retirement: A Cross-Sectional View of White Married Men." *Journal of Human Resources* 12 (Summer 1977): 329-347.

_____ . "Labor-Force Participation Patterns of Older Self-Employed Workers." *Social Security Bulletin* 43 (April 1980): 17-28.

_____ . "The Extent and Correlates of Partial Retirement." *The Gerontologist* 21 (December, 1981): 634-643.

_____ . "Retirement Income Rights as a Component of Wealth in the United States." *The Review of Income and Wealth* 31 (September 1985): 223-236.

_____ . "Economic Status of the Elderly: Beware of the Mean." *The Review of Income and Wealth* 33 (March 1987): 63-82.

Quinn, Joseph F. and Richard V. Burkhauser. "Influencing Retirement Behavior: A Key Issue for Social Security." *Journal of Policy Analysis and Management* 3 (Fall 1983): 1-13.

Ransom, Roger L. and Richard Sutch. "The Labor of Older Americans: Retirement of Men On and Off the Job, 1870-1937." *The Journal of Economic History* 46 (March 1986): 1-30.

_____ . "The Decline of Retirement in the Years Before Social Security: U.S. Retirement Patterns, 1870-1940." In *Issues in Contemporary Retirement,* edited by Rita Ricardo-Campbell and Edward P. Lazear, 3–37. Stanford, CA: Hoover Institution Press, 1988.

_____ . "The Trend in the Rate of Labor Force Participation of Older Men, 1870-1930: A Reply to Moen." *Journal of Economic History* 49 (March 1989): 170-183.

Rebitzer, James. "Establishment Size and Job Tenure." *Industrial Relations* 25, 3 (Fall 1986): 292-302.

Reimers, Cordelia and Marjorie Honig. "The Retirement Process in the United States: Mobility Among Full-Time Work, Partial Retirement, and Full Retirement." In *Redefining the Process of Retirement: An International Perspective,* edited by Winfried Schmahl, 115-131. Berlin: Springer Verlag, 1989.

Reno, Virginia. "Why Men Stop Working At or Before Age 65: Findings From the Survey of New Beneficiaries." *Social Security Bulletin* 35 (June 1971): 3-17.

Rhine, Shirley H. *Managing Older Workers: Company Policies and Attitudes.* New York: The Conference Board, 1984.

Rones, Philip L. "The labor market problems of older workers." *Monthly Labor Review* 106 (May 1983): 3-12.

Ruhm, Christopher J. "Bridge Jobs and Partial Retirement." Mimeographed. Department of Economics, Boston University, August 1988.

_____ . "Why Older Americans Stop Working." *The Gerontologist* 29 (June 1989): 294-299.

Ruhm, Christopher J. "Job Stoppping: Career Employment and Retirement in the United States." *Industrial Relations* (1990) forthcoming.

Rust, John P. "A Dynamic Programming Model of Retirement Behavior." In *The Economics of Aging,* edited by David A. Wise, 359-398. Chicago, IL: The University of Chicago Press, 1987.

Sammartino, Frank J. "The Effect of Health on Retirement." *Social Security Bulletin* 50 (February 1987): 31-47.

Sandell, Steven H. "Public Policies and Programs Affecting Older Workers." In *The Older Worker,* edited by Michael E. Borus et al., 207-228. Madison, WI: Industrial Relations Research Association, 1988.

Schiller, Bradley R. and Randall D. Weiss. "The Impact of Private Pensions on Firm Attachment." *Review of Economics and Statistics* 61 (August 1979): 369-380.

Schulz, James H. "The Economics of Mandatory Retirement." *Industrial Gerontology* 1 (1974): 1-10.

_____ . *The Economics of Aging.* New York. Van Nostrand Reinhold Co., 1988.

Shank, Susan E. "Women and the labor market: the link grows stronger." *Monthly Labor Review* 111 (March 1988): 3-8.

Shapiro, David and Steven H. Sandell. "The Reduced Pay of Older Job Losers: Age Discrimination and Other Explanations." In *The Problem Isn't Age: Work and Older Americans,* edited by Steven H. Sandell, 37-51. New York: Praeger, 1987.

Sherman, Sally R. "Reported Reasons Retired Workers Left Their Last Jobs: Findings From the New Beneficiary Survey." *Social Security Bulletin* 48 (March 1985): 22-30.

Sickles, Robin C. and Paul Taubman. "An Analysis of the Health and Retirement Status of the Elderly." *Econometrica* 54 (November 1986): 1339-1356.

Starr, Paul. "Social Security and the American Public Household." In *Social Security: Beyond the Rhetoric of Crisis,* edited by Theodore R. Marmor and Jerry L. Mashaw, 119-148. Princeton: Princeton University Press, 1988.

Stecker, Margaret L. "Beneficiaries Prefer to Work." *Social Security Bulletin* 14 (January 1951): 15-17.

_____ . "Why Do Beneficiaries Retire? Who Among Them Returns To Work?" *Social Security Bulletin* 18 (May 1955): 3-12, 35-36.

Steiner, Peter O. and Robert Dorfman. *The Economic Status of the Aged.* Berkeley: The University of California Press, 1957.

Stern, Steven. "Measuring the Effect of Disability on Labor Force Participation." *Journal of Human Resources* 24 (Summer 1989): 361-395.

Stock, James H. and David A. Wise. "The Pension Inducement to Retire: An Option Value Approach." In *Issues in the Economics of Aging,* edited by David A. Wise. Chicago: University of Chicago Press, 1990, forthcoming.

Sundberg, Heimer. "The Flexible Pensionable Age in Finland." In *Redefining the Process of Retirement: An International Perspective,* edited by Winfried Schmahl, 84–89. Berlin: Springer Verlag, 1989.

Svahn, John A. and Mary Ross. "Social Security Amendments of 1983: Legislative History and Summary of Provisions." *Social Security Bulletin* 46 (July 1983): 3-48.

Sweeney, George, J. S. Butler, Kathryn H. Anderson, and Richard V. Burkhauser. "A Life Cycle View of Work after Retirement." Vanderbilt University, Department of Economics Working Paper, May 1989.

Tobin, James. "The Future of Social Security: One Economist's Assessment." In *Social Security: Beyond the Rhetoric of Crisis,* edited by Theodore R. Marmor and Jerry L. Mashaw, 41-68. Princeton: Princeton University Press, 1988.

Tuma, Nancy Brandon and Gary D. Sandefur. "Trends in the Labor Force Activity of the Elderly in the United States, 1940-1980." In *Issues in Contemporary Retirement,* edited by Rita Ricardo-Campbell and Edward P. Lazear, 38-75. Stanford, CA: Hoover Institution Press, 1988.

Turner, John A. and Daniel J. Beller. *Trends in Pensions.* Washington, D.C.: U.S. Government Printing Office, 1989.

U.S. General Accounting Office. *Retirement Forecasting* (GAO Report GAO/PEMD-87-6A). Vol. 1. Washington, D.C.: U.S. Government Printing Office, December 1986.

_____ . *Retirement Forecasting* (GAO Report GAO/PEMD-87-6B). Vol. 2. Washington, D.C.: U.S. Government Printing Office, December 1986.

_____ . *Social Security: The Notch Issue.* Washington, D.C.: U.S. Government Printing Office, March 1988.

U.S. Social Security Administration. "Old-Age and Survivors Insurance: A Report on the Retirement Test." *Social Security Bulletin* 23 (October 1960): 4-8.

_____ . *Social Security Bulletin, Annual Statistical Bulletin.* Washington, D.C.: U.S. Government Printing Office, 1986, 1990.

U.S. Special Committee on Aging. *Aging America: Trends and Projections (1987-88 edition).* Washington, D.C.: U.S. Department of Health and Human Services, 1988.

Viscusi, W. Kip. "Job Hazards and Worker Quit Rates: An Analysis of Adaptive Work Behavior." *International Economic Review* 20 (February 1979): 29-58.

Wentworth, Edna C. "Why Beneficiaries Retire." *Social Security Bulletin* 8 (January 1945): 16-20.

Wolff, Edward N. "The Effects of Pensions and Social Security on the Distribution of Wealth in the United States." In *International Comparisons of the Distribution of Household Wealth,* edited by Edward N. Wolff, 208-47. Oxford: Clarendon Press, 1987.

Woods, John R. "Retirement Age Women and Pensions: Findings From the New Beneficiary Survey." *Social Security Bulletin* 51 (December 1988): 5-16.

Ycas, Martynas A. "Recent Trends in Health Near the Age of Retirement: New Findings From the Health Interview Survey." *Social Security Bulletin* 50 (February 1987): 5-30.

Ycas, Martynas A. and Susan Grad. "Income of Retirement-Aged Persons in the United States." *Social Security Bulletin* 50 (July 1987): 5-14.

INDEX